Complete Yorkshire

© 1973 Ward Lock Limited

Reprinted 1976

ISBN 0 7063 1530 8

Drawings by Cetra Hearne

Photographs by Peter Baker, Roy Westlake, Tony Kersting,
Geoffrey Wright and John Edenbrow.

Text filmset in Times New Roman by Technical Filmsetters Europe Ltd.,
Manchester.

Plans based upon the Ordnance Survey map with the sanction
of the Controller of Her Majesty's Stationery Office.

Printed and bound by Editorial Fher S. A., Bilbao, Spain.

RED GUIDE

Complete

Yorkshire

The coast resorts, the
dales, main centres and
places of interest.

Edited by Reginald J. W. Hammond F.R.G.S.

WARD LOCK LIMITED

116 Baker Street, London W1M 2BB

Maps and Plans

Contents

CONTENTS

Illustrations

7

THE RED GUIDES

Edited by Reginald J. W. Hammond

Bournemouth, New Forest

Channel Islands

Cornwall : North

Cornwall : South

Cornwall : West

Cotswolds

Devon, South

Dorset Coast

Isle of Wight

Lake District

London

Norfolk and the Broads

Peak District

Wales N. (Northn. Section)

Wales N. (Southn. Section)

Wales, South

Northern Ireland

SCOTLAND

Highlands of Scotland

Northern Scotland

Western Scotland

RED TOURIST GUIDES

Complete England

Complete Scotland

Complete Ireland

Complete Wales

Lake District (Baddeley)

Complete Devon

Complete West Country

Complete South-East Coast

Complete Yorkshire

Complete Scottish Lowlands

Complete Cotswolds and
Shakespeare Country

Complete Wye Valley,
Hereford and Worcester

Complete Dorset and
Wiltshire

Complete Thames and
Chilterns

WARD LOCK LIMITED

Introduction

Yorkshire is not only the largest county in England, to those born within its boundaries it is unquestionably the greatest. Whether this pride is justified or not, it would surely be difficult to find a county with more claims to the visitor's interest.

Few would argue that foremost among Yorkshire's many attractions are the incomparable Dales. Here, in one of the grandest areas of unspoiled country in the whole of England, are mountains and moorland, as well as peaceful villages, waterfalls and awe-inspiring caverns. Excellent centres for touring the Dales include Harrogate, Settle, Skipton and Ilkley.

The Dales constitute one of Yorkshire's two National Parks the other is the North York Moors, again one of the loveliest parts of England. It is bounded on the east by the splendour of the Yorkshire coast, which rivals that of Devon and Cornwall along its hundred miles of variety – with towering cliffs, secluded fishing villages and splendid sands. Resorts like Whitby, Scarborough and Bridlington cater for all possible tastes in accommodation and entertainment.

Yorkshire, besides being very much concerned with the present day, is rich in an eventful history to which many monuments, glorious cathedrals, magnificent houses, castles and some of the most beautiful ruins in England bear eloquent witness – Fountains Abbey, Castle Howard, Richmond Castle, the Minsters of York, Beverley and Ripon, Nostell Priory, Temple Newsam – these are only a few of the famous names that spring to mind. Battlefields, too, like Towton, scene of one of the bloodiest conflicts ever seen on English soil, are evidence of the county's often tumultuous past.

Yorkshire is really three counties in one, for each of the three Ridings has still its own county capital and county council. The word Riding itself is evidence of Yorkshire's antiquity, for it is derived from an Old Norse word dating back to the Vikings, who settled here and divided Yorkshire into "thridings", or thirds. That is why there is no "South Riding" – except as the title of a novel by Winifred Holtby, one of the many writers of distinction who have kept Yorkshire's literary tradition alive.

From the Brontës, through J. B. Priestley and Phyllis Bentley, this tradition seems as strong as ever in the newest generation of Yorkshire writers; there must be something in the air or scenery of Yorkshire that impels its denizens to write about it. And this is particularly true, perhaps, of the West Riding – the greatest of the three in population and area, and itself bigger than any other English county.

Indeed, the West Riding is almost a country in itself. It contains not only a large part of the Dales, but also the industrial areas which, though they cover but a comparatively small area of the Riding are sometimes the best known to those who still think of Yorkshire in terms of mills, muck and money-grubbing millionaires! '

While few tourists will choose to spend a holiday in the heavily industrialised area dominated by Bradford, Leeds and Sheffield, these districts are by no means lacking in interest or beauty for those with receptive minds and eyes to see. Sheffield with its steel, Bradford with its wool, Leeds with its multifarious trades, and the coal towns – Barnsley, Pontefract, Doncaster – have a proper pride in their rôle in the industrial life of Britain and in the centuries of craftsmanship which are their heritage.

Very different is the North Riding, which has itself all the requirements for a splendid holiday, with superb coastal scenery as well as excellent walking country in the North York Moors and the Cleveland Hills. North Yorkshire contains some of Yorkshire's – and indeed England's – loveliest villages like Hutton-le-Hole, Castleton, Hovingham and Lastingham. Forests and waterfalls, old market towns, splendid ruins as well as fine old houses and, of course, the beautiful coastline – all these, together with friendly and hospitable people, make a North Riding holiday uniquely memorable.

The East Riding, too, has its share of the Yorkshire coast, stretching from Filey, an ideal family resort, down to the lonely promontory of Spurn Head. In between are Bridlington with its bay, Hornsea, famous for its Mere, and Withernsea. There are many reasons why no visitor to Yorkshire should miss visiting the East Riding – Holderness, flat and quaint; rich farmland; the spacious Wolds; Beverley with its glorious Minster, and Hull, one of the country's leading seaports.

Situated where all the Ridings meet, yet a part of none of them, York can surely claim the title unique. York Minster, the greatest medieval church in Europe north of the Alps, is breathtaking in its majesty, yet York has even more to offer – excellent museums to remind us of the time when England's Second City was a centre of Roman life; boating on the river Ouse; fine old halls; beautiful churches and the wonderful medieval walls, the most complete in England, with their four "bars" or gateways ... these are only a few of York's attractions.

We have already mentioned Hull as a tourist attraction in its own right, but it must be considered again when we look at Yorkshire's accessibility by sea, land and air.

Hull may well call itself the "Gateway to Yorkshire" for visitors from the Continent. There are regular passenger services between Hull and Rotterdam and Gothenburg which have done much to open Yorkshire to Europe. Car ferry services with drive-on drive-off facilities are an obvious attraction to the foreign motor-tourist.

Visitors travelling by air arrive at the Leeds/Bradford Airport at Yeadon or at Teesside, the biggest jet airport in the North of England.

Many of the county's holidaymakers still arrive by car of course, and in these days of fast motorway travel, Yorkshire can no longer be considered as a remote northern fastness. The M1 and the A1 (the Great North Road) offer access from London and there are many quick and easy routes from all parts of Britain.

For those who prefer train travel, British Rail now links the county with the whole of Britain by means of the Inter-City network. From King's Cross, London, there are fast regular and frequent services to Bradford, Leeds, Hull, York and Doncaster and other parts. Between St. Pancras and Sheffield runs another Inter-City express service. On most of these trains seats may be reserved and on some overnight services sleeping berths are provided. Inter-City services cannect with local trains to reach more remote places. Circular tour tickets are available from the point of entry to the point of departure.

There is accommodation in Yorkshire to suit every taste and pocket, from camp and caravan sites or homely farmhouses in the Dales to the most luxurious hotels. Throughout this Guide we have listed some of the establishments known to give good service, but the Yorkshire Tourist Board, 312 Tadcaster Road, York Y02 2HF, will be pleased to supply more detailed information.

Youth Hostellers will find Yorkshire a splendid place for holidays. Details of Yorkshire hostels may be obtained from Dept. 1, Y.H.A., 96 Main Street, Bingley, Yorkshire.

Hornsea and the Mere

Hornsea

Car Parks. – Several facing the Promenade.
Hotels. – *Alexandra*, Railway Street; *New*, Market Place; *Marine*, Victoria Avenue; *Seaforth*, Esplanade; *Victoria*, Market Place; *Rose and Crown*, Market Place.
Population. – 7,140.
Camping Sites. – Four recognized sites in Cliff Road, and two at South Cliff.

Hornsea is a bright and bracing little resort which is very popular with Hull and Beverley folk. There are splendid sands and excellent sea-bathing.

In the Victoria Gardens there are putting and bowling greens and pitch-and-putt courses, a **Floral Hall** (used for dancing, stage shows and concerts), sun verandah and café. For the children there are sports, dress-parades, sand-building competitions, concerts and other amusements.

Hall Garth Park is a fine open space of over 20 acres in the centre of the town. Here are more putting greens, a children's corner, a kiosk and a 9-hole golf course where equipment may be hired.

The Hornsea Golf Club Course of 18 holes is about 1 mile to the south of the town centre – frequent bus service.

The Promenade extends for about a mile, with gardens.

Hornsea Mere. The chief attraction of Hornsea for many is its Mere, the largest freshwater lake in Yorkshire. It is nearly 2 miles long and 1 mile broad. Yacht racing is popular, and the Mere is noted for its fishing – especially for perch and pike. Licences should be obtained in advance, as the number is limited. A motor-boat makes frequent trips and there are rowing-boats for hire. On the shores are facilities for putting and refreshments, and on the thickly wooded banks cormorants, water hen, coot and heron are to be seen.

Parish Church. Although Hornsea is mentioned in Domesday Book, and was a seaport of some importance in the days of Queen Elizabeth, the only truly mediaeval structure is its large Parish Church, the site of which has been similarly occupied from very early times. The present building was erected about 1430 and is almost entirely in the Perpendicular style. It was restored in 1868 by Sir Gilbert Scott, R.A., and since then there have been other additions and restorations to the interior. There are three fine windows in the chancel forming a lantern and some interesting effigies, some of which came from nearby Nunkeeling Priory. An alabaster tomb of the last Rector of Hornsea, Anthony St. Quentin, shows curious scratchings in the outlines of various designs of footwear, probably of the Commonwealth period.

In the churchyard is an ancient market cross, much restored. Another cross, probably erected by the Abbot of St. Mary's, York, stands in Southgate.

The principal street of Hornsea bears the curious name of **Newbegin** (biggin means building).

Behind the esplanade is the **Town Hall,** standing in the beautiful Elim Lodge gardens. The grounds are open to the public.

A walk of a couple of miles, partly across fields, brings one to **Goxhill,** with a pretty little church surrounded by trees. A couple of miles north of Hornsea and reached by shore, cliff, or road, is **Atwick,** with an ancient market cross. By continuing for another 4 miles the energetic walker will arrive at **Skipsea,** mentioned on page 33, and **Ulrome,** where the site of prehistoric lake dwellings has been discovered. In the opposite direction one may go by cliff or road to **Mappleton,** 3 miles, and to **Aldbrough,** a much larger village, 4 miles farther. Other villages worth a visit are **Sigglesthorne,** pleasantly situated amid rolling country and possessing a fine old church; **Rise,** a pleasant village 6 miles SSW of Hornsea; and **Burton Constable,** famous for its magnificent baronial hall in a beautiful park of 750 acres.

Burton Constable Hall

Beverley

Car Parks. – The Market Place (except Saturdays), and Morton Lane.

Distances. – Doncaster, 44 miles; Driffield, 13; Hull, 8; London, 201; Scarborough, 34; Selby, 29; York, 29.

Banks. – *Barclays, Lloyds, Midland, National Westminster, York County, Yorkshire.*

Early Closing Day. – Thursday.

Golf. – 18-hole course, Westwood.

Hotels. – *Beverley Arms* (58), *King's Head* (9), *Lairgate* (30), *Angel, North Bar.*

Market Days. – Wednesday, Friday and Saturday.

Population. – 17,320.

Post Office. – Register Square. Several small offices.

Racing. – Meetings from early April to September.

Tennis. – Beverley and East Riding Club, Seven Corners Lane.

Beverley is the county town of East Riding. It is an attractive market town with a wealth of fine Georgian buildings. Although mainly concerned as an agricultural centre, there are several light industries now well established.

At one time the relative positions of Hull and Beverley were the reverse of what they are today, Beverley being the great town and Hull the unimportant suburb.

The town grew up at the gates of the Minster church, and derives its name from Beaver Lea or meadow. The beaver is displayed on the town arms.

The town was at one time protected by a ditch, or fosse, portions of which may yet be seen. This was crossed by five drawbridges, each defended by a bar or gate. One of these gateways, the **North Bar,** is still standing. It dates from the early fifteenth century and is built of brick, not stone. It is two storeys high and has stepped battlements. The archway is wide and groined, and still retains the groove for its portcullis. The massive oak gates also remain, but the side portals are modern.

In the Market Place, or **Saturday Market,** stands a fine **Market Cross.** It is an open octagonal structure, consisting of a base of three stone steps, from which rise eight stone columns. These support a cupola, on which are the arms of England and France, of the town, and of the builders of the cross – Sir C. Hotham and Sir M. Warton, M.P.s for Beverley, 1714. At the top of each column is a stone urn, and the structure terminates in a turret, surmounted by a cross and gilded ball.

Beverley Minster

The Minster is at the south end of the town, about five minutes' walk from the railway station. John of Beverley, fifth Bishop of York, founded a monastery here about A.D. 700. He is traditionally stated to have been born at Harpham. He died

Beverley Minster

in 721 and was buried in the monastery. At his tomb miracles were alleged to have taken place, and he was canonized in 1037. The original building was destroyed in 866 by the Danes. About A.D. 938 the church was rebuilt by King Athelstan as a College for Secular Canons and granted the right of sanctuary, setting up the Fridstool (*see* page 17). Athelstan's building was damaged by fire in 1188 and rebuilding started in A.D. 1220, although the work was not completed until nearly 1400. It is considered to be one of the most beautiful examples of Gothic architecture in Europe. Not only is it, in point of significance, the second ecclesiastical edifice in Yorkshire, but it stands on the site of one of the most ancient religious establishments in the kingdom. Notwithstanding the mixture of Early English, Decorated, and Later English architecture, there is a wonderful unity in the design, giving the impression that the building was the work of one period, though, like other great structures of the kind, it took two centuries to complete. The building is 333 ft. long, the transept measuring 167 ft. The nave and side aisles are 64 ft. wide, measured internally, the height of the nave being 67 ft., and that of the aisles 33 ft.

The **West Front** is one of the most magnificent in Europe, and was declared by no less an authority than Rickman to be the finest example of the Perpendicular, as that of York Minster is of the Decorated, style. The noble towers, 163 ft. high, which grace its angles are supported by elaborately ornamented buttresses, and surmounted by an extremely rich and varied cluster of pinnacles. The great west window, of nine lights, is unusually fine. Its arch is bounded by a sweeping canopy, crocketed, and terminating in a finial. The whole front is panelled in three divisions; the buttresses are ornamented with tiers of niche-work of excellent composition and most delicate execution; the gable above the window is filled with

16

fine tracery; and the top is finished with a raking battlement, delicately pierced and ornamented with pinnacles.

The **Nave** and **Transepts** are Early English, of which style the fronts of the transepts are remarkably pure specimens.

The **Choir** is divided from the nave by a carved **Oak Screen,** completed in 1880. The sixty-eight **Stalls** and other fittings of exquisite working were completed about 1520. The reredos, of stone, erected in 1826, is a restoration of the original Decorated one, mutilated during the Protectorate. At the right of the altar is a curious relic of the old days of Sanctuary, the **Fridstol,** Freed Stool, formed of one entire stone, which, according to Leland, once bore in Latin the inscription, "This stone chair is called Freed Stool (*i.e.* the chair of peace) to which what criminal soever flies hath full protection." The register of fugitives between 1478 and 1539 is in the British Museum.

The **Percy Tomb,** to the left of the altar, is an exquisite specimen of Decorated work, believed to be a monument of a Lady Percy who died in 1365. The richly decorated canopy is a masterpiece of medieval art. The east window is filled with some medieval glass, collected from various parts of the church, and the other windows contain modern stained glass of considerable merit. The **Percy Chapel,** of Perpendicular architecture, contains the altar tomb of Henry Percy, fourth Earl of Northumberland (1489). Between the clergy desks in the nave is the grave of *St. John of Beverley*. Other points of interest are the west doors with their Georgian carvings, the Norman font with a Georgian cover, the reredos screen at the back of the altar, the misericords, the soldiers' chapel in the south transept, and the reredos gallery with its wonderful ceiling carvings.

Under the supervision of Sir G. Gilbert Scott, the Minster underwent a thorough restoration from 1866–1880.

St. Mary's Church

almost rivals the Minster in dimensions and in beauty of architecture. It is situated in the north part of the town, about half a mile from the Minster. It was founded in the twelfth century, and was primarily the church of the Guilds and Freemen. The only visible remains of the Norman church are the plinths of its external buttresses, seen in the chancel, the interior arch of the doorway to the south porch, and the zigzag ornament over the arcade in the north transept. In the second quarter of the thirteenth century the nave was rebuilt with aisles, and the chancel was extended to its present length. These additions involved cutting arches through the walls supporting the tower, which so weakened it, that, in 1520, the upper part of the tower fell on the nave, killing a number of the worshippers.

The wooden ceilings of the various parts of the church, which have been restored and repainted, are of considerable interest and display a great variety of interesting bosses.

The north arcade bears on each pillar interesting tablets regarding the donors with figures which may well be actual portraits in stone.

The eastern pillar of the north arcade is known as the Minstrels' Pillar. It has on one side five coloured figures of minstrels with their instruments. It was constructed by the Guild of Minstrels operating between Trent and Tweed, which met annually at Beverley to choose an Alderman.

The North Chapel, now set aside as a vestry, has a newly restored gilt and coloured roof which is a particularly fine reproduction of early sixteenth-century woodwork. It contains many interesting bosses. On one is a fox in a pulpit preaching to geese; on another a miller on horseback. The roof of the chancel contains forty representations of the Kings of England. To complete the required number, some legendary monarchs, such as Brutus and Lud, have been included, for the latest king of the series is Henry VI, in whose reign the work was done. The ceilings of the nave and chancel have been restored. The stalls in the choir are of early fifteenth-century work. In the string course above the north arcade of the chancel is the unusual nail-head ornament which has been called "the Beverley stud-moulding". The eastern portion of the north aisle of the choir consists of St. Michael's Chapel, "the crowning glory of the church, a masterpiece of English Gothic architecture, carried out in miniature". Above this chapel and the adjoining chantry chapel is an upper storey that now serves as a museum and contains the stocks, pillory and other interesting relics. The seventeenth-century parish library is housed in the south transept in a display cabinet incorporating parts of fifteenth-century oak screen-work. The church plate includes two sixteenth-century chalices, also silver chalices and a flagon of the seventeenth century.

Bridlington

Banks. – *National Westminster, Midland, York County,* King Street; *Barclays* and *Lloyds* in Manor Street; *Yorkshire* in Queen Street.

Bathing. – Extensive sandy beaches. Tents for hire. Modern swimming pool.

Boating. – Steamer, motor-launch and speedboat trips from the harbour, and rowing boats may be hired.

Boating Pools: Model yacht pools on Princess Mary Promenade and in Beaconsfield Gardens. Motor-boat pool at the Spa.

Bowls. – Crown greens in Duke's Park Recreation Ground, off Quay Road. Also at Sewerby Park, Avenue Park (old Town); Beaconsfield and South Marine Drive.

Buses. – Buses link Bridlington with Flamborough, Filey, Scarborough, Hornsea, Driffield, Beverley, York and Leeds, etc. *Bus Stations:* Promenade.

Caravan Sites. – There are a number of sites available at which fully furnished caravans may be hired. Application should be made to the respective managers at: *Marton Road Camp; Limekiln Lane Camp; Shirley Camp,* Jewison Lane, Sewerby. The Corporation maintain a site on South Cliff for private caravans: application for space to Town Hall.

Cinema. – *Winter Gardens,* Promenade.

Distances. – Filey, 11; Hornsea, 15; York, 41; Hull, 19; Scarborough, 18; London, 221.

Early Closing. – Thursday.

Entertainments. – Dancing at the Spa Royal Hall most weekday evenings. Annual International Dance Festival and Championships held in June at Spa Royal Hall. Wrestling. Dancing also at Burton's Buildings; Baron's Studio. Stage plays at the Spa Theatre. Daily concerts at the Floral Pavilion, Royal Prince's Parade. certs. Daily concerts at the Floral Pavilion, Royal Prince's Parade.

Fishing. – First-class facilities available throughout the year from South Pier, beaches and boats. From North Pier in winter only.

An annual Fishing Festival is held about the middle of September. Particulars from the Information Bureau, Garrison Street.

Freshwater fishing at Driffield Beck, Leven Canal and Hornsea Mere. Season: June to February.

Golf. – The 18-hole course of the *Belvedere Golf Club* is situated close to the South Cliff and adjacent to Kingsgate. There are numerous competitions open to visitors. Sunday play. There is a delightfully situated 12-hole course in Sewerby Park, and an 18-hole course at Flamborough Head.

Hotels. – *Expanse,* North Marine Drive; *Brockton,* Shaftesbury Road; *Spa,* South Marine Drive; *Southcliffe,* South Marine Drive; *Shirley,* South Marine Drive; *Alexandra,* Sewerby Terrace; *Heatherlands,* South Marine Drive; *Regent,* North Marine Drive; *Wyngrove,* South Marine Drive; *Revelstoke,* Promenade; *Monarch,* South Marine Drive; *Ryburn,* Flamborough Road; *Shellbourne,* Summerfield Road; *Gainsborough,* South Marine Drive; and many others.

Information Bureau. – Garrison Street.

Library. – King Street.

Market Days. – Wednesday and Saturday. The market is in King Street.

Museum. – At the Bayle Gate.

Parks. – *Sewerby Park* – with its golf course, putting and bowling greens, archery, croquet and a well-stocked aviary. *Duke's Park* – cricket, putting, tennis and recreation grounds. *Avenue Park* – bowls, tennis, putting; and *Queen's Park.*

Population. – 26,370.

Postal. – Head Post Office, Quay Road. There are other offices in Princess Street and High Street, Old Town.

Sailing. – Excellent facilities for private yachts. For many years Bridlington has been the racing centre of the *Royal Yorkshire Yacht Club.* The Club's Annual Regatta is held usually in August.

Steamer Excursions. – Regular summer trips around Flamborough Head.

Tennis. – Duke's Park Recreation Ground. Entrances from Quay Road, Victoria Road and Trinity Road. Avenue Park Recreation Ground, Westgate.

There are excellent facilities for horse-riding, cricket, croquet, archery, rifle-shooting, etc.

Bridlington, like many another ancient town, has its older part a mile inland and its modern offshoot by the sea. It is still quite usual to refer to the latter as the "Quay". The railway station is about midway between the two portions, a long thoroughfare known as Quay Road and St. John Street connecting them.

The **Royal Prince's Parade** overlooks a coast which suffers constant erosion. The elaborate series of sea-defences sweeps northward, under various names and at varying levels for a considerable distance towards Flamborough. In places two or more promenades run side by side, shelters being built below the higher one; elsewhere the walks are divided by colourful flower-beds. The walk to the end of the promenade and on to Sewerby, with its parks, is one of continual interest.

In the **Floral Pavilion** orchestral concerts take place daily during the season. The gardens contain a Floral Clock. Overlooking the Parade is the **3 B.s Theatre Bar** used for concerts, revues, etc.

The 3 B's Theatre Bar stands between the Royal Prince's Parade and the Promenade which runs parallel to the sea and is the widest and straightest thoroughfare in Bridlington. Here are shops, cinemas and other entertainment.

Holy Trinity Church, the spire of which shows up so prominently, stands at the far end of the Promenade, where the Flamborough Road turns inland towards the railway. The church dates from 1871.

The North Sands. Bridlington Sands, like all those on this coast, are firm and extensive. There are no rocks; and tidal currents are practically unknown. Both the north and south sands are swept by the tide right up to the sea wall and as a result the beaches are clean and form an excellent natural playground.

The **Harbour** divides the north and south sands of Bridlington and is formed by two substantial stone piers, the space enclosed being about twelve acres. Being tidal, the harbour is not so much used as it would otherwise be, but it provides useful shelter in foul weather and during northerly gales. In fact, a number of coasting vessels and yachts are generally moored within. The Harbour is kept free from silt by a stream of spring water, known as the *Gypsey Race*, which rises north-westward near Wold Newton and flows to the town through Rudston and Boynton. In the centre of the harbour basin is an *Ebbing and Flowing Well* of fresh water. The water begins to flow when the level of the tide has reached to within four feet of shore and continues till the tide has ebbed to the same level.

The **North Pier,** 670 ft. long and from 25 to 30 ft. wide, dates from 1818. The **South Pier,** over a quarter of a mile long, is a favourite resort for amateur fishermen.

South of the harbour is the **Spa** where one can enjoy good music and entertainment while sitting in full view of the bay and the harbour entrance, where there is a never-ending movement of yachts and small boats.

The **Spa Royal Hall** is a magnificent concert hall and ballroom. Daily amusements are provided during the season, and there are often special shows featuring famous stars of the entertainment world.

At the **Spa Theatre,** adjoining, are staged dramatic and music hall presentations.

Opposite the Spa entrance are the **Pembroke Gardens** and the **Yorkshire Yacht Club House,** as distinct from the Royal Yorkshire Yacht Club which

In Bridlington Harbour

is slightly nearer the harbour, and adjoining is the **Lifeboat House,** generally open for inspection.

The **South Marine Drive,** which starts near the principal entrance to the Spa, runs southward until, at Kingston Road, its line is continued by the **Belvedere Parade.**

The **South Sands** are equal to those north of the Harbour. They are as firm, level and clean, as safe and pleasant for bathing and boating, and as safe a playground for children, who have here their "corner" with its donkeys, suntraps, and other attractions. There are deck-chairs and tents for hire, and various stalls supply refreshments, etc.

Immediately north of the railway, close to the Quay Road level-crossing, is the **Dukes Park Recreation Ground.** Here cricket and lawn tennis players are provided for and there are bowling greens. If we follow Quay Road inland from the crossing we at once have on our left the **Town Hall.** We pass the **Lloyd Hospital,** and arrive at St. John's Avenue, which goes off to the left and would also take us to the vicinity of **Bridlington School,** founded in the reign of Henry VI (1422–61) and revived in 1899.

Continuing along Quay Road, we soon pass the **Baptist Chapel,** notable because the church fellowship is the oldest but one in Yorkshire, having been formed in 1698. The old Chapel, restored by the Corporation, is in Applegarth Lane, near the Priory Church.

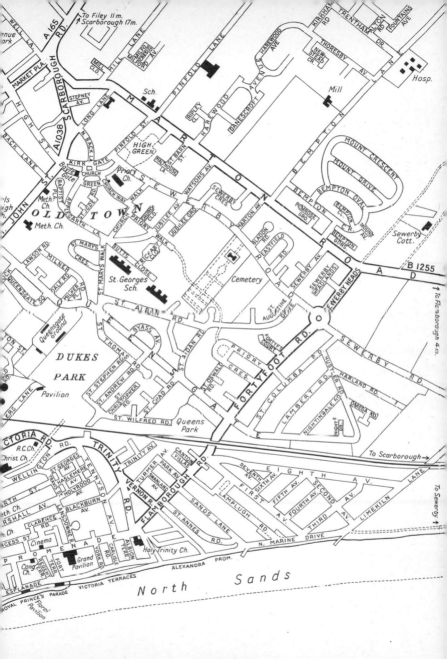

Sewerby

A short bus ride, a pleasant walk northward along the cliff-top or a saunter along the beach and up the concrete steps brings one to **Sewerby Hall** and **Park** *(admission charge)*.

Owned by Bridlington Corporation, the fine Georgian mansion is now in use as a restaurant, where meals may be enjoyed in the beautiful old rooms. An art gallery on the first floor displays a number of exhibitions throughout the season. In a separate room is a collection of trophies and awards of the pioneer airwoman Amy Johnson. Surrounding the house are forty acres of lawns, ornamental gardens and fine parkland. Close to the main entrance gate is an enclosure with wallabies and Formosan deer. There is a small zoo *(admission charge)* and an attractive aviary, as well as a "Pet's Corner". The deck-chairs are free, there is a car park, cafés and a milk bar. The excellent sports facilities include archery butts, putting greens, a crown bowling-green and croquet lawn. In addition there is a 12-hole golf course. The Children's Corner provides roundabouts, swings, and a model traffic layout.

The Danes' Dyke Estate and the Flamborough Head Estate adjoin the Sewerby Park.

At Danes' Dyke are attractive woodland walks while a road to the beach provides a route for cars to the water's edge. From Danes' Dyke are pleasant walks to Flamborough Head either along the cliff top or by the road.

The Old Town

Old Bridlington has the characteristics of a market town and some resemblance to a cathedral city. Its narrow High Street and the dignified, shuttered residences and bow-fronted shops which abut on it are by no means without charm.

Bridlington for more than two centuries has enjoyed a curious kind of self-government. Charles I granted a charter, establishing a sort of corporation, known as "Lords Feoffees", with control over market tolls and other matters. This body consisted, and still consists, of twenty-five freeholders, thirteen being called lords, and twelve assistant lords. They hold office for life, annually electing from among themselves a kind of mayor, who bears the title of Chief Lord. Until 1863 the Lords Feoffees had the general control of public matters.

The Priory

The manor belonged to the Earl of Morcar. The Conqueror, however, bestowed it on one of his friends, Gilvert de Gant (or Gaunt), whose son Walter, in 1113 founded the priory for canons of the order of St. Augustine. Successive endowments rendered the monastery one of the most powerful and wealthy religious establishments in the north. John de Bridlington (1366–79), the most famous of the thirty-one priors, was so renowned for sanctity and learning that at his death he was canonized, his grave behind the high altar being resorted to as a shrine, where miracles might be confidently expected. The stately pile appears from the earliest times to have been the home of persons of distinction. It was the Alma Mater of William de Newburgh, the monkish historian; of Robert the Scribe, whose works are enumerated by Leland; of William of Longtoft, the author of a *Chronicle of England* in French verse; of Sir George Ripley, the alchemist; and

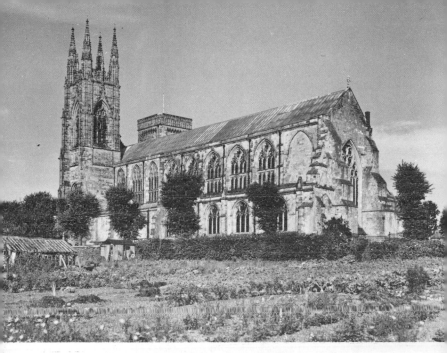

Bridlington Priory

many others. The last prior, William Wode, was executed at Tyburn in 1537 for his share in the Pilgrimage of Grace.

So, for four centuries, the Priory increased in importance and in riches; but the end came with the Dissolution in 1539, its great possessions probably assisting its downfall. The stately priory buildings were all razed to the ground. Had not the nave been set apart as a parish church it would, no doubt, have shared the fate of other portions. As it is, the only parts of the monastery now in existence are the Church and –

The Bayle

This stands some hundred yards away from the entrance to Kirkgate and Baylegate. It was the original gate-house of the monastery. In addition to the main gate, there is a small postern. The three "B's" on the shield on the west side are the arms of the Priory, incorporated in the present arms of the town and are generally taken to be the initial letter of Bridlington repeated three times. (The monks were fond of threes, as symbolical of the Trinity. Whitby Abbey had three ammonites, Fountains Abbey three horseshoes, Selby and St. Mary's at York three swans, and Kirkstall Abbey, Leeds, three swords.) The arch is a good specimen of fourteenth-century architecture.

In the Bayle is a **Museum of Antiquities** *(Thursdays* 2.30–4.00, *or by appointment, fee)*. The collection includes prints, drawings and paintings of the Priory, harbour and town, ships' models, old implements and an important collection of Valentines and spectacles.

Leaving the gateway, we cross the close-like Green to –

The Priory Church. The Church is dedicated to St. Mary, as was the Priory of which it formed part. For a long time after the Dissolution the Church was scandalously neglected, but a restoration, under Sir G. Gilbert Scott, extending over a period of thirty years (1850–80), left us the present imposing edifice.

The **West Front,** with its rich window and profuse decoration, is the most imposing portion of the exterior. The north-western tower, with its plain, flat-topped parapet, is in the Early English style. The intended spire was never added. The other tower with its crocketed pinnacles, forms one of the most attractive features of the edifice. It has a fine peal of eight bells.

The **West Window,** by Wailes, is one of the largest and finest Perpendicular windows erected in England during the last three hundred years.

At the other end is a Jesse window, containing thirty faces. The windows on the north side of the church are beautiful specimens of the Early English style. The windows on the south side, are all of very early type, their tracery consisting of combinations of trefoils and quatrefoils.

The parapet is ornamented by a border of unusual design, which is continued round the top of the north-west tower. The North Porch is a splendid specimen of architecture with fine mouldings.

The proportions of the interior of the church are very striking. The nave is divided from the aisles by ten noble arches and the chancel is formed by enclosing three of the bays. The clustered pillars of the arches are extremely fine.

At the west end of the north aisle are two sections of the cloister arcade, dating from the last quarter of the twelfth century and one of the most beautiful things of its kind and date which we now possess in this country.

In a case at the west end are various ancient books, and the gravestone of Walter de Gaunt. The upper part exhibits an elaborate architectural design, with the figures of two wyverns in fighting attitude; below them is a vase, with a fox on one side and a goose on the other. The lower part of the stone contains a representation of a cat or a lion rampant, crosswise on the stone.

Flamborough

Distances. – Bridlington to Flamborough Village by road, 5 miles; by cliff path, 4 miles. Flamborough Village to North Landing, 1¼ miles; to Lighthouse, 2 miles; to South house, by cliff path, 1½ miles.
Hotels. – Ship; Rose and Crown; Thornwick; Thornwick Bay; Sea Birds; North Star; Dog and Duck.

Flamborough, the fascinating and ever-changing capital of what is often called "Little Denmark", is well known to all Yorkshiremen and visitors from many parts of the country. In winter it is grey, grim and wind-swept with angry waves pounding ceaselessly against the foot of the towering white cliffs, or shrouded in fog and silence, except for the drone of a siren warning shipping of the dangerous headland. Springtime brings the clear bracing air and primroses and gorse bloom resplendent amid the soft green grass that caps the white cliffs. Far out to sea, coasters pass, signalling to the coastguard station.

The headland is practically cut off by –

Danes' Dyke

an immense grass-grown entrenchment, extending for about 2½ miles from the south to the north shore of the promontory and completely severing from the mainland an area of about 5 square miles. Some people have favoured the opinion that the entrenchment was the work of the Danes, others that the Brigantes, the Celtic tribe which formerly peopled Yorkshire, were responsible for it.

Danes' Dyke attracts visitors by its beautiful woodland walks and a perfect picnic beach.

Flamborough

On the whole, the visitor will do best not to stop at Flamborough itself on the outward journey, but to proceed at once to the North Landing and devote any spare time he may have at the end of the day to an inspection of the village and the church. There are small hotels in the village and near the North Landing are the *Old Thornwick*, *North Star* and *Thornwick Hotels*.

The North Landing

Flamborough Head, bare, bleak, precipitous and forbidding, is at no pains to conceal the fact that it does not exist for the encouragement of seafarers.

Flamborough Head

But man, ingenious and determined, has contrived from the earliest dawn of history to make use of two "landings" even on inhospitable Flamborough. Of these the North is by far the more important.

It was here, according to the story, that Robin Lythe, the pretty baby boy and embryo smuggler, was found and adopted by the kindly fisherfolk; and at low water one may walk out to **Robin Lythe's Cave,** on the right-hand side of the Landing as one faces the sea. This is the principal of the many caves in the headland, the central part of the roof being nearly 50 ft. high.

On the other side of the precarious "landing" one can scramble at low water through cloister-like pillars and arches; and from the scars at the seaward end of the cliff the amateur fisherman may cast his line with every chance of success.

Many of the caves are only to be seen from a boat. The cliffs gain much in dignity and height when seen from below.

Briefly, the objects to be seen to the south on leaving the North Landing are the seaward entrance to Robin Lythe's Cave; the King and Queen Rocks, only the latter of which remains standing, and around which, when the wind is in certain quarters, the breakers dash with uncontrolled fury; the Breil Cave, which can be entered only at low tide; St. George's Hole, just under Breil Point, which can sometimes be entered at high tide; the Eve Rock, in Selwicks Bay and lastly, near the fog-signal station, the Common Hole, the Dovecot, or Pigeon-Hole, and the Kirk Hole. What a happy hunting ground for smugglers this coast must have been in days of old, and how small a chance could the revenue officers have stood against men who knew every nook and corner in the honeycombed headland!

To the north of the Landing, in the direction of Thornwick Bay, are the Church Cave and the Smugglers' Caves. It is worth while to land here if tide and weather permit. The interior of the caves is like marble, dazzlingly white, but veined here and there with rich colours.

The Flamborough lifeboat "Friendly Forester" is stationed at the North Landing. Originally there were two stations at Flamborough but that at South Landing was closed in 1938.

The Flamborough Fisheries. The principal season begins about the middle of October. The fishing is of the long-line variety. There are no drifters, no trawlers. The fish mostly caught are cod: but haddock, ling, skate, etc., are common. Crab-fishing by means of pots lasts from Easter to July, or even later. The herring-fishery is now a thing of the past. The fishermen often sell their catches on the beach to local dealers, who have the fish packed and conveyed to the station.

But the North Landing, after all, is only a small part of Flamborough. From the head of the Landing, where the road ends amid a clutter of bungalows, caravans and cafés (the steep road down to the Landing is *not* for cars), there are footpaths along the top of the cliff on either side. That to the left leads to Thornwick Bay, Bempton, and Speeton (see page 31) but there is not time to go in both directions in a single visit. We will assume, therefore, that the southward path is taken.

North Landing to the Lighthouse

This walk of a mile and a half would be hard to beat anywhere on the Yorkshire coast. The cliffs, from a hundred and fifty to two hundred feet above the sea, are broken into a succession of charming little bays and inlets, necessitating many deviations of the path.

The **Lighthouse**, 92 ft. high and 214 ft. above sea-level, stands some way back from the extreme point. It was built in 1806 by John Matson, a Bridlington builder, who used no scaffolding and completed his work in nine months. The light is visible for 21 miles and shows itself in groups of four flashes every fifteen seconds. Previous to its erection in 1806 the wrecks averaged five a year. Even now casualties occur and the lifeboat at the North Landing is often called out. In foggy weather the siren emits two blasts of two seconds every $1\frac{1}{2}$ minutes. The tiny bay below the lighthouse is guarded by the sentinel-like **Eve Rock.** Visitors may view the lighthouse on weekday afternoons (except when the fog-signal is sounding).

Close to the lighthouse is the memorial to the battle off Flamborough Head between the American and British forces in 1779. The memorial takes the form of a bronze plaque and also a toposcope – a squat concrete column inset with local cobblestones with a brass plate on the top showing compass points and distances to places and countries across the North Sea or along the coastline.

Not far away is **H.M. Coastguards' Station,** a very interesting and important establishment. A constant visual and radio watch on shipping is maintained. It is also the Coastguard Rescue Headquarters for the Flamborough district. The lofty four-storeyed, hexagonal Tower that forms a landmark only less prominent than the lighthouse was probably built as a beacon lighthouse about 1673. It is now in dis-repair and not safe to ascend.

The South Landing

resembles the North in many respects, although the cliffs are lower and the situation less striking. The outlook over the Bay is good, and the views of Bridlington decidedly pleasing.

North Landing, Flamborough

Flamborough Village

is chiefly inhabited by a small fishing and agricultural community. In recent years a number of houses, some of which are let as apartments in summer, have been built. Some of the farms also provide accommodation.

The population of the whole headland is only about eighteen hundred, of which about fourteen hundred live in the village.

Flamborough Church, dedicated to St. Oswald, was restored in 1864–69. Most of the church belongs to the thirteenth century, but there are traces of older work.

The nave arches are of the thirteenth century, the first church being a single aisle, which accounts for the "Leper Squint", on the north side of the pulpit, now being inside the church. The chancel arch and the font also are Norman. The oak rood screen is of great historical interest. It was at one time elaborately painted and gilded. Within the Communion rail is an ancient inscribed brass to the memory of Sir Marmaduke Constable, who, at the age of seventy, fought at the stricken field of Flodden. Interesting recent additions are the Flamborough Book of Service, depicting the various Services of the recent war, and a bronze sanctuary lamp. During the church repairs in 1969 a medieval window was discovered at the west end of the north aisle. This in fact is the oldest window in the church. It is filled with clear glass with leaded lights in the form of a viking ship.

From that part of the churchyard, separated from the church by a road, there may be seen the ruins of an ancient –

Keep or Tower

frequently spoken of as the "Danish Tower". In the year 1326, Sir Marmaduke obtained authority from Edward III to crenellate (fortify) his manor-house at Flaynburgh, and this was probably the place referred to.

A little further on and close to the Post Office is the red **Fishermen's Memorial.** This commemorates three fishermen drowned in 1909 in an unsuccessful attempt to save the crew of a fishing coble wrecked in a gale.

Flamborough to Bempton and Speeton. – Instead of turning towards the Lighthouse from the North Landing by the route described on page 29 take the cliff path in the other direction, northward. After descending a small ravine, ascending on the opposite side, and then crossing a headland, we are faced with one of the grandest views to be had on this wild and broken coast. Two hundred feet or more below is **Thornwick Bay.** Then comes Little Thornwick Bay, with its massive overhanging rocks, backed by the straight walls of Bempton and Speeton Cliffs. Good walkers should continue by the path along the edge of the cliffs for 2 or 3 miles to the **Bempton** and **Speeton Cliffs.** In spring thousands of sea-birds line the cliffs for miles. It is a common impression that the cliffs on this part of the coast reach their loftiest altitude at Flamborough Head, but this is not so. The culminating point is an immense, nearly perpendicular precipice near Bempton, upwards of 400 feet high. From this point the cliff slopes downward, until at Flamborough Head the height is only 150 feet.

Bempton *(see page 39)*, which with its station stands about a mile inland, and almost due north of Flamborough village, has a Norman and Decorated church, rebuilt in 1829. It possesses a fine Early English font. Near by on the Speeton–Flamborough road is **Buckton Hall.** This old family mansion has associations with many eminent men.

31

Walks and Drives around Bridlington

To Boynton and Carnaby. From the Old Town to Boynton is a straight road of less than 3 miles. About a mile from Old Bridlington is the tiny hamlet of **Easton,** interesting on account of its connection with Charlotte Brontë, who stayed here on several occasions.

Just beyond Easton, on the left, is a stone lodge with red tiles. Here a public footpath will be seen leading near the delightful park surrounding **Boynton Hall** *(open by appointment)* long the home of the Strickland family, a Tudor-style red-brick mansion.

Close to the park gate is the **Church,** an excellent and unspoiled example of the Classical style. The nave and chancel were built in the eighteenth century (1769), the handsome tower in the fifteenth.

Turning off opposite the church and vicarage is a bridle-path to Carnaby. This leads past the west side of the Hall over the stream and through the beautifully wooded groves. The path presently reaches a road. Beyond the gateway opposite, the path leads past Carnaby Temple to **Carnaby.**

The church tower is very similar to the one at Boynton. Here, however, is a good south arcade and aisle with twelfth-century windows. The font, like so many in this part of the country, also belongs to the twelfth century.

The main road from Carnaby to Bridlington passes on the right the hamlet of **Bessingby.** Two side-tracks lead to the village. Bessingby Hall is a finely situated mansion, sheltered on north and east by trees.

To Rudston and Burton Agnes. This is a popular drive, the round being about 18 miles. Generally speaking, this excursion is simply an extension of that above, the first and last portions of the journey being the same.

Rudston is noted for the prehistoric Monolith in its churchyard. This huge block of moorland grit is 29 ft. high, and about the same length underground and is computed to weigh about forty-six tons. It is of glacial origin and was probably deposited on the valley by a melting glacier, to be subsequently erected on the hill. The name of the village is possibly derived from the stone.

The **Church,** amid a circular churchyard, stands on the brow of the hill, and, though mainly Decorated in style, has a Norman tower. The building was restored and in part rebuilt in 1861. The twelfth-century font is enriched with curious diaper-work.

Winifred Holtby, the Yorkshire novelist, is buried in the churchyard.

A short distance to the west, on the Kilham road, the site of a *Roman Villa* was discovered in 1933. During excavations a Roman workshop, a hypocaust and remarkably fine tessellated pavements were uncovered. They were subsequently removed to Hull Museum.

Burton Agnes, 5½ miles south-west of Bridlington, is the prettiest village in the district.

Burton Agnes Hall *(open May to mid-October daily, Saturdays excepted. Also Easter Monday and Saturdays by appointment. Charge. Free car park. Teas).* There is a bus stop (half-hourly services from Bridlington and Driffield) about 200 yards from the Hall. The Hall, the seat of the Boynton family, is a fine example of late Elizabethan architecture, dating from 1600, with an addition made by Inigo Jones in 1628. It is entered by a stately gate-house bearing the arms of James I. Within is a fine collection of old and modern pictures, antique furniture, beautifully carved ceilings and overmantels in oak, stone and plaster.

West of the present building are the remains of the old Hall, a Norman manor-house built about 1170. This is now in the care of the Department of the Environment. Nearby is the church, which has been much restored, but is probably of Norman foundation. There are interesting tombs in the North Chapel.

Harpham lies half a mile south-west of Burton Agnes. This ancient place was, in the seventh century, the birthplace of St. John of Beverley, to whom the church is dedicated.

The **Church** has a massive square fourteenth-century tower, surmounted by pinnacles. The windows of the Lady Chapel display a pedigree in stained glass, including 28 knights and baronets (the latter dignity was conferred by Charles I) with their arms and those of their wives.

Great Driffield (pop. 7000) is a busy centre on the edge of the wolds. Its church has a high Perpendicular tower.

To Barmston and Skipsea. From the south side of Bridlington a modern road known as Kingsgate leads towards Carnaby Moor, Fraisthorpe, Barmston, and on by the coast towards Hornsea. A favourite walk is by Kingsgate, across the fields to the seaside and sands, and back again to Bridlington by the cliffs, or, when the tide is out, by the sands, which attract thousands of holiday-makers in the summer months.

At **Barmston** are some fine stretches of firm sands, cliff nooks, a caravan park, café and shop, water ski-ing and sailing (East Riding Sailing Club) are popular. There is a frequent bus service to Bridlington.

The **Church,** to the west of the village, is largely fifteenth-century and its walls are constructed of typical East Riding glacial boulders. It has one of the most beautiful Norman fonts in Yorkshire, a squint, and a blocked-up doorway through which the devil and his imps used to be driven by the priest. There is a list of rectors in an unbroken line from 1240.

Barmston succeeded Skipsea as the military capital of East Yorkshire. The castle moat may still be seen. The area covered by the stronghold was very extensive, as can be seen from the scanty remaining traces. In the middle of the fifteenth century a hall, of which a part is still standing, was erected in the fortified enclosure. In the reign of Elizabeth I there was more building, either as an addition to the mansion, erected about 1450, or in substitution of a portion of it. That, too, is standing.

After Barmston comes **Skipsea,** with fine level sands a mile from the village. There is a bus service to Hull and Bridlington. It was important at one time as the seat of the Beveres, Lords of Holderness. The remains of their castle can be traced on a mound (Albemarle Hill) at Skipsea Brough. The ancient Church, Early English and Perpendicular, dates from 1196.

Six miles beyond Skipsea is Hornsea *(see page* 13*)*

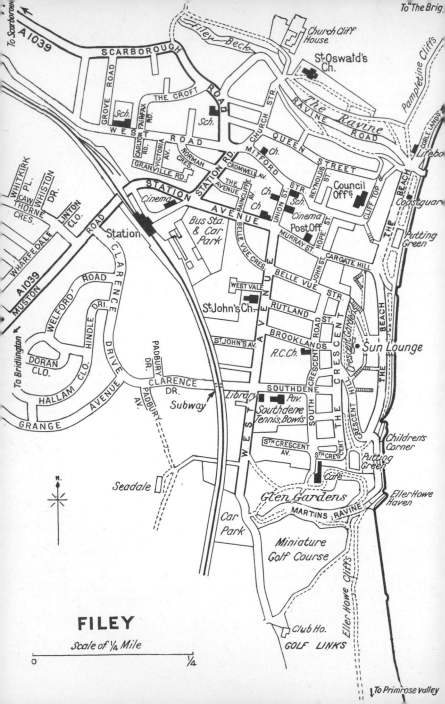

FILEY

Scale of ¼ Mile

Filey

Angling. – From July to the end of September there is good sport from boats, and also from the Brigg. Codfish, coalfish, mackerel and pollock furnish the biggest catches, and dab and gurnard are quite common.

The Angling Festival, held early in September, is perhaps the most important event of this kind on the north-east coast.

Archery. – There are ranges on the Foreshore and in Glen Gardens.

Banks. – *Barclays, Midland, Yorkshire* and *York Trustee Savings Bank*.

Bathing. – Excellent. On the beach with its six miles of sand the water deepens very gradually and there are no holes or currents. Deep water near the Brigg. Beach tents available for hire.

Bowls. – At Southdene.

Buses run between Filey, Bridlington and Scarborough. There are two routes to Scarborough: one via Gristhorpe and Cayton Bay, and the other through the villages of Lebberston and Cayton. Similarly the route to Bridlington may be through Reighton or through Hunmanby and a number of Wold villages.

Caravan Site. – North Cliff.

Cinemas. – *The Grand*; the *Brigg*.

Distances. – Bridlington, 12 miles; Hornsea, 25; Hull, 42; London, 238½; Pickering, via Scarborough, 25; Scarborough, 7½; York, 40.

Early Closing Day. – Wednesday.

Golf. – 18-hole course on cliffs, south of the town, about a mile from the station. There are Putting Greens in the South Crescent Gardens, Glen Gardens and on Foreshore.

Hotels. – *Hyland's*, Crescent; *Southcliffe*, Primrose Valley; *Victoria*, Crescent; *White Lodge*, South Crescent; *Beach*, The Beach; *Foord's*; *Belle Vue*, Crescent; *Three Tuns*, Murray Street; *Downcliffe*, The Beach; *Sea Brink*, Beach; *Southdown*, The Beach; and numerous others.

Population. 5,120.

Post Office. – Murray Street.

Riding. Ponies on the sands, Stables at Hunmanby.

Tennis. – Grass and hard courts in Southdene, at rear of Crescent.

Filey, with its magnificent and safe sands, its cliffs, caves, rocks and pools, is an ideal place for children and for those adults who prefer a quiet yet bracing resort. There are good facilities for bathing, boating, fishing, archery, riding, tennis, golf and bowls, and the town is a splendid centre for walks and numerous excursions.

The greater part of the town stands high above the sea on a somewhat precipitous cliff with a superb outlook over the expansive bay, with the Brigg as northern boundary and the chalk cliffs of Speeton, Bempton and Flamborough Head tapering away south-eastward. Like Bridlington, Filey glories most in her magnificent bay, which has an almost semi-circular sweep, and is girdled by 6 miles of hard, tide-washed sands. There is a children's corner at the south end of the Promenade.

Overlooking the bay on the seaward side of The Crescent are the **Crescent Gardens,** the North and South. The former has a sun lounge where concerts and concert party shows are given daily. The building incorporates a café.

In the South Crescent Gardens there is a putting green. From here there is a fine view of the bay.

Still further south are the **Glen Gardens,** picturesque grounds which include an archery range, a café and motor-boating pool.

Church Ravine. The wooded Ravine, which runs steeply up from the sea at the northern end of the town, contains several sheltered nooks.

St. Oswald's Church. The Parish Church, dedicated to St. Oswald, the patron saint of Northumbrian (or North of the Humber) fishermen, stands just above the Ravine.

The church was granted to the Augustinian Canons of Bridlington by Walter de Gaunt in his foundation charter of the Priory, and was served by clergy appointed by the Canons up to the suppression of the Priory in 1537. The earliest parts of the existing church, the nave and its aisles, were begun towards the end of the twelfth century.

The walls of the nave aisle were originally much lower than they are now, and the aisle roofs were of steeper pitch. The walls were raised to their present height in the thirteenth century.

In the second quarter of the thirteenth century the original chancel and the eastern bay of the nave were taken down to make way for an eastward extension on a much larger scale, consisting of the chancel, the crossing with central tower and the north and south transept.

It is a peculiarity of the church that the chancel is on a lower level than the nave. This is a feature found in very few churches.

The clock is the work of that famous timepiece-maker, James Harrison, immortalized by Byron.

The massive church tower is appropriately surmounted by a weather-fish, if the word may be used, instead of the conventional cock.

The **Roman Catholic Church** stands at the junction of Brooklands and Crescent Road. It is a small but remarkable building erected in the style of the earliest basilicas. Outside, it is a plain but striking little church, with its tower of antique pattern, buttresses adorned with monograms, and a mosaic on the east end. The M. R. on the flat turret is of course an abbreviation of Maria Regina, the church being dedicated to the Virgin Mary. Inside, a baldachino shelters a copy of a sixth-century altar preserved in the Rimini Museum in Italy.

Old Filey

The old fishing quarter of the town, with its queer "yards" and houses, is interesting, and can show some curiosities in the way of street nomenclature. The Ship Inn, now a private residence, had a convenient secret chamber, hollow beams and a secret sliding panel, and immediately in its rear were cottages with mysterious hiding-places.

Charlotte Brontë ("Currer Bell") often stayed at Cliff House, then the most southern house in the town. It is situated in Belle Vue Street, and is now an attractive café with a glass verandah extension hung with grape vine. In her letters the authoress of *Jane Eyre* often mentioned Filey.

Here in Filey the old fishing families still persist, the Camishes, Jenkinsons, Boyntons – the war memorial commemorates many – and still the nicknames of various members of each family are carried on from generation to generation.

The Sands at Filey

Filey Brigg. The Brigg is a great reef of rock jutting out into the sea for nearly a mile, forming a fine natural pier and breakwater. It is a bracing, breezy spot. In rough weather it is a grand sight to watch great waves pounding the rock and forming gigantic fountains of spray. On the north side are caves and deep caverns, around which many tales of smugglers have been woven.

The Brigg is quite dry for several hours on each side of low water, and one can clamber among the great boulders, or explore the pools left by the receding tide. Or one can scramble round the lower edges of the cliff, and note how the sea has scooped great semi-circular openings in the rock, with a deep pool for flooring. The largest of these pools is called the "Emperor's Bath", since it is said a Roman Emperor used it for bathing. There are ledges on which the patient angler can sit, there are sheltered pools for bathers, and there are cosy nooks. Care is necessary in visiting the Brigg in rough weather, and the warning tablet let into the rock by the Paget family should be regarded. At low water the Brigg can be reached by a short walk along the sands, or at high tide by boat. Anglers favour the route along Carr Naze to Pampletine Cliff and descend by means of the cliff ladder. Good fishing can be had at this part of the Brigg.

The cliff path can be followed for some distance in the direction of Cayton Bay, but it entails some rough scrambling, and is not without danger on account of crumbling cliffs. *(But see page* 39.*)*

Jutting out at right angles to the Brigg there have been found some traces of an artificial pier, supposed to be Roman.

The dangerous reefs of the Brigg are marked, for the safety of shipping, by a light-and-whistle buoy giving a white flash every 5 seconds and a whistle operated by the movement in the water.

A Geological Note

To the geologist the cliffs in the neighbourhood of Filey form a rich field for study. The soft clayey cliffs are known as "Speeton Clay", and are in marked contrast to the solid chalk rampart presented by Flamborough Head. Northward of the town another contrast is presented in the shales and sandstones of Gristhorpe Bay.

In a single morning's exploration of the Brigg a party of scientists found no fewer than twenty different kinds of fossils. In many ways Filey Brigg is an interesting field for geological study. It is formed of coralline oolite capped with boulder clay, beautifully weathered by rain. The lower stratum is calcareous grit.

The peculiar weathering of the various kinds of rock in Gristhorpe Bay gives a unique appearance to the landscape, the calcareous grit at the top forming a flat table, and then a long slope of Oxford clay resting on another bed of Oxford clay, which in its turn weathers perpendicularly. At the southern point of Gristhorpe Bay is the celebrated plant bed which occurs in the upper part of the Estuarine series.

View from Filey Brigg

Excursions from Filey

To Gristhorpe and Cayton Bays. Bus to Gristhorpe, or walk or drive for $2\frac{1}{2}$ miles along the Scarborough road *(bus route)*. Another alternative is to follow the cliff-path northward from Filey Brigg. On no account attempt to get from Filey to Gristhorpe by the shore, no matter how low the water may seem. It simply cannot be done, for the cliffs descend sheer into deep water just south of Gristhorpe Bay.

In 1834, a tumulus on Gristhorpe Cliff was opened up. Six feet below the surface was found a great oaken log split with wedges to form a coffin. Within the coffin lay the bones of a six-foot man, with a bronze weapon, bone pin and wrapped in a skin cloak. Five similar burials have been found in Yorkshire. They belong to the period 1750–1500 B.C. The Gristhorpe burial is exhibited in the Scarborough Museum and is famous among archaeologists.

Gristhorpe Bay is worth visiting, on account of its rugged escarpments and boulder-strewn beach. It is a favourite ground for fossil-hunters, ferns and plants being very abundant in the shales. The prominent headland to the north of the bay is **Red Nab** (280 ft.) and at low water this may be rounded by **Cayton Bay,** described on page 55.

To Scarborough. Those who desire to go farther than Cayton Bay in the direction of Scarborough have two alternatives: (a) the high road (3 miles); (b) the cliff path, entering Scarborough by the Holbeck Gardens. It is extremely dangerous to walk along the shore and attempt to round the headlands south of Scarborough.

To Primrose Valley, Bempton and Flamborough. Primrose Valley (*Southcliffe Hotel*), or Mile Haven, 1 mile south of Filey, is well worth the short stroll along the sands, or can be reached by road. It is a spot greatly favoured by picnic parties and campers. There is a car-park, and refreshments can be obtained.
Butlin's Holiday Camp lies to the east of the main Bridlington road and covers 800 acres of cliff-land overlooking Filey Bay. The cliffs here are low, and give access to a great stretch of level beach. There are frequent buses. Non-residents are admitted from 10 a.m. to 6 p.m. *(Saturdays excepted).*
Hunmanby Gap, south of Butlin's Holiday Camp, is easily reached from Filey by the sands (*see* above). Refreshments are obtainable at the Gap and there is a car-park.
From **Bempton** station it is a quarter of a mile to the village. The lane leading to the cliffs goes straight ahead, presently passing between two gates arched by whale ribs. The outlook from the highest part of the cliffs (400 ft.) is grand. To the south brown cliff changes to white and continues to Flamborough, though the Head itself is not visible. Northward one commands the whole sweep of Filey Bay and the coast towards Scarborough.

Speeton Church

From Bempton it is a walk of about 3 miles to the North Landing, crossing the northern termination of the Danes' Dyke.

To Hunmanby. It is a pleasant walk or drive of 4 miles from Filey to **Hunmanby** *(White Swan)*, or the village may be reached by rail or bus. It is situated at the foot of the Wolds, and has become an agricultural and shopping centre of some importance. The imposing Early English-style gateway seen from the railway is the entrance to **Hunmanby Hall,** and dates only from the early part of the last century. It was built of stones taken from Filey Brigg, and the extensive and alarming erosion of the coast during the last century has been attributed in part to such despoiling of the Brigg, which, of course, forms a natural breakwater. The Hall was long the seat of those famous hunting squires, the Osbaldestones. It became a boarding-school for girls in 1928.

The **Church** boasts a Norman tower and chancel arch. The north arcade is twelfth-century. The armorial bearings, so conspicuous, are those of the Mitford and Osbaldestone families, for many generations Lords of the Manor. Noteworthy also are the old headless market cross on the village green, the ancient pinfold (the word "pinfold" means pound for stray cattle) and lock-up, and the cottage architecture.

To Reighton and Speeton. Reighton, 5 miles south of Filey, on the Bridlington road *(bus route)*, has a church dating from the twelfth century, erected on the site of a previous Saxon church. Restorations since 1890 have produced an interior of great charm. The Norman font, in the shape of a Roman altar, with a shaft at each corner and surmounted by scalloped capitals, has sides carved with rich diaper work. Cobblestones from the beach form the floor of the tower. A small mass clock or scratch dial in a fair state of preservation may be seen on the Norman buttress of the south wall of the nave.

Reighton Gap goes right down to the water's edge, and is said to have been the haunt of smugglers. Good bathing. Car-park, caravan site and refreshments.

Half a mile south of Reighton lies the *Dotterel Inn*. The dotterel, formerly, like the great bustard, common on the unenclosed sheepwalks of the Wolds, is now locally extinct.

Two miles further along the Flamborough road is **Speeton,** where the church stands isolated in a field, enclosed in a wall of local stone.

The earlier Saxon church was used by the Danes, and restored by the Normans. The mass clock on the south wall is a good specimen, having thirty-one lines and holes.

To Folkton Brow and Staxton. This is a good drive or walk westward of about 7 miles. The breezy heights of the Wolds afford fine prospects of the surrounding country, and the air is delicious. There are traces of many entrenchments on the heights, and the long barrow on Folkton Wold is famous among students of archaeology. The road lies through **Muston.**

To Sledmere, Kirkham and Castle Howard. If the road route via Hunmanby *(see* above*)* and Weaverthorpe is used this will involve a round trip of some sixty miles.

Sledmere House *(open afternoons in summer, except Monday and Friday; Charge)*, situated on one of the highest points of the Wolds, is the seat of Sir Richard Sykes, Bart. The Georgian house was built in 1751; the gardens and park were designed by "Capability" Brown.

From Sledmere there follows a delightful run to Castle Howard via North Grimston and Langton, crossing the river Derwent at Kirkham.

Kirkham Priory was a house of Augustinian canons and the remains include a fine Decorated gateway, part of the cloister, and fragments of the church. The site is now in the care of the Department of the Environment. *(Standard hours of opening.)*

The Gatehouse, Kirkham Priory

Castle Howard

Castle Howard

Admission charges to house and grounds or to grounds only. Open from Easter to early October, every afternoon except Mondays and Fridays.

"A palace, a town, a fortified city . . ." so Horace Walpole described Castle Howard, second only to Blenheim in size among Vanbrugh's creations, and his first building. This magnificent house, containing fine tapestries, furniture, and pictures by Rubens, Gainsborough, Reynolds and others, should on no account be missed by visitors to this part of Yorkshire.

Castle Howard was begun in 1701 and was still building at Vanbrugh's death in 1726. The Park, mostly bounded by a wall, covers over 1,000 acres. There is a lake of some 70 acres in which bathing and fishing are permitted.

The Mausoleum and the Pyramid are by Hawksmoor, Vanbrugh's co-architect. The Temple of the Four Winds is by Vanbrugh himself, and the fine stable block (1781–4) is by John Carr of York. In the stables is the Costume Museum.

The return journey is usually made via **Malton,** a market town on the west bank of the *Derwent*. Its site was occupied by the Romans, of whose presence many traces are preserved in the local museum. On part of the site of the Roman fort a Norman castle once existed. There are two churches, St. Michael's and St. Leonard's. Each has a Norman arcade.

Green fields separate New Malton from **Old Malton,** a quiet village 1 mile north-east. Its parish church consists of a portion of the nave of a Gilbertine Priory, founded between 1147 and 1154. Only one of the two west towers is standing.

From Malton the return route is along the York-Scarborough road through Sherburn and Ganton.

Scarborough

Angling. – The **Mere** (23 acres) is the property of the Corporation of Scarborough but the fishing is controlled by the *Mere Angling Club*, who issue day and evening tickets from the Boathouse or Bailiff. Coarse fish are abundant – roach, perch, bream, tench and pike with an occasional carp. Fishing from the bank only, early morning and late evening being the best times. Frequent bus service.

An Open Peg-down Match is held on the last Sunday of the Angling Festival.

Within easy reach of Scarborough are numerous streams where good trout and grayling fishing may be had.

An International bait and fly-casting competition is held each year at the Mere during September.

Banks. – *Lloyds, Midland, Barclays, National Westminster, York County, Yorkshire.*

Bathing. – Good bathing from beach. Three bathing pools. It is dangerous to bathe in certain parts when the sea is rough, there being a strong undercurrent at such times. Red flags are flown when bathing is unsafe.

Overlooking the Valley Gardens, in their own pleasant grounds, are the **Municipal Medical Baths**, including provision for electrical treatments, Aix and Vichy Douches, a Needle Bath and Turkish Baths. There is a café.

Boating. – Motor, rowing, and sailing-boats can be hired in both bays. There is safe boating on the Mere and on the Peasholm Park Lake.

The *Rowing Club* has its headquarters on the Foreshore Road, and members of recognized rowing clubs are welcomed as visitors.

The *Yacht Club* headquarters are on the Lighthouse Pier. The *Model Yacht Sailing Club* at the Mere.

From the Lighthouse Pier there are sea trips daily. Pleasure craft provide short excursions along the coast.

Bowls. – Crown greens at Alexandra Gardens and Manor Road Recreation Ground. Flat greens at Seacliff Gardens and South Cliff Bowling Club. Beginning in June, and with the Finals in early September, the tournament for the Gambart Baines Challenge Cup attracts competitors from all parts of Britain.

Buses afford speedy access to all parts of the town, and there are connections with all places of interest and centres in the district.

Cliff Tramways. – The *Central Tramway* is between the Grand Hotel and the St. Nicholas Gardens. The *South Cliff Tramway* is at the southern end of the Spa grounds. The *St. Nicholas Tramway* is near the southern end of the Grand Hotel. *North Bay Cliff Lift* is near the Corner Café.

Cinemas. – *Capitol,* Albemarle Crescent; *Odeon,* Westborough; *Futurist,* Foreshore Road; *Olympia,* Foreshore Road.

Distances. – Ayton, 5 miles; Bridlington, 18; Castle Howard, 27; Cayton, 4; Filey, 7½; Flamborough, 19; Forge Valley, 4½; Hackness, 5; Hunmanby, 9; Kirkham Abbey, 27; Pickering, 18; Ravenscar (Peak), 10½; Rievaulx Abbey, 34; Robin Hood's Bay, 14; Sledmere, 18; Thornton Dale, 16; Whitby, 21.

London, 230; Edinburgh, 227; York, 42; Newcastle, 89; Manchester, 109; Birmingham, 162.

Early Closing. – Wednesday.

Entertainments. – Plays at the Library Theatre; various productions at the Open-air Theatre; all-star variety and musical shows at Floral Hall, Futurist and Spa Theatre; band concerts at Peasholm Park; dancing in Spa Ocean Room, galas and fireworks in Northstead Manor Gardens on Wednesday evenings.

Golf. The links of the *South Cliff Golf Club* (18 holes) are situated near Oliver's Mount, astride the Filey Road, about a mile and a quarter from the station.

The course of the *North Cliff Golf Club* occupies an ideal site overlooking the North Bay.

Hotels. – *Royal,* St. Nicholas Street; *Grand,* St. Nicholas Cliff; *Crown,* Esplanade; *Park Manor,* Northstead Manor Drive; *Southlands,* West Street; *Prince of Wales,* Esplanade; *Castle,* Queen Street; *Villa Esplanade,* Esplanade; *Bedford,* The Crescent; *Granville,* Esplanade; *Clifton,* Queen's Parade; *Astoria,* Esplanade; *Majestic,* Northstead Manor Drive; *Breece,* West Street; *Carlton,* Belmont Road; *Gibson's,* Queen's Parade; *Elizabethan,* Albion Road; *Brooklands,* Esplanade Gardens; *Esplanade,* Belmont Road; *Fairview and Ann's Garden,* South Cliff; *The Mount,* Cliff Bridge Terrace; *Norbreck,* North Cliff; *Princess Royal,* South Cliff; *Holbeck Hall,* Sea Cliff Road; *Crescent,* Belvoir Terrace; *Riviera,* St. Nicholas Cliff; *Sefton,* Prince of Wales Terrace; *Palm Court,* St. Nicholas Cliff;

St. Nicholas, St. Nicholas Cliff; *Salisbury*, Huntriss Road; *Brunswick Lodge*, Brunswick Terrace; *Central*, The Crescent; *Commodore*, South Cliff; *Cumberland*, Belmont Road; and many others.

Information Centre. – Harcourt Place, St. Nicholas Cliff.

Library. – Vernon Road.

Museums. – The *Scarborough Museum of Regional Archaeology* is in Museum Terrace at the foot of Vernon Road. The *Museum of Natural History*, The Crescent, is at Wood End, *St. Thomas's Museum*, East Sandgate.

Population. – 43,061.

Post Office. – Aberdeen Walk.

Putting. – Clarence Gardens and Royal Albert Drive.

Sea Angling. – Whiting, gurnard, codling, billet and dab are the commonest kinds, but plaice, brill and flounders may also be caught. In summer good sport comes from spinning and float fishing for mackerel, pollock and billet from the Marine Drive and piers or from boats (tackle and bait provided).

The rocky foreshore north and south of the town is one of the finest rock angling grounds in England and the two angling societies hold frequent competitions throughout the year. There is also a Boat Angling Society which admits temporary members.

An angling festival, extending over eight days, is held annually in September.

Tennis, etc. – Public hard courts in Northstead Manor Gardens, Clarence Gardens. At the *Scarborough Lawn Tennis Club* on the Filey Road, 12 grass and 7 hard courts are available. There are two squash courts.

Other Sports. – Motor-cycle road races on Oliver's Mount circuit in June and September. Water ski-ing on the Mere. A yachting regatta is held early in August.

Scarborough first came into prominence as a health and holiday resort late in the seventeenth century. Before that time it was chiefly noteworthy as a fishing port and a refuge in times of storm for coastal sea traffic.

The following summary will give some idea of the various quarters into which the town is now divided.

First, there is the **South Cliff,** a highly favoured, fashionable residential quarter, with many hotels and boarding houses, and for which, on leaving Central station, arrivals should take the first turning on the right and cross the Valley Bridge. **Westborough,** the street in which the Central station stands, is, with its continuations and the streets leading from it, the principal business quarter of the town. A walk of half a mile down Westborough, Newborough and Eastborough brings one to the Harbour, above which nestles the picturesque **Old Town,** the Scarborough of history and the home of the fishers and boatmen. A climb up the hill by any of the streets which run at right angles to Sandside or more directly from the railway station by way of Aberdeen Walk and Castle Road will bring one, after passing near the ancient Parish Church, to the **North Cliff,** with its hotels and boarding-houses and holiday amenities.

The South Bay

Turning right from the Central station, along Valley Bridge Road, a few yards brings us to **The Valley Bridge** which saves a descent to the Valley, a deep ravine which cuts off the South Cliff from the centre and north side. The central portion is about 70 ft. above the road in the Valley Park.

Immediately below the bridge are the **Valley Gardens** one of the beauty-spots of Scarborough. From the west side of the bridge the eye follows the winding paths and the road till they become merged in the town; on the other side the vista is closed by the sea, set in a framework of foliage.

Above the Valley Road, on the left-hand side as one faces the sea, are three fine mansions, the most easterly of which is *Londesborough Lodge*, now the **Municipal Medical Baths Establishment,** equipped for the administration of electrical treatments, Aix and Vichy Douches and Turkish baths. A café is available.

The Sands, Scarborough

The **Art Gallery** occupies the adjoining house. A permanent collection of pictures of local interest is housed here, and there are frequent loan exhibitions. The third house is *Wood End*, formerly the home of the Sitwell family, and which is now open to the public. The main block is used as a natural history museum, the conservatory as a tropical garden and aquarium. The library wing houses a collection of MSS., printed books, portraits, drawings, etc., associated with the Siltwell family.

Easy slopes lead down to the Gardens from the Valley Bridge. Walking seawards, we notice that the ravine is spanned at its commencement by another bridge. This is the **Spa Bridge,** which affords easy access to the South Cliff, but is more generally used in connection with the Spa. Beneath the Spa Bridge is an underground car-park.

The bridge forms the principal entrance, for foot-passengers only, to –

The Spa

The Spa waters are no longer available. The attraction of the Spa, however, chiefly lies on its situation and its social amenities. Set in lovely surroundings, with tree-lined walks, beautiful gardens and promenades overlooking the sea, the Spa offers to visitors a choice of orchestral concerts, stage productions, dancing on a perfect floor, or enjoying the magnificent floral displays, the shops and the cafés. For children there are special shows.

The town owes its present position and popularity in great part to the saline and mineral springs first noted in the seventeenth century. More than seventy years after the discovery of the springs, a cistern covered by a wooden house of primitive construction was erected for the convenience of persons drinking the water. This speedily became a popular morning lounge. The old Spaw House was destroyed by a landslide in 1737, and the waters were for a time lost. In 1739 a new and more pretentious pump-room was erected.

The successive Spa buildings seem to have suffered in turn the catastrophes of landslide, storm and fire. The last building to suffer was that erected in 1839, and transformed and added to by Sir Joseph Paxton in 1858. Paxton's work included a fine music-hall, and the gardens are still much as he designed them. Fire, however, played havoc with the place, the greater part being destroyed in 1876. From designs by Thomas Verity emerged a **Grand Hall**, seating over two thousand persons, with a roomy promenade around it, a gallery of considerable dimensions, and a **Theatre**, where more than seven hundred spectators can be accommodated, and where first-class concert parties perform. In 1913 came a new bandstand, marble forecourt, colonnade and Grand Hall café, and afterwards the Roof Garden, Ballroom, etc. The **Ballroom** (now known as the **Ocean Room**) accommodates fifteen hundred dancers while on the floor below is a café and bar. The Open-air Bandstand has balconies and seats on each side, forming a terrace on which visitors can lounge or promenade while listening to the band and watching the crowd on the lower promenade. In a wing are a number of useful shops.

The stretch of sand immediately under the South Cliff, protected by the wall of the Spa, is commonly known as the **Children's Corner.** A raised promenade runs at the foot of the cliffs between the Spa and the Bathing Pool, forming an irregular wall with many a cosy corner and sheltered nook.

The sands, both in the South and North Bays, though covered at high tide, extend far seaward and are delightfully firm. The tide recedes a considerable distance, but equally at high and low water bathers highly appreciate **The South Bay Bathing Pool** approached from the sands (at low tide), from the Esplanade, and through any of the entrances to the South Cliff Gardens, from which footpaths lead down to the sea, or by way of the Spa Promenade. The pool can accommodate 1,200 bathers at one time and an equal number of spectators. The depth varies from 3 ft. to 6 ft. and there are a diving pit 15 ft. deep and shallow sections reserved for children.

The South Cliff Tramway at the southern end of the Spa grounds is useful both for frequenters of the Spa and persons wishing to reach the South Cliff quarter quickly from the sands. It runs up the face of the cliff, at an incline of about one in three, terminating at a point nearly opposite Prince of Wales Terrace.

There is another cliff tramway near the Grand Hotel, and a third, the Central, between St. Nicholas Gardens and the Grand Hotel.

The South Cliff Gardens consists of a stretch of beautifully wooded undercliff some 19 acres in extent, between the Spa and the Holbeck Gardens. Gently sloping paths lead to and from the **Belvedere Rose Garden,** and connect the high ground with the shore at the point where the beach bungalows, for bathing, etc., are placed. The view from the summit of this part of the cliff, 175 ft. above sea-level, is very fine.

Linked up with the South Cliff Gardens are the pretty **Holbeck Gardens** with an area of about 15 acres, and extending from the top of the cliff nearly down to the sands. Terraced walks have been constructed on the slopes.

At the Esplanade entrance is a massive arched Clock Tower, in classical style, and close by is a public putting green.

The **Italian Gardens** are very attractive.

Red Court Gardens. On the other side of the Esplanade from the Clock Tower of Holbeck Gardens is the rectangular Red Court Garden, sometimes referred to, after its donor, as the Shuttleworth Garden. It is a sunny and secluded spot, with smooth lawns and beds of named varieties of roses. The rock garden is interesting, but the most fascinating part is the miniature rock and water garden.

South of Holbeck Gardens is Wheatcroft Cliff; a pathway running along the top of the cliff forms a boundary for part of the South Cliff Golf Links.

Returning to the Spa area, and going along Albion Road, we come to the Church of **St. Martin's-on-the-Hill,** a beautiful stone building consecrated in 1863. The narthex and last bay of the nave were added in 1879 and the Lady Chapel in 1902. G. F. Bodley, R.A., was the architect and the church is full of the work of his pre-Raphaelite companions, Burne-Jones, William Morris, Rossetti and others.

Leaving the church, turn right into Ramshill Road, and leaving the Valley Bridge on the left, we descend into the valley to

The **Archaeological Museum** *(open weekdays)* occupies a curious rotunda-shaped building dating from 1860. Its collections are devoted to archaeological and historical material relating to the Scarborough district and is arranged in chronological order, one wing of the building being devoted to prehistory and the other to medieval history. The Rotunda Gallery contains relics of later times.

One of the most interesting cases in the Prehistoric Gallery is that containing the finds from the Star Carr area in the vicinity of Seamer and Flixton. This site was first opened up by a local archaeologist, and excavations in 1949–51 disclosed a remarkable mesolithic lakeside camping site, completely preserved by the wet peat bog.

Just south of the Grand Hotel are **St. Nicholas Lift** and a zigzag path which takes the foot-passenger from St. Nicholas Cliff to the Foreshore Road. Near the foot of the lift is a terminal of the bus services to North Bay via Marine Drive and various parts of the town. Past the foot of the lift we reach **Foreshore Road** a busy promenade with restaurants, cafés, snack bars, theatres, and fun shows extending for about half a mile round the curve of the South Sands from the Spa Bridge to the Harbour. It is then continued as Sandside and Marine Drive right round the foot of the Castle Cliff to the North Sands.

The **Central Tramway** runs up St. Nicholas Cliff and places Foreshore Road and its attractions within easy reach of the town centre and the Railway Station.

The **Town Hall** is a handsome Jacobean-style mansion comprising extensions to the former St. Nicholas House. The adjoining **St. Nicholas Gardens** overlook Foreshore Road.

The Harbour

There are three piers or arms, the outer East and West Piers and the Vincent Pier dividing the harbour into two parts. The East Pier extends from the foot of Castle Hill for a distance of 1,380 feet. Many of its stones weigh from 20–30 tons each. The Vincent Pier dates from 1732. From the lantern platform *(fee)* of the lighthouse at its end is a good view of the town.

The **West Pier,** called also the Fish Pier, is 140 ft. wide. Here are a useful Car Park and the offices of the fish merchants and salesmen, and when an auction is in progress the scene is lively.

Very fair rod and line fishing is to be had from the piers, whiting, codling, coalfish, and flatfish being plentiful when the conditions are favourable.

For many centuries Scarborough was an important haven and trading town. It sent ships to the Iceland fisheries. It built cobles, barques, brigs and brigantines. It traded with Russia and the Baltic ports. Coasting vessels called here with general cargo and passengers. The herring fishery was always of considerable importance, especially when the barrels of salted herrings were loaded straight on to German and Russian boats lying alongside the quays. The harbour is still busy with fishing boats, and cargo boats from Baltic ports. It is also a haven for private yachts, motor boats and dinghies. The Scarborough Yacht Club welcomes visitors from other clubs and holds sailing regattas during the summer.

From the Foreshore Road a network of steep and narrow thoroughfares, with stairways in places, leads up the hill between the brick dwellings with red roofs of **The Old Town** lying between the harbours and the green dikes of the Castle. Visitors with time and inclination should certainly inspect some of the quaint courts and streets.

The Foreshore Road is continued by **Sandside,** which may be described as the High Street of this locality. In East Sandgate, a few yards from Sandside, is –

St. Thomas's Museum *(open on weekdays and Sunday afternoons, May to September; in winter on Wednesdays only).* In 1970 the former Church of St. Thomas (the "Fisherman's Church") was opened as this museum for the display of historical material relating to the town.

No. 23 Sandside is labelled **King Richard III Café and Steak House,** a building converted in 1964 for use as a restaurant. Here King Richard may have stayed, once when visiting Scarborough with his fleet, and possibly on other occasions.

This old stone-built high-gabled building is an interesting link with the historic past of Scarborough. Reputed to date in part from 1350, it is but one wing remaining of what has undoubtedly been a fine mansion of considerable size, standing along and dwarfing all the neighbouring houses. When it was restored in 1914, the building was modernised both inside and out.

The ornamental ceiling, of sixteenth-century Italian plaster work, in the top room of the house, is beautifully decorated in high relief, and contains representations of the Rose of York, the Bull of the Nevilles at each corner, and three rabbits placed back to back forming a triangle. In reality they only have three ears among them, yet so skilfully executed is the deception that few persons would notice that they have not two each.

The stone figure of the hunchbacked dwarf near the door outside the building was brought from the neighbourhood of Newark.

Some 150 yards farther is the corner around which one turns to enter the passage where stands the former *Three Mariners Inn*, a reputed haunt of smugglers which has four entrances, including one below ground.

Harbour and Sands, Scarborough

Though no longer an inn the building is open to visitors and contains some fine panelling and carving.

Eastborough is a busy thoroughfare, the continuation of which up Westborough leads directly to the station.

The smaller thoroughfare bearing almost at once to the right is **West Sandgate.** A few steps up it brings one to a relic of great antiquarian interest standing at the corner of a shop opposite the Leeds Hotel. The relic is the shaft of a very ancient cross, at which it was long customary to read all proclamations. It is named the **Butter Cross,** and is frequently mentioned in old Corporation records. The market, too, was formerly held near it, in the neighbouring Princess Street.

Ascending Eastborough which shortly becomes Newborough, we come to **St. Nicholas Street,** on the left, and **Huntriss Row.** No. 14 St. Nicholas Street was built about 1750 and was at one time the mansion of the Bell family. The front is flanked by two fluted Ionic pilasters rising to support a stone entablature.

At the bottom of Huntriss Row is the garden known as **St. Nicholas Cliff.**

Between the upper ends of St. Nicholas Street and Huntriss Row the name of the main thoroughfare changes once more to **Westborough.** In Aberdeen Walk, which branches northward from it, is the **General Post Office.**

51

North Bay from Scarborough Castle

In Vernon Road, running southward from Westborough, are **Christ Church** and the **Public Library**. It contains a large Lending Library, Reference Library, and "Scarborough Room", and a Children's Library, together with reading rooms open to all.

In York Place, near by, is the **Friends' Meeting House**.

St. Mary's Church stands on the tongue of high land separating South Bay from the North Side. Most of the present structure including the tower is a rebuilding of 1669 on the foundations of a twelfth-century church, a restoration having been carried out in 1850. The windows at the east end of the church were destroyed by a parachute mine during the war. A very beautiful stained-glass window by Stammers depicting the Benedicite was inserted in 1958. The church is unique in England for the row of chantry chapels on the south side and shows the continental influences of the day. Amongst a number of mural monuments there is one to Roubilliac, the eminent eighteenth-century French sculptor.

In the churchyard beyond the tower will be seen the gravestone of Anne Brontë ("Acton Bell"), sister of the better-known Charlotte.

St. Peter's Roman Catholic Church, in Castle Road, is worth visiting on account of its stained-glass windows. One, erected by public subscription in commemoration of Queen Victoria's Diamond Jubilee, has three lights, depicting St. Augustine, St. Andrew and St. Patrick. Another window is a memorial to deceased pastors of St. Peter's, the saints depicted being St. Vincent de Paul; John Fisher (a native of Beverley), Bishop of Rochester, who was martyred with Sir Thomas More, under Henry VIII, in 1535; and St. Philip Neri.

The North Bay

The North Bay is one of the most attractive parts of Scarborough. The first step in its development was the construction of the **Marine Drive and Promenade,** a fine drive, passing round the base of Castle Hill and linking the North Bay with the South. Almost throughout its length the Drive is overlooked by more or less steep cliffs – below the Castle they are precipitous, but northward the slope of the Castle Holmes becomes more pronounced, and farther north has enabled the cliff to be laid out with the lawns and walks of the **Clarence Gardens** and the **Alexandra Gardens,** with Floral Hall, tennis courts and bowling greens and putting. Running along the cliff-top are **Queen's Parade** and various terraces of hotels and boarding-houses commanding fine views of the Bay.

The **Alexandra Gardens** are surrounded by high mounds, which afford protection from wind. Within the enclosure are pleasant walks, flower-beds, rockeries, a miniature stream for water-lilies, three crown bowling greens, and tennis courts. On a terrace facing the sea, but outside the Gardens, is a large shelter, much used during the season.

Of note in the gardens are the **Floral Hall,** in which spectacular shows are presented, and a Planetarium.

A cliff tramway connects the cliff-top with the Promenade to the **Corner Café,** which is an important landmark, being a bus terminus (service to South Bay via Marine Drive and harbour) and providing a nucleus for the various developments at the end of the North Bay. The most recent of these is the **North Side Bathing Pool** with capacity for 800 bathers and 700 spectators, with sunbathing terrace, promenade and cafés.

Northstead Manor Gardens are beautifully laid out between the main road and the sea.

In several respects these grounds comprise the most interesting additions to the amenities of Scarborough in recent times. The Gardens themselves have been laid out and developed with skill and amenities include a children's boating pool and water chute, a café, a miniature railway, and the popular **Open-air Theatre.** Part has also been developed as a Marineland, Zoo, and Adventure Playground. Some 6,000 seats are available at the theatre. Each gives a clear view of the stage. And, thanks to Nature's remarkable acoustic workmanship, even a stage whisper can be heard in the back rows.

The **Miniature Railway** runs every 20 minutes from the station beside the Burniston Road, alongside the lake and then along the cliffs towards Scalby Mills Hotel.

The ancient manor of Northstead, like the better-known Chiltern Hundreds, provides an appointment under the Government by means of which members of the House of Commons who wish to be released from their legislative duties are enabled to resign their seats. The appointment of steward and bailiff of the manor was first made for this purpose in 1844.

Peasholm Park and Lake lies inland from the Bathing Pool. The large ornamental lake has inlets and a waterfall, and a chain of miniature lakes extends at different levels up the glen. The Fall, 45 ft. in height, can be illuminated at night by hidden lights. The Lake, which has an average depth of 3 ft., is fed from the brook which rises in Raincliffe Woods and runs through the ravine, entering the large Lake over a double waterfall, some 9 ft. in height.

The large **Island** in the Lake is of natural formation, and rises above the water-level to a height of some 45 ft. Winding walks lead to the top, from which a pleasing view is gained. There is a tree walk with models and figures illuminated at night. The smaller island was formed out of material excavated to form the Lake, and is intended as a natural refuge for the water-fowl.

Music is provided daily. The seating is, in the main, placed on terraces opposite the widest portion of the lake and the "floating" bandstand. Spectacular shows, such as the reproductions of famous naval battles with scale models of ships, are given twice weekly during the season. On the topmost terrace is a café.

At the upper end of the Park are a **Miniature Golf Course** and a Putting Course.

The Castle

Open daily, charge. The promontory on which the ruins of the castle, the curtain wall, the fosse and the dike stand is nearly 300 ft. above the level of the sea, and inaccessible on all sides but the west. The fosse or moat which cuts off the height from the mainland is very deep and has beyond it, as an extra protection, the castle dike, a ridge formed of the material thrown up when the moat was dug. The sole approach is by a narrow stone causeway across the fosse, a steep ascent with a barbican, repaired in the seventeenth century, at its foot. The remains of the once noble stronghold are very few, the tall battered Norman Keep being the only remnant of consequence. The walls are about 12 ft. thick but the west side has entirely gone. The Keep must have been originally at least 100 ft. high; it is now barely 80 ft. The building has consisted of three storeys, with an underground dungeon. The western half of the Keep was largely destroyed in the Civil War siege of 1644–45. Leland tells us that the approach was defended by two other towers, with a drawbridge between; and some remains of these are still traceable.

Beyond the Keep and on the right as one enters the Castle Yard are the ruins of **Mosdale Hall,** which is believed to have been built during the reign of King John as an official residence. The name of Mosdale Hall was acquired from John Mosdale, who was appointed life-governor of the castle in 1397 and in whose period of office it was rebuilt.

The site of the castle is in the care of the Department of the Environment. Excavations from 1921 onwards on the seaward extremity of the hill led to the discovery of three types of ancient remains: undermost the remains of a late Bronze Age and early Iron Age village of the fifth century B.C.; above these the remains of a Roman signal station; nearest the surface, the remains of three chapels, one earlier than the Norman Conquest and two later.

In 1925 the Roman Signal Station excavations were opened to the public. A model of this, together with finds from the excavations, is in the Archaeological Museum. The public are allowed to walk about the whole site, which is 260 feet above sea level, and commands an especially fine view extending northwards to Ravenscar (9 miles) and southwards to Filey Brigg (7 miles) and Flamborough Head (17 miles).

Walks and Excursions from Scarborough

To Oliver's Mount. The Mount is reached by Ramshill Road and Filey Road *(bus route)*, turning off to the right at Queen Margaret's Road or Mountside. **Oliver's Mount** is the prominent hill overlooking the southern part of the town and is distinguished by the impressive stone obelisk which serves as the town's war memorial. There is a good road to the top and coaches make daily trips in the season. The central part of the plateau is hedged in, being partly occupied by a reservoir. There is a café and on the slopes a motor-cycle circuit for road racing competitions. On the west side is an artificial ski-slope.

To the Mere. Like Oliver's Mount, this is owned by the Corporation. The most pleasant way is by the Filey road *(bus)* and Queen Margaret's Road. The Mere is a popular picnic spot. There is fishing and small boats may be hired. There is a café and a Model Yacht Club.

To Cornelian and Cayton Bays. This walk should be varied by taking the cliff-path one way and the sand the other, according to the state of the tide. As an alternative one may follow the coast road by bus or car. Visitors cannot be too often reminded that in order to pass the headlands south of Scarborough into the bays beyond, and to return dry and in safety, it is *essential* to select a time between two and three hours after high water. If it is intended to make the outward journey by the cliffs, it is best to proceed by the Esplanade above the Spa to the beautiful Holbeck Gardens. (The terminus of the Town Centre bus is only a short distance inland from the Clock Tower.)

A wide path flanked by flower borders leads south from the Tower, running parallel to the Esplanade. Continue past the grounds of the Holbeck Hall Hotel, out of the gardens and on to the open cliffs, where there is a signpost "Cayton Bay". The path keeps to the cliff edge skirting the South Cliff Golf Course, until after passing the promontory known as the White Nab we are above –

Cornelian Bay. The bay is so named because carnelians (the name was originally spelt thus) are to be found among the pebbles. Jaspers, agates, and several kinds of sea-shells will reward the diligent seeker. Keeping to the cliff-path, we reach **Osgodby Nab,** a much-worn, pointed headland, and can scramble by a rough path through stunted, wind-blown trees down to the sandy strand of Cayton Bay.

It is possible to clamber round the shore of the Nab, but unless the tide is far out it is better to re-ascend the cliff and keep to the path.

Cayton Bay is a favourite spot for bathing, picnics and camping. There are shops, cafés and holiday camps. One can sit for hours on the sands or the fallen rocks, watching the waves and the spindrift. From the higher ground, if the tide is up and the wind is in the proper quarter, the sea can be seen splashing over Filey Brigg, sending up great columns of spray like a school of whales "blowing".

The return to Scarborough (3 miles) can be made by the road or, if the tide allows, by the sands.

To Falsgrave Park. The best way to reach Falsgrave Park from central Scarborough or the South Bay is by bus along Westborough, past the station and All Saints' Church, to where the Seamer Road turns off on the left. The fourth turning on the right in Seamer Road is Spring Hill Road, leading to **Falsgrave Park,** a pleasant open space of about 13 acres rising to a point from which the view is rivalled only by that from Oliver's Mount. The Park is sometimes known as Spring Hill, from having been the source of Scarborough's first water-supply.

To Raincliff Woods. During the season cars and coaches pass through Lady Edith's Drive on their way to and from Forge Valley; but the Drive, pretty as it is, gives only a hint of the beauties of this region. The bridle-paths may be followed in any direction: there is little chance of losing one's way, as the woods clothe a slope. The trees are of all kinds – beech, oak, ash, fir and larch – and in the spring and early summer the banks are covered with primroses, violets, and bluebells.

Lady Edith's Drive starts in the Scalby road near Throxenby, about 1 mile north of the junction of that road with the Ayton road and just past the Technical College. (Buses pass the end of the drive.) It is named after Lady Edith Somerset, daughter of the seventh Duke of Beaufort, and widow of the first Earl of Londesborough. At the end of the avenue follow the road to the right and then round to the left as it skirts the weed-grown lake known as **Throxenby Mere.** Open country is passed and then the road enters **Raincliff Woods.**

A pleasant walk of some five miles may be taken from Throxenby Mere through the Woods and along the river to Ayton Castle. A path leads from the far (westernmost) end of the Mere, leading up to the crest of the hill. About halfway up the side of the slope a second path runs away to the right, through the wood, roughly parallel with both the crest of the hill and the road below. After crossing a field the path gradually loses height and rejoins the main road near the junction of the roads to Hackness and Ayton. A walk of about 500 yards in the Ayton direction brings the walker to a bridge. Cross this and follow the river in the original direction on the opposite side. The path climbs slightly to Ayton Castle, on the farther side of which a gate leads on to the lane to West Ayton. *(Bus service.)*

Between 2 and 3 miles from the Scalby road one comes to a fork; to the left is the road through Forge Valley to East Ayton; to the right is the road to Everley and Hackness.

To Forge Valley. For the foot of the Valley follow the Pickering road from Falsgrave to East Ayton, where turn sharply to right at the Methodist Chapel. For the upper end of the Valley follow Lady Edith's Drive as in foregoing excursion.

Forge Valley – the name is derived from an old forge, demolished about 1800 – is a beautiful glade, 1½ miles in length, formed by the river *Derwent*. It is the most picturesque portion of the river's course. Steep slopes – in places almost perpendicular – rise on either side, and are clothed with trees from top to bottom. Road and river keep close company all the way.

Near the southern end of Forge Valley is a square ruin standing solitary in a field on the western side of the river. This is all that remains of **Ayton Castle,** a fortified manor-house built in the late fourteenth century.

Near the upper end of Forge Valley **Lady Edith's Drive** goes off on the right through **Raincliff Woods** and is a good route back to Scarborough; but for a longer excursion keep to the Derwent valley at least as far as Hackness.

Troutsdale

To Hackness, Silpho Moor and Harwood Dale. The road is via Forge Valley or Lady Edith's Drive (*see* above) or via Scalby and Suffield, though this is preferable as a return route. This excursion and that to Forge Valley, are frequently taken in conjunction, either when motoring or walking. The more open portion from Lady Edith's Drive to Hackness is well worth seeing – the views of the wooded hills across the valley are very lovely.

Following the road northward from the end of Lady Edith's Drive, we come to a farm where the road makes a sharp bend to cross the **Sea Cut,** a waterway constructed to carry the surplus waters of the Derwent after heavy rains directly to the sea, instead of by the circuitous course of the river. Next the prettily situated *Everley Hotel* is passed, and in another three-quarters of a mile a stone bridge at **Hackness.** Near the bridge the road divides. The right-hand branch leads to Hackness Church and village. That to the left follows the main stream northwestward for 2 miles to **Langdale End,** passing a lane climbing to the lofty village of **Broxa** (535 ft.) and another leading back to the Pickering road at Snainton by way of **Troutsdale.**

From Broxa there is a forest drive connecting up with the top of Reasty Hill with magnificent views over Harwood Dale.

From Langdale End another forest drive is via Bickley through beautiful woods and lovely valleys to Dalby, and then on the Pickering or Thornton Dale road to Whitby *(toll charge for cars.)*

From **Langdale End** there are several routes up to the moors which are best followed with the aid of the map. The best of these walks is that over Allerston Moor to **Saltersgate,** on the Whitby-Pickering bus route.

For **Troutsdale,** *see* page 59.

From almost opposite Hackness Church a road climbs steeply with dangerous hairpin bends to **Silpho Moor,** a fine spot for walking or riding.

Hackness is a pretty village surrounded by lofty, wood-crowned hills. **Hackness Hall,** the seat of Lord Derwent, was built in 1795, and is an imposing family mansion in a lovely setting. The Hall is regularly occupied and is rarely open to the public. Motorists and others are allowed to use the road through the park but must go straight through. The grounds are private and picnicking is not allowed.

The Church is an ancient structure, with a sturdy tower capped by a small spire. The building retains several Norman arches, of which the earliest is the plain chancel arch. The nave and chancel were built in 1050.

Several interesting monuments are to be seen in the church. The remains of an eighth-century cross, at the east end of the south aisle is believed to have been erected by the monks of Whitby.

Beyond the church the road passes beneath an arch and enters the Park, through which it climbs to Suffield.

Suffield, a small hamlet of farms and cottages, is perched high (538 ft.) above the sea and commands a fine view over Scarborough. From Suffield the road now descends steeply for $1\frac{1}{2}$ miles to –

Scalby, a place of considerable antiquity, mentioned in Domesday Book as **Scallebi.** The Church, in the centre of the village above the stream is ancient, having been presented to the Priory of Burlington (Bridlington) by Eustace FitzJohn about 1150. There is a curious poor box and an old sundial near the porch.

Brompton Church

Silpho Moor and Harwood Dale. At Suffield take the road ahead, which presently turns to the left among trees. This road runs almost straight for some 3 miles across **Silpho Moor,** passing through woods and across expanses of heather beyond which are lovely views across to the coast. Many will agree that this is the best 3 miles near Scarborough. It is a very popular spot for coach-trips and picnics (but see warning on page 58). At the northern end of the moor, at **Reasty Bank** (650 ft.; car park), the ground falls away, and instead of heather and pine-trees we are gazing at a great display of green fields and thick woods, beyond which are the moors over by Robin Hood's Bay.

In the middle distance is the village of **Harwood Dale,** with an inn, a church built in 1862, and a derelict older church built in 1634 by Sir Posthumus Hoby, who is commemorated in Hackness Church, and a variety of walks. The winding road past the inn continues to the main road about half-way between Whitby and Scarborough.

A more direct approach from Scarborough is by the main road *(bus route)* to Burniston, at the end of which turn left and in about 150 yards to left again – the Hackness road. This begins to climb and soon the wooded edge of Suffield Moor is displayed on either hand. Pass a cross-road and at the next turning go to the right and through a farm gate. This track leads along the edge of the moor and can be so followed, or an early opportunity may be taken to getting on to the top. Reasty Bank is to the right as one faces the edge, and Suffield to the left.

Motorists must follow the Hackness road to the top of the hill, there turning right along the road to Reasty Bank.

To Thornton Dale. This is an excursion westward of Scarborough to a village considered by many to be the prettiest in the county. It can be reached by road, and much interesting scenery lies along the route *(bus service)*.

As a rule the coaches leave Scarborough by way of Falsgrave for Stepney Hill, at the end of 5 miles reaching Ayton, where the *Derwent* is crossed at the south end of Forge Valley and a glimpse may be had of the ruins of Ayton Castle on the right.

Passing **Hutton Bushel** (to the right of the road) and **Wykeham** (where the church has a detached belfry, probably part of a much older building) we come to **Brompton,** 8 miles from Scarborough. The village is of note as the native place of Mary Hutchinson, wife of William Wordsworth. The pair were married, on October 4, 1802, in the Parish Church. A copy of the marriage certificate hangs in the vestry. Brompton Hall, now a school, was the home of Sir George Cayley (1773–1857) the "father of aeronautics".

We next pass through **Snainton,** in a fruit-growing district. Snainton Church, at the end of the rather straggling village, is Victorian, but beside the road is the lych-gate, a striking Norman arch from the original building.

The road turning up beside the inn climbs steadily to the moors and then with dramatic suddenness discloses a splendid view of **Troutsdale,** by which one can return to Scarborough *via* Hackness. Less than 400 yards past Cockmoor Hall, on the right-hand side of the road, at the car park and view-point (650 ft.), will be seen **Cockmoor Dikes.** The date and purpose of these multiple earth works has yet to be determined. Walkers can keep westward where the road elbows its way down into Troutsdale, and in a mile or so join the road through **Netherby Dale** to **Ebberston** (*see* below). At the far end of Snainton bear to the right, and in a mile or less Ebberston is reached, an attractive village at the foot of Netherby Dale.

A lane up the Dale runs off to the right at the cross-roads in the village. Fork left after about 1 mile. Shortly afterwards the road turns to the left at a disused quarry and then right again in the original direction. In half a mile we reach **Scamridge Dikes,** which run away from the road on either side. A fine stretch of the **Oxmoor Dikes,** another large earth work, lies one mile to the north-west of the point we have now reached. Motorists must retrace the road to Ebberston but walkers can turn right after another mile and thus down into Troutsdale and so to Hackness, or they may continue past Givendale Head turning left and southwards along Givendale Rigg and so down to Allerston.

Another route along the higher ground to the east will strike the long straight road from Cockmoor Hall to Snainton. There are also routes westward to Thornton Dale.

On the west side of Ebberston is the *Bloody Field*, the site of a battle in 707 between King Alfrid of Northumbria and his relative Oswy. There is an opening in the rocks called *King Alfrid's Cave*, where it is said the king died of his wounds.

A short way beyond Ebberston is the parish church which dates from Norman times. A short distance away is **Ebberston Hall** *(open from Easter to September on Saturday and Sunday afternoons)*. It is a charming and elegant small villa built in 1718 in the Palladian style. The architect was Colin Campbell, who also remodelled the front and built the main gateway of Burlington House in Piccadilly, London.

A mile or so from Ebberston we pass the ancient village of **Allerston,** and **Wilton,** and then descend into charming **Thornton Dale,** 16 miles from Scarborough. With its wide, tree-shaded street, on one side of which a clear stream flows, Thornton Dale is always picturesque, and it is becoming popular as a headquarters for walkers and cyclists. The best of the village lies off the main road. The Market Cross on the village green is probably over 600 years old, but the stocks are of comparatively recent date. The almshouses on the main road were founded by Viscountess Lumley in 1657.

The road to the right at the cross-roads in Thornton Dale is that via Saltersgate to **Goathland** and Whitby.

To the east of this road lies the **Fylingdales Early Warning Station.** A fork to the right on the way up the hill from Thornton Dale leads round through beech woods on the left (do *not* descend to the mill) to **Ellerburn,** with a quaint little church, dedicated to St. Hilda. It contains both Saxon and Norman work.

Ellerburn is a pleasantly situated little hamlet from which there are some good walks. Motorists, cyclists and walkers can follow the road beside the stream through the **Thornton Dale.** It is a pretty route which takes on a new interest as the vast area of a state forest is reached. A mile or so beyond, it is possible, by courtesy of the occupants of *Dalby House*, to descend to and cross the river, thence ascending to the Thornton Dale-Saltersgate road a little north of its junction with the road from Pickering.

Pickering, Helmsley, Rievaulx

Two miles west of Thornton Dale is the old-world market town of –

Pickering

Distances. – Helmsley, 13 miles; London, 222; Malton, 8; Scarborough, 17; Whitby, 21; York, 26.

Early Closing Day. – Wednesday.
Hotel. – *Forest and Vale* (10).
Population. – 4,500.

Pickering stands at the head of the Vale of Pickering, a remarkably flat tract stretching 30 miles along its greatest length from east to west and 7 miles across its greatest breadth.

The **Parish Church** is dedicated to SS. Peter and Paul. The nave arcades are Norman, as is also the lower part of the tower, but the clerestory is Perpendicular. Above the arcades of the nave is a wonderful series of wall-paintings, believed to date from the middle of the fifteenth century. They were discovered in 1852, but were almost immediately again hidden by whitewash. Thirty years later they were cleaned and restored. They depict scenes from Bible history and the lives of the saints.

Upon the capitals of the north transept arch are grotesque heads. On the north side of the chancel arch is the recumbent figure of a knight, supposed to be "William de Bruys (Bruce) of Pykering", who founded a chantry in 1337. The truncated effigy is reputed to be that of John of Gaunt. In the Bruce Chapel lie the effigies of Sir David and Dame Margery Roucliffe.

Pickering Church is a place of pilgrimage for American visitors to Yorkshire, for in the sanctuary is a memorial to Walter Hines Page, unveiled in 1924 by William Kellogg (the author of the "Kellogg Pact"); this and another brass together commemorate the wartime association of Great Britain and America in 1917. The panelling in the chancel was given by Mrs. Page and members of another famous family associated with the American Embassy – that of Choate. The piece of old panelling is a memorial to Henry Ware Clarke, an American of Yorkshire origin, who was killed at Cantigny in 1918. The church also contains an old memorial tablet in commemoration of two surveyors named King, both of Pickering, who helped to plan the City of Washington.

The **Castle** *(admission charge: open daily)* is north of the town. It is an attractive relic of great historical interest, and is well preserved by the Department of the Environment. The older parts of the castle date from the twelfth century. The circle of walls is complete, with three towers; the area within is divided into inner and outer wards, and contains the Keep (standing on a fine motte), Chapel, and traces of the Hall. Henry II visited the castle, and there gave a charter to the weavers of York; he is said to have been accompanied by Fair Rosamund, after whom one of the towers has been named. King John and the first three Edwards also visited Pickering Castle, and Richard II was confined here before his removal to Pontefract Castle. Among other royal visitors were Henry IV and Richard III.

North of Pickering a few miles are the **Cawthorn Roman Camps.** The Camps are four in number, and were built around the year A.D. 100, their occupation being only temporary. The Camps are on the brow of a 650-ft. hill midway by road between the villages of Cawthorn and Newton. They are considerably overgrown and the spot is difficult to trace. Whatever one's interest in antiquities, the spot is worth visiting for the splendidly wide view of the northerly moors, and of Elleron Lodge in the foreground below eye-level. Even more to be recommended is the extension of the excursion to Stape and Wheeldale Moor, for here begins one of the finest stretches of **Roman Road** in Britain and incidentally one of the most enjoyable moorland walks (which can be terminated at Goathland where there is a bus connection). A portion of the roadway has been preserved by the Department of the Environment.

Westward along the main road from Pickering are the villages of **Middleton,** with its quaint Norman church containing fragments of Saxon work including some fine wheel crosses; **Aislaby, Wrelton** and **Sinnington,** where there is a Maypole on the village green. **Cropton,** north of Wrelton, was the birthplace of William Scoresby (1760), the navigator and Arctic explorer. The Castle Mound at Cropton gives a splendid view of the lower end of Rosedale and the moors to the north. Only slight traces of the castle building remain.

Lastingham. Rather less than 7 miles north-west of Pickering, and reached by lanes leaving the main road at Wrelton or Appleton Common, is the delightful little village of Lastingham *(Blacksmith's Arms)*. It is an excellent place for a quiet holiday, with good walks and rides and some fishing, but it is principally visited on account of its church.

Lastingham Church is in every way interesting and its crypt is unique. It probably occupies the site of a stone church in which the bones of St. Cedd, Bishop of the East Angles, were buried after they had lain for some time in open ground. St. Cedd, later succeeded by his brother, St. Chad, had founded a monastery at Lastingham in 654. In 664 he visited it and here he died of the yellow plague.

The present building dates from the close of the eleventh to the close of the thirteenth century. With its stone-vaulted roof, the interior is a lovely harmony of curves.

The crypt is entered by a flight of stairs from the middle of the nave and lies beneath the east end and chancel. It was built during the period 1078 to 1088. It remains today practically in its original state, and is the only one in England which is complete with chancel, nave and two side aisles. In the crypt are beautiful fragments of crosses and an ancient altar.

Just over a mile west of Lastingham is **Hutton-le-Hole,** a pretty village at one time a centre of the early Quakers. From here the moors to the north are easily gained and there are some splendid panoramas to be seen from Blakey Ridge. This road rises to 1,350 feet where it meets the road from Rosedale. Near the junction stand the two ancient stone Ralph Crosses. An old custom, now unhappily forgotten, required a few coins to be left in the hollow at the top of one cross, for travellers.

A mile or more south of Lastingham is the trim village of **Appleton-le-Moors.** Its church described as a "little gem of moorland churches" is a good example of ornate Victorian Gothic.

From **Sinnington** (above) the main road continues through picturesque scenery and over a stretch of moor into **Kirby Moorside,** which once had two castles of which no trace remains.

Kirkdale Church and Cave. – Between Kirby Moorside and Helmsley, by the road which leads to the right a mile beyond Kirby, the traveller reaches **Kirkdale.** Here, at the concrete crossing of the beck (which has swallow-holes), to the right stands the little minster of St. Gregory, quiet and secluded, with a Saxon sundial and inscription telling how, at some time between 1050 and 1065, St. Gregory's Minster was all to-fallen, and was rebuilt by Brand and Hawarth, priests, in the days of Tosti the Earl. And, of the sundial, "This is day's sun-marker at each tide." Just before the ford, to the right of the road, are the remains of the famous hyena-den and bone-cave explored by Buckland. Many museums, including those of York and Scarborough, have specimen bones taken from the cave.

Farndale. – From Kirby Moorside take the road to **Gillamoor,** a quiet upland village. At Gillamoor turn right, and stop at the crest of the hill overlooking Farn dale. Through the wide, shallow dale runs the *Dove,* and away to the north lies the hamlet of Farndale. In and beyond stand some cottages of very ancient design. On the moor above stands the great rock-tumulus called *Obtrush,* home of a goblin. The return journey may be made by the road crossing the *Dove* in Farndale village and running along the daleside to Hutton-le-Hole, where a main road runs north to Castleton or south to Kirby Moorside. The dale is famous for its profusion of daffodils.

Pickering Castle

Helmsley

is a pretty little town on the river *Rye*, with one or two old houses, the ruins of a fine castle, and an ancient church, largely rebuilt in 1867, but with its original Norman porch and chancel arch. The attractive historical murals and windows are modern.

The remnant of **Helmsley Castle,** built between 1186 and 1227 and surrounded by fourteenth-century ramparts, stands in Duncombe Park, the seat of the Earl of Feversham. It is noteworthy for its double rock cut ditches, huge keep and the west tower. Being held for Charles I, the castle was besieged by Fairfax, who obtained its surrender on terms which allowed the garrison to march out with flying colours, but provided for the slighting of the fortress. *(Open same times as Rievaulx Abbey except that it is closed Sunday mornings.)*

The present house (Dunscombe Park), probably by William Wakefield (*died c.* 1730) is now a school and not on view, but the school gardens are open to the public on Wednesdays during the months of May to August.

The little town is becoming increasingly popular as a holiday centre. The best trout fishing is at Shaken Bridge, up the Rye beyond Rievaulx.

About 3 miles north-west of Helmsley is –

Rievaulx Abbey

Rievaulx Abbey

Admission *charge. Open daily throughout the year.*

The Abbey is a beautiful ruin in a charming glen. It was the first large Cistercian monastery established in England, having been founded by the Lord Helmsley in 1131. In recent years the site has been systematically excavated by the Department of the Environment, and measures have been taken to preserve the ruins, which are among the most beautiful in England. They consist partly of the remains of the church and partly of the remains of the monastic buildings. Owing to the nature of the site the builders were obliged to make the length of the church run north and south. Its ruins are those of its nave, chancel and transepts. The greater part is Early English, but portions are Norman, being the remains of an earlier church. On the west of the nave was the cloister square, and to the west of that is the refectory of Early English architecture. Southward of this are many other domestic buildings. At the Dissolution, Rievaulx Abbey was surrendered by an abbot and twenty-three monks. With the lands appertaining to it, it was granted to De Roos, Earl of Rutland.

Southward of Helmsley is a picturesque and wooded district. The road runs through the village of **Oswaldkirk** – the church of St. Oswald, king and martyr – and next **Stonegrave,** possessing a small but interesting church (restored). The oldest part of the tower is said to be Saxon and in the church, among other fragments of Saxon work, is an exceedingly good example of a wheel-headed cross.

Two miles south-east is –

Hovingham Spa

one of the prettiest villages in Ryedale. In the vicinity have been found important Roman remains, including a hypocaust and bath and a tessellated pavement near Hovingham Hall. The church has a fine Saxon tower, some Norman work and some early carvings

Hovingham Hall, built in 1760, is the seat of Sir William Worsley, Bt. The main approach to the house is through the Riding School which serves as a concert hall for the famous Hovingham festivals. In the ground *(occasionally open for charity)* is a beautiful cricket field.

Some $2\frac{1}{2}$ miles north of Hovingham is the little village of **Nunnington** with its Hall, now the property of the National Trust and open to view May to September, Wednesdays and Sundays, 2–6. It is a large manor house, mainly late seventeenth-century but with a West Wing dating from 1580. Nunnington Church was built mainly in the thirteenth century and possesses notable features in woodwork, stonework and monuments.

Returning through Hovingham Spa we soon pass through the charming stone-built village of **Slingsby,** consisting of a single street, at the bottom of which stands the church, rebuilt in 1867–69, and the shell of a castle intended to be a country house. It was begun by Sir Charles Cavendish, brother of the Duke of Newcastle, about 1642.

From Slingsby the road south-eastward runs to **Malton** (page 42) on the York-Scarborough Road.

North from Scarborough

The coast north of Scarborough closely rivals that of Cornwall in its bold and rugged beauty. The main road runs a considerable way inland and misses the many beauties of the cliffs.

At the extreme end of the North Bay Promenade is **Scalby Mills** with a narrow glen with rugged boulders and steep banks between which a beck tumbles to the rocky shore. From the high ground above the hotel a peep can be had along the stream, with the weir in the mid-distance.

Cloughton is a pleasant village 6 miles north of Scarborough. The **Church** is an ancient building restored. The east window was erected by Sir Frank Lockwood to the memory of his father and mother. There is another window in memory of Sir Frank himself.

Opposite the junction of the Whitby and Ravenscar roads is the bus terminus where a lane leads to Salt Pans, a small rocky bay. **Cloughton Wyke** is a pretty shingly inlet to the south and reached on foot only by a winding path from the 100-foot high cliff surrounding the Wyke.

At **Hulleys,** about 1 mile NNW of Cloughton, a "stone circle" has been cleared of undergrowth by the Scarborough Archaeological Society. The building of which the remaining stones formed part is thought to have been at one time the smithy of the British settlement on the plain above. Other prehistoric remains, including a stone circle belonging to a Bronze Age burial mound, stand on Cloughton Moor about 200 yards to the west of the main road to Whitby (A171).

Hayburn Wyke is a popular place for a picnic. From the hotel winding paths (sticky in wet weather) lead steeply down through a long dell to the sea, where is a stony beach backed by cliffs. Trees planted by the Forestry Commission will soon grow to make this an attractive woodland spot. The Wyke is formed of two streams which rise on the moors above and join at the pretty **Waters Meet.** The stream at its mouth tumbles down to the sea over great gritstone blocks in a fine cascade. Those who are willing to risk a sprained ankle may scramble round to the north headland, for the sake of the fine view of the tiny bay with its fern-clad slopes. Far southward, Scarborough Castle stands boldly out against the sky.

The term wyke or wick, common along the coast, is Norse for a small creek or bay, and the openings to which it is applied in the north correspond to what are known in the south, particularly in the Isle of Wight, as "chines".

Ravenscar stands on a plateau 600 feet above sea level and commands a vast panorama of moorland, cliff and sea. Tradition says that the Danes here hoisted a standard on which was depicted a raven – from which the present name is derived. It is more certain that a Roman signal station stood here – possibly one of a chain of forts for coast defence. In the seventeenth century, alum was discovered, and the industry flourished for a time until superseded by alum discoveries elsewhere. The abandoned workings are clearly visible. Ravenshill Hall, where now stands *Raven Hall Hotel*, was built in 1774, when the Roman stone (now in Whitby Museum) was unearthed. Golf, tennis, bowls, fishing, riding, putting, dancing and an excellent modern swimming pool are available. There are several good walks, one of the prettiest being to **Tan Beck,** a miniature glen.

The Cliffs at Ravenscar

Robin Hood's Bay

Banks. – *Barclays, Midland, National West-minster.* 10.30–12.30 Tuesdays.
Boating. – Pleasure and fishing.
Early Closing. – Wednesday.
Golf. – At Whitby (6 miles) and Ravenscar.
Hotels. – *Victoria, Grosvenor.*
Guest Houses. – *Storra Lea, Fyling Villa.*
Parking Place. – Bank top and at old railway station.

Population. – About 1,200.
Post Office. – King Street and at Station Road.
Reading Room, Library and Museum. – Fisher Head. Open Mondays and Thursdays.
Tennis, Putting and Bowls. – Club opposite the Grosvenor Hotel. Hard courts and crown greens.
Riding. – Along beach. Horses may be hired.

Robin Hood's Bay is 6 miles from Whitby and 14 miles by road from Scarborough. This picturesque district with its quaint little "town", is almost as much a show place in the touring season as Clovelly in North Devon. There is excellent accommodation in both parts of the village, while many of the old cottages in the older part are available for letting in the summer. There are tennis courts, bowling-greens and putting greens.

The bay sweeps in a wide curve from the 600-foot cliff at Ravenscar north-westward to end in its northern headland, North Cheek or Ness Point. In the background there is a steep rise of several hundred feet to the Fylingdales moors. The village nestles in a stream-cut ravine at a point where the cliffs drop to their lowest, about a hundred feet above sea-level. The structure of the lower village reflects the atmosphere of centuries before town-planning was thought of. So narrow and so steep are the little streets that it must have been difficult in the past even for a horseman to thread his way through some of them. On the right-hand side of the slipway to the beach are the Marine Biological Laboratories of the University of Leeds.

The new part of the village, on the higher ground farther from the coast, has developed on modern lines and presents a distinct contrast to the picturesque clusters of houses below.

The **Old Church** of Fyling was probably erected by the Abbot of Whitby shortly after the place came into his possession. It was dedicated to St. Stephen and was no doubt an appanage of Whitby Abbey till the dissolution of that monastery. In 1822 the church was rebuilt, but is now little used, owing to its remote position. A new Church, also dedicated to St. Stephen, stands near the station. A link with the original church is supplied by the Norman font which was found in 1898, buried in a field.

No good walker having quarters at Robin Hood's Bay will refuse the challenge flung out by the lofty point at the southern extremity of the bay –

the point now commonly called **Ravenscar.** The easiest way of gaining it, *but only when the tide is on the ebb*, is to walk along the beach to the extreme limit of the sands, and then to ascend the zigzag track which will there be found. There are other routes by cliff- and bridle-paths, but these paths are broken by the mouths of several becks.

The cliff-path starts from Albion Road and presents no difficulty until *Mill Beck* is reached. *(Bathing in Mill Beck is dangerous though there are some safe places in the vicinity.)* Then a steep descent is made to the Youth Hostel and a continuing footpath will be found on the other side of the deep lane.

Another descent must be made at *Stoupe Beck (Dangerous to bathe)*. Re-ascend by a bridle-path running obliquely inland and at the farm turn to the cliff-path again. This presently winds inland through fields towards the quarry on the hillside and may easily be mistaken. There is no direct path to Ravenscar by cliff-top.

By Path or Road to Whitby. – Whitby can be reached from Robin Hood's Bay by a popular walk along the top of the cliffs. The distance is 8 miles, but ample time should be allowed. The footpath leaves the main street on the right, near where the latter bends inland. At a distance of about 6 miles the High Lighthouse is reached. Then Saltwick Nab is seen below on the right and the Abbey ruins almost face one.

Those who drive must go by the high road through Hawsker.

Do not try to walk to Whitby by the beach. It cannot be done.

Robin Hood's Bay

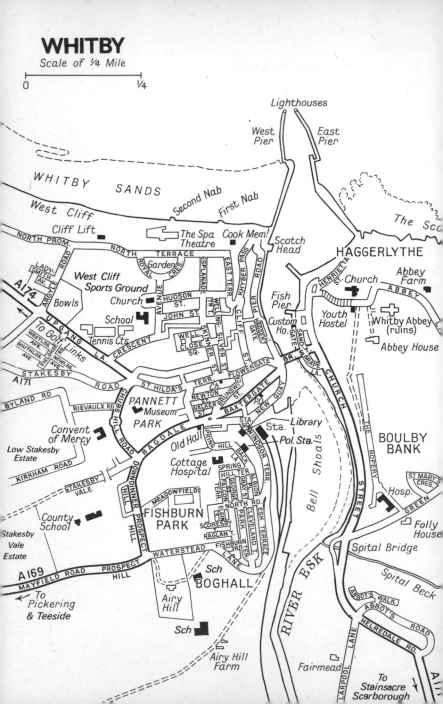

Whitby

Angling. – The Esk, which falls into the sea at Whitby, is a famous river for salmon, sea-trout and brown trout. From August onwards, whenever there is enough rain to cause a freshet down the river, thousands of fish can be seen making their way over the salmon passes at the weirs at Ruswarp and Sleights. The visitor who finds pleasure in angling will have no difficulty in obtaining the right to exercise his skill in the Esk, and as the railway follows approximately the whole course of the river, it is easy to get from Whitby to any desired angling ground. The best stretch of water is preserved by the Esk Fishery Association, and extends, except from Egton Bridge to about Grosmont, both sides, from beyond Glaisdale to Whitby, 11 miles. Information regarding angling in the Esk generally, may be obtained of the Secretary, Esk Fishery Association, Danby.

Banks. – *National Westminster, Yorkshire, Barclays, Midland* and *York County.*

Bathing. – From the West Pier to Sandsend is a fine three-mile stretch of gently sloping sands. As there are strong currents in parts care is desirable. Some of the municipal tents furnished with deck-chairs and other fittings, are reserved for weekly hire. These are erected and kept on part of the sea-wall at the base of the cliffs.

There is a well-equipped Bathing Pool on the cliff-top near Happy Valley.

Boating. – Sea and river boating. There are coastal excursions daily by motor boats from Fish Quay. Cobles may be hired but a boatman should always be taken.

Bowls. – One crown green and one flat green at the Sports Grounds on the West Cliff.

Buses run to Sandsend, for Mulgrave Woods; Aislaby, for the Moors; Beckhole, for Thomassin Foss; Goathland, for Mallyan Spout; Littlebeck, Falling Foss, Blue Bank, Sleights, for the Moors, and other beauty spots. There are also services to Thorpe and Robin Hood's Bay, and to Middlesbrough via Hinderwell, Loftus, Skelton, and Guisborough.

Main routes: United Automobile Company buses in Station Square. There are numerous private coach tours.

Distances. – Bristol, 320 miles; Egton, 7; Goathland, 9; Grosmont, 7; London, 245; Mallyan Spout, 10; Pickering, 21; Ravenscar, 10; Robin Hood's Bay, 7; Scarborough, 21; Staithes, 11; York, 48.

Early Closing Day. – Wednesday.

Golf. – At Upgang, a mile west of the town, the finely situated course leased to the Whitby Golf Club. Visitors are admitted as temporary members. Sunday play.

On the Sports Ground, on the West Cliff, is a Miniature Course, and a Putting Green. Crazy golf in Spa Top.

Hotels. – *Royal*, West Cliff; *Metropole*, West Cliff; *Daneholm*, North Promenade; *Kirby's*, West Cliff; *Saxonville*, Ladysmith Avenue; *Marvic*, West Cliff; *Beach Villa* (Private), Esplanade; *Esplanade House*, West Cliff; *Riviera*, West Cliff; *George*, Baxtergate; *Albany* (Private), 3 Royal Crescent; *Queen's* (Private), North Promenade; *Plough*, Baxtergate; *Langley House*, Royal Crescent; *Carlton* (Private), Royal Crescent; *Haven Crest* (Private), West Cliff; *Amalfi* (Private), Royal Crescent; *Beach Cliff*, North Promenade; *Sea Crest Guest House*, North Promenade; *White Point*; and many others.

Information Bureau. – New Quay Road.

Library. – Public Library, Station Square.

Museum and Art Gallery in Pannet Park.

Population. – 12,130.

Postal. – The Head Office is in Baxtergate, Branch offices in Skinner Street, the Parade, Abbots Road, Fishburn Park, Church Street and Ruswarp.

Railway Station. – The Town Station is on the west bank of the Esk, and in the low-lying part of the town. It has direct line communication by diesel services from Middlesbrough along the Esk Valley, stations in the National Park served being Kildale, Commondale, Castleton, Danby, Glaisdale, etc.

Sea-fishing. – The lower deck of the extended Piers is reserved for fishing. There is a small admission fee. Motor-boats with tackle and bait are available for fishing parties, and fair catches of whiting, gurnet, cod, mackerel and flatfish, etc. may be generally relied upon a short distance from land.

Special fishing competitions are organised for visitors during the season both by the Whitby Yacht Club and the Whitby Sea Anglers' Association.

Tennis. – Grass courts on the West Cliff Sports Ground, opposite the Spa. There are also a number of excellent hard courts, entrance at the corner of Crescent Avenue and Upgang Lane.

As a town, Whitby is undeniably picturesque, particularly the old quarter. The whole town lies on both sides of the River Esk, which, in its lower reaches, becomes the Upper and Lower Harbour. The mouth of the river points due north, with the old town on the East Cliff and the modern town on the West Cliff. For several generations Whitby has been highly popular as a holiday resort though its pleasures are not stereotyped. The West Cliff residential quarter is sober and dignified; the hotels stand on bold yet accessible heights; the business and shopping centre is still faintly Victorian; and the old town never fails in picturesque appeal. While living its own eager, tenacious life, Whitby is full of tradition and history. By the bridge that spans the Esk the whaling captains used to gather, in parts of the old town the jet industry flourished. Whitby Town railway station is built upon the site of the former shipyards.

The **Old Town** is served by streets that are narrow, winding and often steep. The thoroughfare known as **Flowergate** is so ancient that Domesday Book refers to "Flore" and its name occurs in a charter granted in the time of Abbot Roger, whose rule was from 1222 to 1224.

Baxtergate, a few yards southward, is one of the oldest thoroughfares. In it now are some of the older hotels, **St. Ninian's Church,** and the **Post Office.** At the riverside end one may turn leftward up a devious and steep passage (Golden Lion Bank) into Flowergate, rightward over the Bridge, or keep forward by way of **St. Ann's Staith** to the West Pier. The opposite end of Baxtergate is continued by **Bagdale,** in which are some fine Georgian houses. To the junction there comes **Victoria Square** from the station, and here also on the left is the lower end of **Spring Hill,** which leads to the fine **War Memorial Hospital.** At the junction of Spring Hill with Bagdale is **Bagdale Old Hall,** a residence which, in spite of alterations, is one of the most interesting buildings in the town. On the farther corner in Spring Hill is a sixteenth-century sculpture of St. George and the Dragon.

Pannett Park. Bagdale runs alongside Pannett Park, the main entrance of which is in St. Hilda's Terrace. It is a warm, elevated tract commanding lovely views of the town and neighbourhood. In the section adjoining Chubb Hill is an attractive Floral Clock.

The **Museum and Art Gallery** should be visited. Very interesting are its prehistoric remains, collections of "bygones" and ship models. Perhaps the most remarkable exhibit among the fossils is the fossil crocodile, *Teleosaurus,* found in 1824 at Saltwick. There are a number of objects connected with Captain Cook and with the Scoresbys, father and son. In the Museum also is the Roman stone found at Peak (now Ravenscar) in 1774. It commemorates the building of a signal-station at that place about the year A.D. 400.

Chubb Hill Road runs round the park from Bagdale to **St. Hilda's Terrace,** a fine bow-shaped terrace of Georgian houses, and **Flowergate** on the direct line to the bridge across the Esk. At the junction of these two thoroughfares is **Skinner Street,** which contains good shops and is continued by the **Esplanade** to the entrance to the Spa Grounds. Flowergate leads to **St. Ann's Staith,** the Marine Parade and the West Pier. These are among the most frequented parts of Whitby. The Staith is the boating quarter and leads to the **Fish Market.** About midway between the Bridge

East Cliff, Whitby

and the Fish Market is **Haggersgate,** one of the only two streets on the west side of the Esk even as late as the middle of the sixteenth century, the other being Flowergate.

One of the flights of steps which pierce the mass of rock on the left – **Burtree Cragg,** locally the Cragg – should be ascended by those who wish to know Whitby. The steps lead to a characteristic Whitby passage lined by cottages and communicating by a tunnel with the thoroughfare above.

Continuing seaward along Pier Road, the visitor will reach a small projection called the Scotch Head. This river terrace and the continuing pier form a favourite promenade.

The **West and East Piers** are formed of solid stone blocks and paved with weighty flags. The West Pier extends for 2,900 feet and the East Pier 1,400 feet. At low tide the depth of water at the entrance averages 7 feet.

The **Lighthouses** on the pier-heads are quite dissimilar. For two hours before and after high water a fixed green light is shown by night, while during the day a ball is hoisted to the top of the western lighthouse. On the West Pier extension is an occulting green light, and on the East Pier extension an occulting red light. West Pier Lighthouse can be visited, and gives fine views of the harbour and coastline.

From the West Pier extension a good view can be had along the coast to Kettleness. From the East Pier one can see as far as the black, humpy promontory of Saltwick Nab. Whitby is one of the few places on the east coast where the sun can be seen to set behind and to rise from a sea horizon.

At the landward end of the West Pier are the old Coastguard Station and the **Lifeboat House.** Higher up the harbour, on the east side, is housed the Motor Lifeboat *Mary Ann Hepworth*, which already has a record of courageous and arduous service.

The **Sands** have made Whitby famous. They extend from the Pier for nearly 3 miles to Sandsend and are firm and level. The best part for bathing is from below the Spa to the pier.

The Cliff. From the West Pier a winding ascent, cut through the rock, leads to the cliff-top. It goes by the formidable title of the **Khyber Pass,** but brown-faced urchins are the only Afghans likely to be encountered. Jet has been worked here for many years. A shorter route to the top is by the flight of steps. Here stands a bronze **Statue of Captain Cook.** On one side of the pedestal is a representation of the good ship *Resolution*, in which the great navigator sailed from Whitby.

A portion of the face of the cliff is occupied by the **Spa Grounds** which have been developed to include a concert hall, bars and buffets, and ball-room, all surrounded by delightful gardens.

Close by is the upper entrance of the *Cliff Lift*.

On the West Cliff are a number of the largest hotels and boarding-houses, a sheltered public garden with seats, and the **Municipal Sports Ground,** containing hard and grass tennis courts, bowling-greens, a

Whitby Harbour

miniature golf course, putting green, archery butts, boating lake, yachting and paddling pool, and a miniature railway. Beyond are the Cricket and Football Grounds – a 6-acre space with main entrance in Upgang Lane.

St. Hilda's Church, in Royal Crescent, has a fine oak roof, carved pulpit with an oak canopy, a carved oak screen, a carved organ case and magnificent organ, the Bishop's throne, and very fine east and west windows. The Lady Chapel is noteworthy for the decorations by Miss Jessie Bayes.

The **Bridge** works on a swivel and is opened to permit larger vessels to enter the inner harbour. Across the Bridge is the **Old Town Hall** or toll-booth for the market. The building was erected by the Lord of the Manor in 1788. The sittings of Court Leet and Baron were held in the chamber until 1905. The Market Hall at the opposite side of the Square is now used as a factory.

A little further along Church Street, on the opposite side, are the steps leading up to the site on which stood a Methodist Chapel, opened by John Wesley in 1788. The Chapel, becoming unsafe, was taken down in 1953. The pulpit used by Wesley was taken to the Methodist Chapel in the village of Newholm, just outside Whitby, and is used there each Sunday. As one faces the steps, the building on the left is Wesley Hall. It was built in 1901 and all services are now held there.

Near the top of Church Street are the famous –

199 Steps

which form a kind of Purgatorial ascent to the Abbey and are also known as Jacob's Ladder. By the side of the steps runs the "Donkey Road". When the top is reached an excellent view is obtained of the West Cliff and the piers and harbour, but the view is even better from the cliff corner above the East Pier. The height of the cliff is about 200 ft.

The Cædmon Memorial Cross. The cross stands on a solid base of stone, and rises to a height of about 20 ft. On the front are four carved panels, representing Christ in the act of blessing; David playing the harp; the Abbess Hilda; and Cædmon in the stable inspired to sing his great song. Beneath runs the inscription, "To the Glory of God and in Memory of Cædmon, the Father of English Sacred Song. Fell asleep hard by, 680." On the obverse is carved a double vine, symbolical of Christ, and in the loops are figures of four great scholars trained at Whitby under Hilda in Cædmon's time, namely, Bosa, Ætla, Oftor, and John. Beneath are inscribed the first nine lines of Cædmon's Hymn of the Creation, as preserved on the flyleaf of the Moore manuscript of Bede's "Ecclesiastical History" in the Cambridge Museum.

St. Mary's Church. The parish church of Whitby is Norman in origin. Its architecture suggests a date about 1150.

The two lower storeys of the Tower were probably built in the second half of the twelfth century. The belfry stage belongs to the thirteenth century, but its windows, which were formerly traceried, to the fifteenth century. The parapets are even later.

In the early part of the thirteenth century the Transepts were added in the Early English style, and the church retained the cruciform outline thus given to it until the nineteenth century. A model of it as it then was may be seen in Whitby Museum.

In the south-east corner of the South Transept is an altar slab, probably Norman, found under the floor in 1922. (In the medieval church there were at least four altars besides the high altar.) In the south wall of the transept is a piscina. To the south of the Chancel arch is a squint.

Whitby Abbey

The ruins of the Abbey stand on a hill to the east of the river Esk. The Abbey was probably the third or fourth monastery erected on the site. The ruins comprise only the choir of the church, with its north aisle and transept, and parts of the north aisle and the west front. The prevailing style of the ruins is Early English; but there are several Decorated windows, and at the west end is part of the tracing of a Perpendicular window, which was inserted in a Decorated opening. The ends of the choir and north transept are fine specimens of Early English work, enriched with tooth ornament. In the eastern aisle of the north transept was a chapel. The site of its altar is still distinguishable. In the north wall is an aumbry or cupboard. The south transept, though similar in design to the north transept, seems to have been less rich in detail. In it is a passage connecting the cloister with the ground to the east of the church.

The nave fell as long ago as 1763, during a violent storm; and the central tower collapsed in 1830.

During the bombardment of Whitby in 1914, the west front of the Abbey was struck by a shell and badly damaged. The arch of the west door was blown up and all the beautiful interior decoration destroyed. In 1921 the arch was rebuilt and the walls strengthened; the ruins having been recognised as an historical monument and are in the care of the Department of the Environment.

The bases of the piers of the nave arcades, now clearly seen, show the sites of the aisles. Only one pillar of the nave remains complete, and that was rebuilt in 1790. The fallen arches of the nave arcades recovered from the débris may be inspected in the field north of the church.

Excavations made slightly to the north of the ruins revealed the plan of the building of stonework, wattle and daub, constructed by the Lady Hilda. Almost all the Saxon work exposed has been re-covered.

Excavations in the Abbey church led to the discovery of portions of the Norman church which was known to have existed on or near the site of the present walls.

Near the crumbling outer wall of the Abbey are the remains of a fifteenth-century cross. It no doubt once stood within the Abbey enclosure. The shaft is about 10 ft. high, and stands on five circular steps.

The Abbey House near the Abbey ruins was formerly the Manor House of the Cholmleys. The oldest portion, the south side, dating from about 1580, was evidently constructed in great part from the remains of the monastery. The Manor House was enlarged in the seventeenth century but remains a beautiful Tudor-style house. The banqueting hall which was built in 1670 in front of the Manor, collapsed in 1760. The ruins are scheduled as an Ancient Monument. Both buildings were built of stone taken from the Abbey. The Manor is used as a guest house. The former Almshouse of the Abbey is now in use as a Youth Hostel.

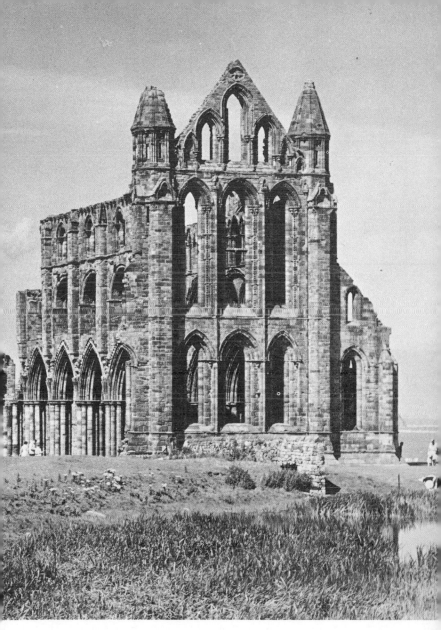

Whitby Abbey

Excursions from Whitby

To Robin Hood's Bay. The road route lies through Hawsker, leaving that village by the road to the left. Robin Hood's Bay will be seen at the foot of a long and, in places, very steep descent.

The walk southward from Whitby to Robin Hood's Bay, though somewhat arduous, is of great interest. The cliffs are in places 300 ft. high, and the outlook seaward is superb the whole distance. Much of the shipping takes a course quite near to the cliffs.

For the cliff-walk of over 8 miles, mount the 199 steps to the churchyard, and then turn leftward to the cliff. After following the path for about half a mile, the almost coal-black **Saltwick Nab** will be seen jutting out seawards and forming the northern protection of Saltwick Bay.

At the Nab, steps lead down to the small plateau and the queer-looking promontory. Some care is necessary in scrambling about the Nab, for the shale is very slippery.

It is dangerous to attempt to reach Saltwick by the shore when the tide is coming in, as the water rises quickly, and the cliffs are unclimbable. When the upper route is being followed, go past the footpath to the tea-garden and continue on the cliff-top through a farmyard, after which take one of the many paths over the grass down to the sands, which are very sheltered. At low water, the slippery Scar and the rough rocks near the East Pier can be explored.

From the point where the descent is made the path is seen to bend slightly inland through a caravan camp site. Follow the footpath – indistinct in places – until the spick-and-span Lighthouse is reached, at a distance of 2 miles from Whitby.

The **High Lighthouse** is itself 44 ft. high, and stands at the cliff-edge, 240 ft. above sea-level. Its purpose on this dangerous and rocky coast is to give warning of the rocks which flank Whitby to the south of the piers within the line of the Bell Buoy. The light is visible in clear weather for 22 miles, and shows a white light every 15 seconds, with a red sector over Whitby Scar. In a building close to the Lighthouse is a powerful siren, giving in foggy weather four quick blasts every ninety seconds. It is jocularly known as the "Whitby mad bull". Visitors are shown over the Lighthouse on weekdays from 1 p.m. to an hour before sunset.

It should be noted that for about a mile either side of the Lighthouse, the cliff path is extremely dangerous. In many places the cliff is under-cut by erosion.
A road connects the Lighthouse with the Scarborough high road at a point about 2 miles from Whitby. The path behind the Lighthouse continues by a somewhat up-and-down course to the **Ness,** which forms the northern horn of Robin Hood's Bay. By continuing along the cliff one finally drops by a somewhat abrupt descent into the main street of the village.

Refreshments can be obtained without difficulty and the return to Whitby made by bus.

To Sandsend and Mulgrave Woods. Bus can be taken from West Cliff to Sandsend. At low tide one can walk the whole distance by the sands.

Sandsend may be regarded as a suburb of Whitby, from which it is 3 miles distant. It has several good hotels *(Sandsend, The Woodlands* (Private), *Bungalow* (Private))*, and is favoured by holidaymakers who like to stay near but not in a town. Owing to the shifting nature of the sands bathers must exercise caution and avoid venturing far out. Two tiny becks, a few hundred yards apart, find an outlet to the sea at Sandsend, scoring deep furrows in the sand in the last part of their course. The ravines running inland are very picturesque, especially the first, where stands the cluster of cottages known as **East Row.**

Mulgrave Woods are available (except for the month of May) *to walkers only,* without charge, on Wednesdays, Saturdays and Sundays. Entrance by the East Row drive where there is a car park. The woods provide a striking contrast to the moorland all around. The visitor is free to follow any of the paths. It may be well, however, to point out that the estate is divided by a ridge, through which the main path passes by a tunnel. This main path connects the entrance at East Row with the main lodge on Lythe Bank. The Old Castle is on this ridge quite close to the tunnel; the eighteenth-century castle is some way northward, on the far side of the valley through which runs the Mickleby Beck.

The building of the present **Castle,** the seat of the Marquis of Normanby, was started by the Duchess of Buckingham, natural daughter of James II. Two wings and a stable block were built by Sir John Soane in 1788 for Lord Mulgrave, and castellation and towers were added by Atkinson in 1812. *The Castle is not open to the public.*

The scanty ruins of the **Old Castle** convey no impression of the former splendour of the place. The parts in best preservation are the west tower of the gateway, an arch at the other end, and a large mullioned window. A dry moat partly encircles the ruins, and they, in turn, encircle a small grass-grown area.

To Lythe and Goldsborough. Lythe is a neat village about a mile from Sandsend or four from Whitby. It is at the summit of the steep hill north-west of Sandsend. The village is 500 ft. above sea-level and commands a fine view over Whitby.

The Parish Church, dedicated to St. Oswald the Martyr, was built in Norman times and is first mentioned in records about 1100. Additions were made in the Early English style in the twelfth century and further restorations in 1788 and 1870. As a result of still further work in 1911 the Church has been restored to much its appearance in medieval days. At this time, some ancient carved stones were discovered. They are known to be of Anglo-Danish origin and were carved in the tenth century and include very fine "hogback" gravestones, incised slabs, crossheads and shafts.

About 3 miles north-westward of Lythe is **Kettleness** (page 89). Rather nearer to Kettleness than to Lythe, the route passes through **Goldsborough,** a hamlet which came into prominence in 1919 through the discovery that it was the site of one of a chain of signal-stations erected along the coast by the Romans to give warning of attack by pirates.

The Goldsborough fort was on high ground about half a mile from the sea. Its outer defence was a ditch 12 ft. broad and about 4 ft. deep. This was crossed by a causeway which gave access to a gateway, the only entrance to the fort. The wall was 4 ft. thick and was strengthened by a bastion at each angle. From the gateway a passage 10 ft. long led between two walls to an unpaved courtyard, in which were a well and an inner building. In a corner of the signal-tower lay the skeleton of a man. The skeleton of a dog was beneath him. His skull bore marks of many sword-cuts. Close by, another adult skeleton lay against the wall. Saxon raiders overwhelmed

Sandsend

the garrison in the early years of the fifth century A.D. A few coins were found, among them being those of the Emperors Eugenius (392–4) and Honorius (395–423).

To Ruswarp. Ruswarp stands on the banks of the Esk, rather more than a mile above Whitby. There are two ways of walking from Whitby:

(a) *By Road.* – Cross the Bridge to Church Street and follow the river, then over the Spital Bridge to the Cemetery and Larpool. The bridge is called Spital because a hospital formerly stood by it. Then the road bends, and an alluring footpath leads leftward to **Cock Mill.** Disregard this, and descend, through Glen Esk, to the river. Ruswarp, with its modern church, has an inviting appearance from this point. There is a path to the Sneaton road.

(b) *By Footpath.* – From the Town Station follow the river on the railway side to the end of Esk Terrace where a stone stile leads to fields. Cross the fields to a foot-bridge over the railway, a little beyond which a junction is effected with another footpath. This second path leaves the high road where it crosses the railway at the top of Downdinner Hill, and is more convenient for West Cliff residents than the first.

The path onwards is somewhat circuitous, but unmistakable. The local custom of partly paving footpaths is worthy of imitation elsewhere. Descending the **Fitts Steps,** Ruswarp is seen below. The River Esk originally flowed past the bottom of Fitts Steps, but when the railway was made its course was diverted.

Ruswarp *(Bridge Inn)* is a place of promise and is growing. Its large cattle market is now a collecting and grading centre, serving an extensive area of country eminently suitable for the rearing of fine-quality cattle. Ruswarp Mill is mentioned in Domesday as being then the property of Whitby Abbey. It was reconstructed in 1752 and again in 1946, and is now equipped with the most modern machinery. The silo, with a capacity of 30,000 bushels, is now a prominent landmark.

A single-span top-arch bridge crossing the Esk was erected in 1936, replacing the one damaged by the great flood in 1930, when Whitby lifeboat came up the river to rescue families marooned by the flood.

Those who wish to return to Whitby by an alternative route should ascend Ruswarp Lane and keep straight on for a mile northward to the four cross-roads below Sneaton Castle. From the high ground there is a good view of Larpool Hall and woods on the other side of the river, and of Whitby and the Abbey. The Abbey is a landmark that can be seen from almost every direction.

Sneaton Castle, on the left of the road is another prominent landmark. The earliest building on record was named Claremont Lodge and when the estate was purchased in 1819 by Col. James Wilson of Sneaton Hall (some two miles to the south) he substantially enlarged the existing building, adding the two massive towers and enclosing the adjacent grounds with substantial crenellated stone walls; he also changed its name to Sneaton Castle. When in 1914 it became the home of an Anglican educational community, it was further enlarged by the addition of St. Hilda's Priory. An outstanding feature is now the beautiful Chapel serving Community and School, completed in 1957. Sunday services are freely available to visitors, 8.00, 9.05 and 6.00.

A few yards further, on the right, a field-path leads back to West Cliff through Stakesby Vale. It is as well, however, to walk a little farther along the high road which runs seaward.

Here, close to the road, stands the **Wishing Chair,** a comfortless stone seat, being the remains of the base of one of the Mile Crosses connected with the Abbey. In 1951, to commemorate Festival of Britain year a new Celtic Cross was carved in stone and erected on the other side of the road. It was said that those who place themselves in the chair, close their eyes, wish for anything reasonable and keep the wish secret will have it gratified. The walk may be continued by keeping straight on to **Upgang,** down Love Lane, returning to town either by the cliffs or the sands. There is a Bathing Pool near Happy Valley on the top of the cliff.

To Sleights Bridge and Aislaby. This is a good extension of the last walk. The round is about 8 miles. Some may prefer to walk to Aislaby, then drop down to Sleights, and take the train or bus home. This misses the best part of the walk, but the scenery is not altogether lost.

For those to whom a walk of 8 miles, including a very steep ascent, is too much, the best plan is to go to Aislaby by bus. From the top of the steep hill at the end of the outward journey here described, one is free to make choice of the way back.

From Ruswarp church the route lies along the riverside road, past the boat-house. The level road hence for 2 miles to Briggswath (the village near Sleights station) is known as **Ruswarp Carrs.** The river is generally dotted with boats. Those who prefer high footpaths to level roads may take the footpath up the hill, entering near the boat-house, and by crossing the fields and climbing many quaint stiles come out into Carr Hill Lane. Downhill then leads to Briggswath, uphill to Aislaby by a footpath a hundred yards higher up the hill, or to Whitby by the road to the right.

At the small village of **Briggswath,** the road abruptly crosses the river. A few yards before the bridge, a flagged bridle-path will be observed leading up the hill on the right. This is known as Featherbed Lane. At the head of the first rise a gate on the left gives on to a field, and a path will be plainly seen. It is a pretty stiff climb to the top. Some distance up a curious rustic arch will be noticed above the hedge. Looking backward, a good view of the valley of the Esk and of the Sleights and Fylingdales Moors is obtained. The last part of the path skirts the grounds of Aislaby Hall, destroyed by fire during the war. The village is reached by turning leftward.

A still more picturesque way of getting to Aislaby is through the **Woodlands,** the entrance to which is seen adjoining Sleights Bridge. The footpath only is public, the road being closed to vehicles. It passes **Groves Hall** and then ascends through a veritable woodland past the back of Woodlands Hall. Here is seen a path leading through Newbiggin to Grosmont. Pass the Woodlands stables, and ascend a narrow bridle-path which comes out close to the unaspiring church of Aislaby.

Aislaby is little more than a cluster of houses, 3 miles from Whitby by direct road, but 5 miles by the way we have come. The local quarries supply stone of great durability, of which many piers on the English coast have been constructed.

The return to Whitby is made by the high road which bends from the village in a north-easterly direction, turning rightward in less than a mile at the next road, and so to the Cross Butts, where a leftward turning winds round to Sneaton Castle, whence the way homeward is plain.

Sleights Bridge to Grosmont. Sleights *(Salmon Leap Hotel)* (connected by bus with Whitby, 4 miles) is one of the prettiest of Yorkshire villages. It stretches along the side of a steep hill which rises from the banks of the Esk and is lined with trees. The village commands extensive and beautiful views, has bracing air, offers boating on the river, and is both close to the moors and within easy access of the sea.

There are River Gardens on the road between Ruswarp and Sleights, and facilities for various sporting pursuits.

Where the new Sleights bridge crosses the river take the path on north side, as far as Woodlands Hall. Instead of turning rightward towards Aislaby, follow the course of the river past Newbiggin Hall to **Grosmont** (page 85). The path strikes the road to Grosmont close to the railway, but it is a roundabout walk of half a mile to the station. From Sleights Bridge to Grosmont is 3½ miles.

An alternative route to Grosmont is through Sleights village as far as the church-yard then turn to right and follow the road along Eskdaleside.

To Glen Esk, Cock Mill and Rigg Mill. Cross the Bridge to Church Street, and follow the road to Ruswarp as far as the lofty viaduct carrying the railway. **Glen Esk**, a little off the road descending rightward to the river, may be reached by road or river.

After passing underneath the railway, and past a farmhouse known as *Crowdy Hall*, where the road bends, a plain footpath is seen on the left, before it descends to Glen Esk, leading through pretty woods. Follow this to a plank bridge above the spot where the Cock Mill Beck and Stainsacre Beck meet and flow henceforth as one stream to the Esk. Crossing the bridge on the left, the path continues through the woods.

Cock Mill, to which we shortly descend by a path through a farmyard, is a delightful picnicking spot. The waterfall has a drop of about 20 ft.

Leaving Cock Mill, the path becomes a road, and mounts high above the streams. In half a mile we leave the wood at **Stainsacre.** Here will be seen a small notice-board – "Road to Rigg Mill". The grassy path bears away with a stream on either side. The village seen to the left is Hawsker, that to the right Sneaton.

About half a mile from Stainsacre, after passing through the second gate on the right, a track leads down to **Rigg Mill Woods.** These woods are also situated on the Cock Mill Beck, but much nearer the source. The visitor may follow the paths in many directions. The fall is rather less than at Cock Mill but there are many trout to be seen in the stream and in the rock pool. There is a picturesque wooden water-wheel. The mill house is occupied as a residence.

Cock Mill to Sneaton. Take the *rightward* path on coming to the twin bridges near the entrance to the woods below Crowdy Hall. This is the old packhorse road, or **Monks' Walk,** and is one of the loveliest in the locality. After crossing the footbridge, the path continues for about a mile by a somewhat devious course across two becks to **Sneaton.** On coming to the hill-top the cart-road must be crossed at right angles. The return to Whitby can be made by this road, leading down to the Esk and Ruswarp.

To Falling Foss. Perhaps the finest walk around Whitby is the stream-side walk between Sleights and Falling Foss. If the excursion includes also crossing the moors from Falling Foss to Robin Hood's Bay, Hawsker or Ruswarp, so much the better.

Train or bus to Sleights, from which Falling Foss is 4½ miles southward. The path to the Foss is somewhat perplexing, and has an awkward trick of dodging from one side of the stream to the other. The rambler should bear in mind that he has to follow the course of the Little Beck, and if he keeps it in sight he cannot go far wrong.

From Sleights station turn leftward, avoiding the road which leads to the village. The path starts directly below the Jubilee Villas, or below the *Salmon Leap Hotel*. In about a mile the path reaches **Iburndale**. About 50 yards south of Iburndale bridge turn up lane on right (by wall letterbox) and in a further 150 yards go through a gate and along the flagged path of a garden, beyond which the path turns left, across the fields.

Ugglebarnby, half a mile from Iburndale, is a place of some interest, and its Church, one of two in the large parish of Sleights Eskdaleside-cum-Ugglebarnby, is well worth a slight detour. The church was rebuilt in 1872, and incorporates remains of a Norman structure. The pews are richly carved, the roof is painted, and the reredos, pulpit, reading-desk, etc., are all in their way works of art.

From Iburndale the path in 1½ miles runs, with sundry crossings and deviations, to the village of **Littlebeck** from which a nature reserve runs through the woods. This last part of the walk through **Newton Woods** to the Foss (another 1¼ miles) is the loveliest of all, but in wet weather one must be prepared for sticky and slippery paths. After winding round a gully, the path gradually ascends to the **Hermitage,** a huge rock which has been hollowed out and within which twenty people could be seated. It is easy to scramble to the top, and here will be found a rough armchair of stone, seated in which one can enjoy a really fine view of the woods and the distant hills.

In another third of a mile the path descends steeply to reveal the **Falling Foss,** or Force. The fall has a drop of from 40 to 50 ft. and has hollowed out a great basin. The effect of the fall is heightened with a background of dense black rock. Fine as the fall is, its setting is also beautiful. There is a profusion of choice ferns in the dell, and most of the boulders are clothed in moss. The scramble down to the Foss basin is steep and after rain is very slippery.

The return to Whitby may be made by the high road from the water-splash via Sneaton, a distance of 6 miles.

To Hawsker. The road to Hawsker and Robin Hood's Bay starts by the Abbey, and gradually turns inland. It may be struck by following Church Street to the right from the bridge for about half a mile and there turning up Green Lane, a steep road opposite the electricity works.

Instead of going on to Green Lane walkers can take the footpath commencing near St. Hilda's Hospital to Hawsker Lane.

Another way of reaching Hawsker is by the cliff-path as far as the High Lighthouse (3 miles). There take the devious road inland to the village, the church of which can be plainly seen.

Yet another way may be taken by passing Green Lane End, crossing the Spital Beck, ascending the hill and keeping left at the road fork. This is the simplest route for motorists, but the least attractive for walkers.

Hawsker is a straggling, picturesque village concerned with agriculture. One of the four sides of the church spire is pierced by a chimney.

The name Hawsker is a corruption of Hawksgarth, though in the Domesday Book the village is recorded as Ghinipe. It has a somewhat dubious claim to fame in connection with Robin Hood.

Newholm, Dunsley, Sandsend, etc. There are a number of pleasant footpaths in the district between Whitby and Mulgrave Woods. A good round of about 7 miles could be had by making for the Wishing Chair, and then through Ewe Cote, a secluded spot with an ancient hall, and Fern Hill, and across the fields to **Dunsley,** about a mile from the coast and once of more importance than now. A Roman road ran from Dunsley across the moors to York. At Dunsley either turn rightward along pretty Dunsley Lane to the sea at East Row, Sandsend; or return to the path skirting Newholm Beck, and walk seaward as far as Raithwaite Hall, where a footpath runs rightward, and comes out in a mile or so at the Golf House, Upgang. The round can, of course, be begun in the reverse direction at Upgang, and the return made *via* Newholm and Stakesby. There is a charming footpath through the fields from Dunsley to Newholm. In the Methodist Chapel at Newholm may be seen the pulpit used by John Wesley in the chapel in Whitby opened by him in 1788.

To Lythe, Ugthorpe and Egton. This is a long round, the walking part being about 12 miles. As Ugthorpe is 5 miles from Sandsend, but only 3 miles across the moors from Lealholm station (book at the Town Station), the walking distance to it may be reduced by omitting Lythe. If Lythe is included, bus (from Whitby) to Sandsend; walk up the steep road to **Lythe** (page 79) and at the village turn southward to one of the lodge gates of Mulgrave Woods. The fine elevated road westward is then fairly straight for 5 miles to –

Ugthorpe which appears in Domesday as Ughetorp. Near the mill Roman coins have been found. The district is said to have been quite untouched by the Reformation and to have maintained its resident Catholic priest all through the era of religious persecution. The Catholic Church (St. Ann) was opened by Cardinal Wiseman in 1857. The Protestant Church (Christ Church) was consecrated in the same year, having been built when the fine old Norman church was pulled down in spite of the protests of all the archaeologists in England.

From the church, a road, a little better than a cart-track, runs southward for 2 miles to Egton Low Moor, joining the main road to Aislaby, 4 miles eastward. On reaching the Aislaby road, turn rightward (west) for a few hundred yards to another road running obliquely southward to **Egton** (*see* page 85). For Egton Bridge station keep straight down the hill for another mile, passing the Protestant Church on the left.

The Esk Valley

From Whitby roads and the railway line follow closely the course of the river.

The lower reaches of the river, from Sleights Bridge to Ruswarp and from Ruswarp to Whitby, have been already described.

Grosmont is the starting-point for several good walks. It is about 6 miles by rail from Whitby, but longer by the charming, though winding, road through Sleights and along Eskdaleside. This road is especially lovely in June. The path through the Woodlands and Newbiggin, on the north side of the river, is preferred by walkers.

Grosmont is a good centre for anglers, being at the confluence of the Esk and its principal tributary.

Egton Bridge is the next station westward. **Egton** village lies to the north and is reached by the uphill road from the station. The village stands over 500 feet above sea level. Above the road on the right is the Church of St. Hilda, rebuilt in the nineteenth century. It retains the Norman shape of the arches of the ancient church. The river is reached from the station by turning downhill.

Arncliffe Woods are reached by crossing the bridge and bearing to the right and in a few hundred yards crossing a brook, the road then following the bank of the stream. At the next stone bridge take the right-hand road uphill. The views of woodland are here very pretty and in marked contrast to the bleak moorland heights around.

Glaisdale. The better part of Glaisdale is known as Glaisdale End, and is situated on rising ground a long half mile from the railway. The village is popular with anglers, and the hunting in the district is famous. It is among meandering streams and wooded vales, and around for miles are the beautiful moors. From the church at Glaisdale End, a good road traverses the broad and beautiful dale which extends at right angles to the railway. The graceful **Beggars' Bridge,** beloved by artists, crosses the river near the station, though a modern bridge rather spoils the romantic aspect.

Lealholm, 10 miles from Whitby, is a very picturesque village in the valley of the Esk, and from which one can explore the beautiful and peaceful **Fryup Dale.** Here several farmhouses and cottages make up the scattered village of Fryup, some 3 miles southwest of Lealholm station.

Danby, $2\frac{1}{2}$ miles westward, is the centre of a pleasant district. **Danby Moor** abounds in tumuli, camps and forts, and has yielded stone implements, sun-dried clay urns containing ashes of cremated Ancient Britons, and various other Early British relics.

Perched on a lofty crag above the river, about a mile short of the station, are the ruins of **Danby Castle,** erected towards the close of the reign of Edward I. The castle consisted of a rectangular block, with a court in the centre and a tower at each angle. The kitchen, with its massive fireplace, a chamber in the western tower, and other portions, are in full repair. The most interesting feature is a vault or dungeon, to which admittance is gained by a flight of stone steps.

In the valley just below the castle ruins an old pack-horse bridge, known as Duck Bridge, crosses the Esk.

St. Hilda's Church, the parish church, is situated in Danby Dale. The village at one time was a very scattered community but at the coming of the railway was rebuilt in the main Esk Valley. The church has a squat solid fifteenth-century tower typical of many dale churches.

On the opposite side of the valley, about $3\frac{1}{2}$ miles from Danby station, is **Danby Beacon** (988 ft.), worth ascending for the good view to be had from it. On the way to the Beacon is *Danby Lodge*, the shooting-box of Viscount Downe, Lord of the Manor, and owner of the Castle.

A charming but strenuous walk from Danby is to pass through **Ainthorpe,** the hamlet near the station; after passing the *Fox and Hounds* follow the road past Danby Castle, through Fryup to Glaisdale.

Castleton, a mile west of Danby, is an attractive place. There is good shooting and fishing and the walks and rides over the moors are excellent. The Church, a good modern structure, stands at the east end of the village. The *Robin Hood Inn* dates from 1671.

On the summit of **Easby Moor** (1,064 ft.), high above Kildale station, is an obelisk, erected in 1827 in memory of Captain Cook. Captain Cook attended the school at **Great Ayton,** a village 2 miles north-west of Kildale as the crow flies. In 1934 the cottage in which he is reputed to have lived was bought by the Government of Victoria, removed and re-erected in Melbourne. An obelisk in Ayton marks the site.

Goathland

Buses connect Goathland with Scarborough, York, Malton and Whitby.

Entertainments. – Concerts, dances, etc., in the Parish Room.

Hotels. – *Goathland Hydro*, Goathland; *Mallyan Spout*, opp. church; *Whitfield* at Darnholm; *Goathland*

Goathland is situated high up among the moors about 9 miles from Whitby. Close at hand is some of the finest moorland scenery, and a region of waterfalls, woods, heather, ferns and mosses. Its air is bracing and fine walks abound in every direction. There are good hotels, and there is a Parish Room in which concerts, dances and whist drives are held.

The principal street is bordered with wide grass margins which push back the broken lines of houses. These margins form part of the Common and are grazed by unattended sheep.

The **Church,** dedicated to St. Mary, is a modern building with ancient associations, a place of Christian worship set up in Goathland many centuries ago. It is constructed of local stone and has a stone tile roof. Between nave and chancel is set a massive squat tower.

Walks from Goathland

To Mallyan Spout. A footpath (an easy 10 minutes' descent) starts from the *Mallyan Spout Hotel*, opposite the church. The Spout is a fine waterfall in a lovely setting of dark rock against which the sunlit spray and the fresh green leaves of trees and ferns form a picture of sheer delight.

To Nelly Ayre Foss. The most direct route from Goathland lies along the road which goes to the right past the church. Where it leaves the moors one must take a footpath on the left. This is followed to the end of a stone wall on the right, and there one drops down to the fall.

There is a Youth Hostel at Wheeldale Lodge.

Beckhole is a hamlet between Goathland and Grosmont, in the beautiful valley through which the Murk Esk winds. It can be made the starting-point of many pleasant walks. There is a fine selection of woodland glens, each with its little stream trickling down, and there are endless nooks and rambles through fields. In the neighbourhood are several pretty falls.

To Water Ark Foss and Walker Mill Foss. – The footpath leading to Water Ark Foss starts at a stile facing the Beckhole Road near Water Ark Lodge. For the first hundred yards or so the footpath is bordered by a tall beech hedge on the west side. The surrounding moorland at Water Ark is moulded into a natural amphitheatre at the base of which the stream cascades majestically to form Water Ark Foss. The Waterfall is not readily accessible at close quarters but can be seen from the top of the ascending path which leads to Beckhole and Green End.

To Darnholm. – A tiny hamlet about three-quarters of a mile from the centre of the village of Goathland. The road to it ends for motorists immediately beyond a shallow ford, and it is here that picnic parties, especially those with children, may spend many happy hours by the side of the pebble-strewn river. Turning to the right pedestrians can reach Goathland village over a pleasant moorland track, or alternatively turn left and arrive at Water Ark from the moor by way of Bradley Hill. Both routes necessitate a rather stiff climb at the outset, but the resulting views are well worth the effort.

Goathland to Grosmont. – The shortest route, 3 miles, between Goathland and Grosmont is by the disused railway line *via* Beckhole. Other routes between the same point are (1) *via* Darnholm and Hawthorne Hill, over Clevel and Dike to Goathland End and Fair Head Farm (4 miles); (2) *via* Bracken Howe and the High and Low Bridge-Stones (4½ miles); and (3) by way of Darnholm and Green End, through moorland, woodland and pasture. The distance is from 4 to 5 miles.

Falling Foss. – A variation of the obvious route can be had turning eastward across the moors at the first branch road nearer Whitby after the junction of the Grosmont road. A line of shooting butts to the right of the road trending downhill gives the opening of the route. In about half a mile the wall of the pastures is reached. Keep to the right until a lane is visible near a larch woodland. This is connected by a cart-track with the moorland. The lane passes a couple of farms, winding gradually towards the Foss Wood and descending steeply to the Foss head, a few score yards above the head of **Falling Foss.**

The North Yorkshire Moors Railway Preservation Society have acquired land and track between Grosmont and Goathland with a view to re-opening this section of the old Whitby/Pickering railway. They own several steam locomotives, and hold "open weekends" during the year. Their headquarters is at Goathland Station.

Further information could be obtained from their Publicity Officer, J. Tindale, 14 Skinner Street, Whitby, Tel. No. Whitby 2084.

Runswick Bay

Whitby to Saltburn

The coast-line north of Whitby is as interesting as that to the south. At first the cliffs are low, but they gradually rise, until at Kettleness they are 375 ft. above the sea, the height increasing still farther at Boulby Cliff, one of the loftiest points on the English coast.

For Sandsend and Mulgrave Castle and Woods, *see* page 79.

Kettleness, 5 miles from Whitby, is a small hamlet in a wild, windswept spot. The headland is nearly 375 ft. high, and affords a very fine view of the pretty bay and of Runswick on the opposite slope. The walk round the bay from Kettleness to Runswick is popular. The safest way round the bay is by the path along the cliff-top. The cliffs between the two places are very rugged and broken in outline, and bear evidence of frequent landslips. Abandoned alum and jet workings may be seen in places. Some caves of considerable extent can be explored by the curious.

Runswick *(Runswick Bay; Cliffemount* (private)*)* is perched on the rugged cliff-side in the most curious and higgledy-piggledy fashion. The "streets" are mere paths leading from one house to another. The soil is wonderfully fertile and the cottage gardens are a mass of flowers from spring to autumn. There are one or two comfortable hotels, and some of the cottages take guests. The tiny village is well sheltered from northerly winds by **Lingra Knowle,** the lofty crag that forms the western extremity of the bay. The outlook is delightful, for Runswick Bay, though small, is one of the best-shaped on the Yorkshire coast. There is good bathing, boating and fishing.

Hinderwell is a large straggling village. The Church occupies the site of an ancient fabric reputed to have been connected with Whitby Abbey. The chalice used in the church is dated *circa* 1420 and as such is one of the three oldest in the country.

Hinderwell to Staithes. – This is a very fine cliff walk. From the church turn to the right for Port Mulgrave ($\frac{1}{2}$ mile), of which a fine view is obtained. From Port Mulgrave there is a path near the cliff edge.

Staithes, one of the most picturesque places in the kingdom, should on no account be missed. Once it was one of the most important centres for fishing in England. There are a few fishing boats still, but in the season pleasure boats operate and the housewives take in summer guests. An estate of new houses has been built on the hill. Buses pass the Lane End and connect with many places. It is the bus service which has been the active agent in destroying the old traditional life, so deeply impregnated with Danish custom and folklore. Staithes was also the headquarters of the famous "Staithes Group" of artists, of whom Dame Laura Knight is the most famous.

To reach the village from the main road it is necessary to go down a break-neck road, skirting a deep ravine formed by the Staithes beck (large car park at bank top). Cars can descend, but the hill is very steep and there is little room for parking at the bottom.

Captain Cook, as a lad, served here for a while in its drapery and grocery shop (one of a row washed away about 1740), until the yarns of the stout old mariners so fired his ambition that he ran off to Whitby in order to become a sailor.

The most striking feature of Staithes is the prominent **Nab,** which shuts in the tiny bay on the north-west side. The extremity is a sheer precipice, and has the appearance of having been cut with a knife.

Two miles north of Staithes is **Boulby Cliff** (666 ft.), with one exception the highest point on the coast of England.

Staithes

Saltburn-by-the-Sea

Amusements. – Dancing in Spa Hall. Miniature railway in Valley Gardens.

Angling. – By permission in Skelton Beck and in the moorland streams. There is good sea-fishing from the pier and boats. Permits for fishing may be obtained from the Council offices, Saltburn.

Banks. – *National Westminster, Midland, Barclays, Yorkshire.*

Bathing. – From the sands, or the Bathing Station at north end of Promenade or the chalets at the foot of Hazelgrove. Tents for hire may be booked in advance.

Boating. – Boating from the beach: short sea-trips. Children's boating-lake in Valley Gardens.

Bus services to and from Whitby, Redcar, Middlesbrough, etc.

Car Parks. – Hazelgrove, Marine Parade, Milton Street and Lower Promenade, Saltburn; the Stray and the Slipway at Marske.

Distances. – Redcar, 5 miles; Whitby, 19; Scarborough, 39; Filey, 46; Bridlington, 57; London, 251.

Early Closing Day. – Tuesday.

Golf. – 18-hole course, half a mile from the town centre.

Hotels. – *Alexandra*; *Zetland*; *Queen*.

Population. – With Marske, 17,820.

Tennis. – 4 grass courts and 2 hard courts on the Cricket Club's Recreation Ground, Marske Mill Lane.

Saltburn is an important holiday resort some 19 miles along the coast northward of Whitby. It is a modern town admirably laid out, and offers not only the charms of the sea, but also those of woodland, meadowland and moorland.

Saltburn is first mentioned in the Register of Whitby Abbey as being the site of a hermitage given to Whitby about the year 1215 by Roger de Argentum. The Saltburn of those days was a settlement of fisherfolk now represented by the beachside cottages known as Old Saltburn, at the foot of Cat Nab. Small as Old Saltburn is, it boasts a substantial public-house, the *Ship Inn*.

Special interest attaches to the slip-way for the fishermen's boats and to the sea-wall of the adjacent promenade, from the fact that their stones originally formed part of the first railway in the world, the Stockton and Darlington.

The modern town occupies a commanding site on a steep cliff more than 100 ft. above the sea, a position which gives it invigorating air and extensive views.

Deep and crooked glens in close proximity to the town form picturesque and shady retreats. The prominent headland, **Huntcliff,** round which the railway has to wind, shuts in the town from east winds, while other lofty hills protect it on the west. On this height, as at Goldsborough, Ravenscar, and probably Filey, stood a Roman signal-station. When it was excavated, fourteen skeletons were found in the well. On the north side of Hob Hill, opposite the golf course, is the site of a Saxon cemetery.

On the verge of the cliff, extending in a semi-circle about a mile in length, is a fine **Promenade,** commanding a marvellous expanse of sea, usually dotted with shipping. At several points it is connected with the beach and the Lower Marine Parade by inclined paths and stairways. There is also a cliff lift.

The **Lower Marine Parade** extends from Old Saltburn to picturesque **Hazelgrove,** a beautiful woodland valley carefully laid out, affording charming glimpses of the sea. One can walk through the valley from the shore to the western side of the town. A miniature railway runs through the gardens from the beach entrance. In the upper part of the glen is a rose garden; at the lower end are bathing chalets available for hire. Spanning the glen at a height of 140 feet is the Halfpenny Bridge, from which there is a fine view. Near by is a beautiful memorial to the war victims of the two world wars.

The beach is part of the stretch of level, hard, golden sands extending from the base of the giant Huntcliff to the estuary of the Tees, a distance of 8 miles. As soon as the tide has left it, the sand can be used for football, cricket, tennis and cycling. Bathers are advised to use the parts of the foreshore opposite the Lifeguard Station. Red flags are flown when bathing is inadvisable. At the north end of the Promenade is a fine **Bathing Station.** There are also chalets at the foot of Hazelgrove, and a municipally-owned caravan site, with direct access to the beach.

The **Promenade Pier,** opposite the lift, is very popular with sea-anglers. At the shore end is a cafeteria.

At the south end of the Promenade are the sheltered **Pleasure Gardens.** Amid trees, shrubs and grassy banks, and past secluded arbours and sheltered nooks, are winding and undulating paths. Here, too, a road elbows its way up the steep cliff, passing the **Spa Pavilion and Italian Garden,** among the most popular of Saltburn's amenities. On rising ground overlooking the valley is a *Corinthian Temple*, noteworthy as having been the entrance to the railway station at Barnard Castle. The laid-out gardens continue to **Riftswood** – a beautiful stretch of woodland with shady walks and secluded seats. Bypassing the railway viaduct, Hob Hill wood and the golf course are reached.

The only public building of note is the stone-built **Parish Church,** a fine building dating from 1868, with handsome tower, 1902.

Excursions from Saltburn

Skelton, a typical Cleveland village, 2 miles south of Saltburn, from which it can be approached through Riftswood, across the bridge, over the stream and onward by wood and field. It is the site of two churches and of Skelton Castle, the seat of the Whartons, has memories of the historic family of Bruce, who held the lordship, and was the birthplace of Commander Wild, leader of the *Quest* Antarctic Expedition.

Upleatham, a delightful village 2 miles south-west of Saltburn. It is renowned for its ancient church, one of the smallest in England.

Marske, about midway between Saltburn and Redcar (*see* page 94). Reached by sands, cliffs, or road.

Redcar, 5 miles to the north-west, can be reached by the glorious sands or by the coast road. (*See* page 95.)

The Moors, 5 miles inland.

Guisborough, the ancient capital of Cleveland, has the ruins of a famous Priory founded in the early part of the twelfth century by Robert de Bruce (or Brus), the second lord of Skelton. The Priory had extensive possessions. The earlier building was burnt down in 1289, and all that remains consists of a twelfth-century gate-house and the east end of the fourteenth-century church, a magnificent relic. The Priory ruins are open for a small charge. The Parish Church, a fifteenth-century (restored) building, stands near the Priory. It contains a richly carved memorial known as the Bruce Cenotaph. This was presented to the Priory probably by Margaret Tudor, daughter of Henry VII, in memory of Robert the Bruce, who died at Guisborough in 1145, and his successors. There are fine carvings portraying the English and Scottish members of the family and various other items of historical interest.

Close to the Priory grounds stands a huge horse-chestnut tree, said to be the largest of its kind in England.

Alum was formerly manufactured in the locality.

Some 3 miles south-westward of the town is **Roseberry Topping,** the most notable, though not the highest, of the Cleveland Hills, that distinction belonging

Guisborough Priory

to Bottot or Burton Head, which has an elevation of 1,485 ft., while Roseberry Topping rises only 1,057 ft. above sea-level, but an exceedingly fine view is obtained from its summit.

The monument seen on a neighbouring height is that to Captain Cook, on Easby Moor. The village of **Marton,** in which he was born, is some 6 miles west of Guisborough, and there he is commemorated by schools bearing his name. A rather shorter distance south-west of the town is the village of **Great Ayton,** to which his parents moved and where he had his schooling, as already noted on page 86.

Marske, the long parent township, occupies the centre of the bay between Saltburn and Redcar, where the cliffs begin to descend to the level of the Tees estuarine region. It has now outstripped Saltburn in size, but has not the amenities of the latter place. A wide coast road, joining Marske to Redcar, is separated from the beach by sandhills, on whose turfy tops is ample accommodation for car parking. Marske forms part of the Marske and Saltburn Urban District. Considerable residential development has taken place in recent years, and with the advent of the great I.C.I. concern and expansion in the iron and steel industry, the whole area is undergoing a remarkable change.

Marske Hall, built in the reign of Charles I, is now used as a Cheshire Foundations Group Home.

The parish church of St. Mark, built over a hundred years ago, contains a carved Norman font from the earlier Church of St. Germain, an early thirteenth-century cross and other relics. Only the steepled tower of St. Germain's remains on the cliff top. In the graveyard is interred the father of Captain Cook.

Great Ayton with Roseberry Topping beyond

Redcar

The most northerly resort on the Yorkshire coast, Redcar is a favourite holiday ground for Northerners. Increasingly popular, it offers colour, music and gaiety to thousands of visitors. Summer attractions include golf competitions, swimming galas, sand competitions and all the fun of the fair for children. There is a cinema showing the latest films and dancing in the Corporation-owned Pier Ballroom with competitions during the season. Racegoers are very well catered for, and Redcar Race Week at the end of July is the most important of some 17 meetings between May and October. The course, noted for its straight mile, is situated approximately a quarter of a mile from the Railway Station, and has an aeroplane landing ground. The modern grandstand incorporates a restaurant, bars and night club.

The glory of Redcar is its magnificent expanse of firm, smooth, level and clean sand. There are three beaches – Coatham Beach, Central Beach and the Stray (30 acres of grass-covered sand-dunes). At one point the beach has a width of nearly a mile at low water.

The **Scars.** Running far out into the sea are masses of rock known as the West Scar, East Scar and Salt Scar. At high tide they are covered by a few feet of water; when the sea recedes they are left bare. Upon them are many varieties of seaweed, and in the pools among them all sorts of marine creatures may be found. The East and West Scars are easily reached from land, but Salt Scar, a mile eastward from high-water mark, can only be reached by boat. About four hours after high-water is the best time to make the expedition. These reefs also form a breakwater, within the shelter of which boating and bathing are particularly safe.

96

From the Promenade there is a fine panoramic view of the extensive **Tees Mouth** and **South Gare Breakwater,** backed by a large expanse of rising hills in the county of Durham, with Seaton Carew and the Hartlepools bordering on the right. Past the headland, Seaham Harbour, about 25 miles distant, may be distinguished with the naked eye on clear days.

In a building on the Promenade just west of the Pier is kept the *Zetland,* one of the oldest lifeboats in the world. She was built at Sunderland in 1802 by Henry Greathead. For the principle on which the Zetland was built Greathead received £1,200 as a reward from Parliament. She was the means of saving no fewer than 350 lives.

Further west is the **Coatham Enclosure** a comprehensive undertaking including a covered sea-water swimming bath, seating 400 spectators, and a boating lake with islands and bridges. There is a large amusement park and a caravan site.

The Cleveland Golf Links immediately adjoin the Coatham Enclosure and stretch 2 miles westward. Immediately south of the Links is the **Locke Memorial Park,** 22 acres, with a boating lake fringed with trees. In the opposite direction, that is eastward of the Pier, is the **Stray,** an extensive track of sandhills and level patches between the beach and the Marine Drive. Here are miniature golf courses, and a Pool where children can paddle at all times and sail their boats in perfect safety.

On the opposite side of the Coast Road is the **Zetland Park,** with tennis courts, bowling greens and an aviary.

Short thoroughfares connect the entrance to the Pier with Redcar Lane, which runs inland past the Cemetery to the **Borough Park,** with its tennis courts and bowling greens.

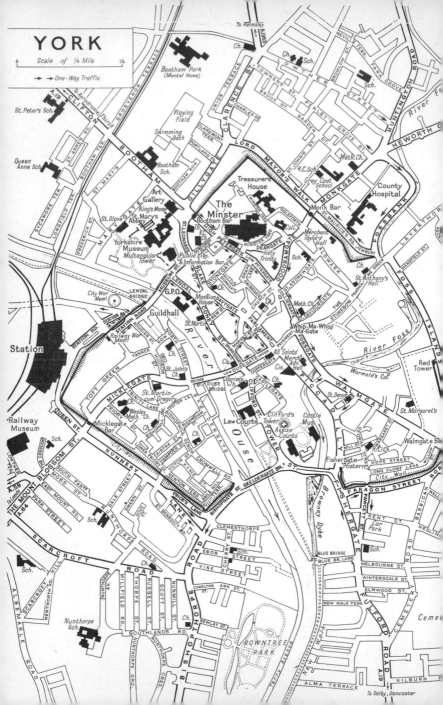

York

Banks. – Branches of main banks in city centre. Exchange Bureau, Coney Street.
Buses. – Main terminals at Rougier Street, Railway Station, Piccadilly and Art Gallery.
Cricket. – *York Cricket Club*, Shipton Road.
Distances. – Bridlington, 41 miles; Doncaster, 34; Driffield, 29; Filey, 41; Harrogate, 22; Hull, 38; Leeds, 24; London, 196; Ripon, 24; Scarborough, 41; Thirsk, 24; Whitby, 46.
Early Closing Day. – Monday or Wednesday.
Entertainment. – Cinemas, theatres, discotheques, music clubs.
Football. – Association: York City F.C., Bootham Crescent; Rugby League: Clarence Street; Rugby Union: Clifton Park.
Golf. – *York Golf Club* (18), Strensall; *York Railway* (18), Pike Hills; *Heworth Golf Club* (9), Muncaster House; *Fulford Golf Club* (18), Heslington.

Hotels. – *Abbey Park* (56), The Mount; *Beechwood Close* (12), Shipton Road; *Chase* (46), Tadcaster Road; *Dean Court* (26), Duncombe Place; *Post House* (104), Tadcaster Road; *Royal Station* (119), Station Road; *Viking* (99), North Street, and many others.
Information Bureau. – Museum Street.
Libraries. – Public Library, Museum Street; Minster Library, Minster Yard.
Market. – Newgate.
Museums. – Castle Museum, Railway Museum, Queen Street; Yorkshire Museum, Museum Gardens.
Population. – 107,150.
Post Office. – 22 Lendal.
Swimming Baths. – Rowntree Park; Yearsley Baths, Haxby Road; Edmund Wilson Baths, Acomb.
Tennis. – Glen Gardens, Rowntree Park, Hull Road Park.

York Minster

Admission. – The whole building (with the exception of the Chapter House, where some of the treasures are stored and for which an admission fee is charged) is open free of charge every day, including Sunday. No sightseeing during service times. Visitors are conducted through the Cathedral at intervals. Cars may be parked in the Minster Yard.

The pride and glory of York is unquestionably the Cathedral, popularly called the Minster in common with a good number of large churches of Anglo-Saxon foundation that were never monastic. This stately edifice, the architectural magnificence of which at once strikes the eye, occupies a site on which a cathedral has stood since the year 627. It is indeed the fifth church that has held this site.

Historical Note. – In 627 – the exact date is known; it was Easter Day, April 12 – Edwin, the first Christian king of Northumbria, was publicly baptized in a small wooden oratory, erected on a spot where, during the Roman ascendancy, the praetorium had stood. Almost immediately he began to build a stone church round it, but the wooden church was left standing until on Edwin's death in battle (633), both were destroyed. In 655, Oswy, the brother of Oswald, and the founder of Whitby Abbey, obtained a signal victory over Penda, who fell fighting at the head of his army; and the conqueror forthwith restored the Cathedral, no doubt to the best of his ability, but, if we are to judge from the rapidity with which it fell into dilapidation, in a not very substantial manner. In 669, Wilfrid, then Archbishop, found it necessary to have the Cathedral thoroughly repaired; the roof was covered with lead and the windows were glazed – an interesting fact, this being the earliest record we have of glass being so used in England. The building was accidentally burnt to the ground in 741, and remained in ruins till 767, when Archbishop Albert employed the celebrated Alcuin to rebuild it in the best Saxon style. Portions of the north and south inner walls of this church remain in the crypt, and the foundations of the apsidal east end and of the north wall were uncovered in 1930.

Early in the eleventh century the Church received permanent endowments from Ulphus, Lord of Deira, but in 1069 it was almost reduced to ashes during the protracted siege that the city underwent at the hands of William the Conqueror. He bestowed the see on Thomas of Bayeux, and the new prelate at once began the erection of a cathedral of Norman architecture, which was, however, much injured by the fire which destroyed a large portion of the city in 1137. The Minster lay in ruins till 1171, in which year it was restored by Archbishop Roger, who rebuilt the choir (the small Norman choir originally built by Thomas of Bayeux) in the Transitional style.

Walter de Gray, archbishop in the time of King John, began the present structure, one of the most magnificent ecclesiastical edifices in England. He lived to see the north transept almost completed, and was buried in the south transept. The erection of the Cathedral occupied about two hundred and fifty years; and throughout this long period the utmost care was taken that the various styles of architecture should blend into the harmonious whole which we see today. It was re-consecrated by Archbishop Neville on July 3, 1472.

Since then, little, if any, structural change has been made in the Minster; and it has suffered less from the ravages of zealots than most of the old churches in this country. In modern times, the fire demon, mindful of his ancient triumphs, has twice attempted the destruction of the pile. On February 3, 1829, the choir was set on fire by a lunatic named Jonathan Martin, and was completely gutted. The beautiful carved woodwork, stalls, pulpit, organ, archbishop's throne, roof and a great quantity of stonework were destroyed. The restoration of the building was immediately taken in hand, and the work was prosecuted with such vigour that the Cathedral was re-opened on May 6, 1832.

On May 20, 1840, the Minster again suffered from fire. The south-west bell-tower, together with the roof of the nave, was almost destroyed. In 1843, through the liberal bequest of Dr. Beckwith, a peal of bells was placed in the south-west tower. In 1845, a monster bell, then the largest but one in England, was purchased by public subscription and placed in the north-west tower. In 1874 and subsequently the south transept, the oldest part of the building, was completely restored. Nearly all the medieval windows of the cathedral have been excellently preserved, and the exterior repaired. During the 1939—45 war many of the windows were removed but are being replaced. The process is slow, as a successful attempt is being made to re-arrange the contents of many panels broken in the fires of 1829 and 1840.

The See of York is one of the most ancient in England.

The Exterior

The Minster is cruciform in plan, its extreme length being 524 feet 6 inches and its width across the transepts 222 feet. Its special features are the fine central tower and the two towers at the west end. The former rises to a height of over 100 feet above the intersection of the choir, nave, and transepts; and is 65 feet in breadth. Each side is pierced with two Perpendicular windows, and the four corners are supported by eight buttresses. A perforated battlement runs round the top. The western towers are each 196 feet high, and surmounted by eight crocketed pinnacles.

The West Front presents the most striking appearance of any part of the building. Between the towers is a very rich window, immediately above the great recessed doorway, in the arch over which are represented, in admirable tracery, the Temptation and the expulsion of Adam and Eve from Paradise. It is in the Decorated English style, while the highest part of this noble façade, being of later date, is in Later Perpendicular. The south side of the nave harmonises with this front, but is not so richly ornamented.

The transepts are of Early English architecture. The south entrance is of more chaste design than the west front, and its decorations, though not so elaborate, are numerous and varied. The circular, or marigold light, surmounting the pointed windows, is particularly worth attention. The east front of the Cathedral dates from the reign of Edward III, and is a superb specimen of the style of architecture in use during the later fourteenth century. The great East Window was considered by Pugin "the finest window in the world." It is indeed superb, and occupies the entire space between the buttresses, which are adorned with niches, canopies and pedestals. This "wall of glass" measures 78 feet in height, by 32 feet in width. The heads of our Saviour and the twelve Apostles are in a row beneath the window; and above it is a representation of Archbishop Thoresby, the builder and benefactor of the Lady Chapel, with a model of the Minster in his hand.

The north side of the building is plainer than the south; but the elegant proportions of the Chapter House and the impressive outline of the grand central tower present, on the whole, a magnificent coup d'œil. It is also celebrated for its beautiful window, divided into five lancet compartments which are known as the "Five Sisters," from a wholly unsubstantiated tradition that the designs were worked in tapestry by five young ladies who lived near the Cathedral, and, having been copied in grisaille glass, were fitted into the window.

On entering the Cathedral we find that, majestic as is the exterior, it is surpassed by the splendour of –

The Interior

The Cathedral consists of Nave, Transepts and Choir, with Lady Chapel between the altar and the east window. There are double aisles throughout. The Nave, one of the longest in England, is 264 feet long, 104 feet wide, and 96 feet high. The Nave is separated from the north and south aisles by seven richly decorated arches, supported by clustered columns, the capitals of which are marvels of sculptured foliage. The Lantern Tower is supported by four massive pillars of similar design, which are connected by lofty arches. The interior of the tower is covered with beautiful tracery, and over the apex of the arches is a stone gallery, running all round. Access to the tower is obtained by a door in the South Transept. The view from the west door is very impressive; it is closed by the beautiful stone Screen which separates the Nave from the Choir, surmounted by the organ. The Screen, of Perpendicular design, is divided into fifteen compartments, containing statues of the English kings from William the Conqueror to Henry VI. Between them, not quite in the centre of the Screen, is the entrance to the Choir; and above are three rows of angels, playing on musical instruments, and representing the heavenly choir. The Screen is the work of William Hindley, master-mason of the late fifteenth century.

The Transepts, like the Nave, are divided from their aisles by pillars and arches of exquisite workmanship. In the South Transept is St. George's Chapel, the War Memorial of the West Yorkshire Regiment, and in the North Transept is St. John's Chapel, the War Memorial of the King's Own Yorkshire Light Infantry. In this latter chapel there is some beautiful medieval glass from the church of St. John the Evangelist, Micklegate, York. Near the North Transept, in the Nave, is the pulpit erected in 1948 as a memory to Archbishops Cosmo Gordon Lang and William Temple. As we enter –

The Choir

our admiration of the majesty of the Minster is heightened. The arcade which runs through the Nave is continued through this part of the edifice; and the spaces

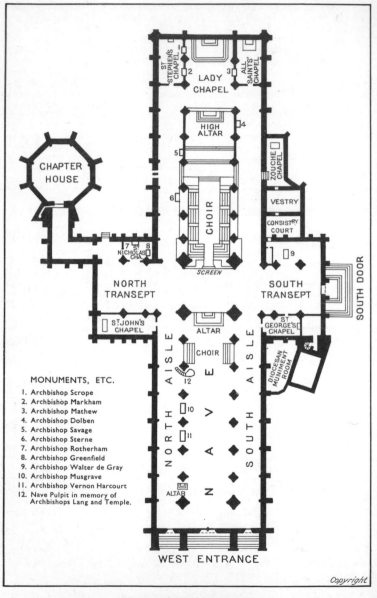

MONUMENTS, ETC.

1. Archbishop Scrope
2. Archbishop Markham
3. Archbishop Mathew
4. Archbishop Dolben
5. Archbishop Savage
6. Archbishop Sterne
7. Archbishop Rotherham
8. Archbishop Greenfield
9. Archbishop Walter de Gray
10. Archbishop Musgrave
11. Archbishop Vernon Harcourt
12. Nave Pulpit in memory of Archbishops Lang and Temple.

PLAN OF YORK MINSTER

between the pillars, the capitals of which are, if possible, more beautifully chiselled than those in the rest of the Cathedral, are filled with the canopied stalls of the members of the Chapter and others, each with the title of the dignitary (in the cases of the Dean, the Precentor, the Treasurer and Succentor Canonicorum), and others with the names of the prebends held by the non-resident canons, the vicars-choral and the Master of the Song School, with the throne of the Archbishop facing the pulpit. The great East Window, that "wall of glass", forms the background to the beautiful picture. As has already been mentioned it measures 78 feet in height by 32 feet in width. There are in all over 200 compartments, 117 about a yard square, and the figures are about 2 feet high. The window is in three divisions – (1) God reigning in Heaven; (2) Old Testament history to the Death of Absalom; (3) the Apocalypse. The whole subject is the Alpha and Omega. Nearby is a screen of stone and glass. Westward of this is the high altar. The pavement of the Sanctuary in the Choir forms a memorial to the first Lord Halifax. What is now called the Lady Chapel, was originally divided into five chapels; these were from north to south on the east wall – St. Stephen's, the Holy Name, Our Lady, St. John the Evangelist, and All Saints.

The Minster is unequalled in the richness and abundance of its Stained Glass. Notice particularly, besides the East Window, the great St. Cuthbert Window in the north Choir transept; the West Window, a masterpiece of Decorated work; the Five Sisters, and the Chapter House windows. There are also two Jesse windows, one in the south aisle of the Nave, and one in the south aisle of the Choir.

The Crypt which is entered from doorways in both aisles of the Choir, consists principally of Transitional architecture. Some herring-bone work has been proved to be Saxon, and a relic of the church built by Archbishop Albert. The rebuilt groined roof in the eastern crypt is supported on six Transitional pillars.

Beneath the Crypt is to be seen a Roman pillar base which is believed to be a portion of the Praetorium.

In the South Aisle of the Choir, and closely adjoining the south transept, are three apartments, the easternmost of which, part of a chapel built under the will of Archbishop La Zouche in 1351, is now used for private prayer and meditation.

The **Monuments** in the Cathedral are so numerous that we can attempt to notice only the most interesting. The Lady Chapel and the north and south aisles of the Choir contain a great many. That of Archbishop Scrope – Shakespeare's Scrope – who was beheaded by Henry IV for high treason, is a plain altar-tomb, under the first arch from the east end, on the north side of the Lady Chapel. Another – perhaps the most curious monument in the church – is in a niche under the east window. It is that of Mrs. Mathew, a daughter of one of the Bishops of Chichester, who was married successively to the Archbishops of Canterbury and York, and who had four sisters, each of whom became the wife of a bishop. The tomb of Archbishop Mathew (*d.* 1628), who was a favourite with both Elizabeth and James I, that of Archbishop Dolben (1686) the standard-bearer at Marston Moor, and that of Archbishop Sharp (1713), a strong opponent of the Romish innovations of James II, and many others, will repay inspection.

The most beautiful monument is the tomb of Archbishop Gray (1215–1255), in the east aisle of the south transept. A spot near the pulpit in the nave is pointed out as the burial-place of St. William, Archbishop of York in the twelfth century, and canonised a century afterwards. In the north transept is a handsome memorial to Rear Admiral Christopher Cradock, who lost his life in a naval engagement in 1914.

The Chapter House

The Chapter House, to the north of the Minster, is octagonal in shape, and lighted by seven Early Decorated windows. The tracery is remarkably rich, and, with one exception, the windows are filled with painted glass of the end of the reign of

Edward I. The roof is vaulted, and ornamented with golden stars on a blue ground. The Chapter House is entered through a vestibule from the eastern aisle of the northern transept. In it are preserved several interesting antiquities.

Now moved to the Undercroft is the Horn of Ulphus, Prince of Deira, the southern part of the kingdom of Northumbria. The horn is 29 inches in length, curiously carved. and was originally ornamented with gold mountings. It forms the title by which the Dean and Chapter used to hold several valuable estates in and adjoining the city. Ulphus was the son-in-law of Canute, and, finding that his two sons were likely to quarrel after his death about their inheritance, resolved to make them both equal by depriving them of the whole. He therefore repaired to the Minster at York, bringing with him the horn filled with wine, and, kneeling before the Minster altar, devoutly drank the wine and dedicated all his lands and revenues to God and St. Peter for ever. During the Civil War, the horn was removed. It, however, ultimately fell into the hands of Sir Thomas Fairfax, the Parliamentary general, whose son Henry, Lord Fairfax, restored it to the Cathedral authorities in 1674.

The Bells of the Minster, twelve in number, and peculiarly rich in tone, occupy the north-west tower.

Big Peter is the third largest in Britain, measuring over seven feet in height, by eight and a quarter in diameter; it weighs ten tons and three-quarters.

The Cathedral is surrounded by the Minster Yard, opened out in 1825 by the removal of the rubbish and buildings which had accumulated in the Deanery Gardens on the north and by pulling down St. Peter's Prison, to the west of the sacred edifice. During the progress of these improvements some of the Transitional arches of the old Palace, were built into the wall of a stable, and may now be seen in the Garden. To the north of the Minster are the Library, formerly the chapel of the old Archiepiscopal Palace, a building of the Transitional period, and the new Deanery and the former Canon's Residence.

Round the City

To the east of the Minster is **St. William's College** *(weekdays, fee)*, home of the Minster Chantry priests from the fifteenth century until the Dissolution when it passed into private hands. Later it was divided into tenements but in the present century it was restored and is now a place for meetings and exhibitions. It is the property of the Dean and Chapter. At the time of the Civil War Charles I set up a Royal Mint and a printing press here. The principal chamber has a fine open-timbered roof. Above the doorway is the seated figure of St. William, a twelfth-century Archbishop of York. The main façade is medieval but the doorway in the picturesque courtyard beyond is Georgian and the main staircase seventeenth century.

Beyond the College is the only surviving gatehouse of those which gave access from Goodramgate into the Liberty of St. Peter, the Minster precincts over which in former days the Minster police had jurisdiction.

The Minster police force today numbers four officers whose uniforms display not the City Arms but the Cross Keys of St. Peter, the Minster's patron saint. It is thought the only ecclesiastical police force outside the Vatican at Rome.

Just inside **Dean's Park** is the **Minster Library** *(free)*. Originally it consisted only of the twelfth-century buildings with lancet windows but over the last few years has been much enlarged and now forms part of the University.

On the right of the cobbled roadway is the garden of the Treasurer's

Blossom time at York

House, and, adjoining, Gray's Court. **Treasurer's House** *(April–October, daily, fee)* together with Gray's Court *(not open)* were once a single building and the home of the Minster Treasurer. After the abolition of the office of Treasurer at the Reformation ("there being nothing left to treasure") it was a private house until the 1930s when the owner gave it to the National Trust. Treasurer's House has a fine collection of period furniture. The present building dates mainly from the sixteenth and seventeenth centuries but it stands on the site of a Roman building and there is the base of a Roman pillar in a cellar. The houses were divided in 1720 and today Gray's Court, taking its name from the last family to live there, is part of St. John's College of Education.

Along Aldwark is **Merchant Taylors' Hall** *(free)*, a medieval building restored in recent years, and showing some seventeenth-century glass and a minstrels' gallery. At the end of Aldwark is **St. Anthony's Hall** *(free)*, formerly the hall of the Guild of St. Anthony but since used for a variety of purposes after the guild dispersed. It is now the Borthwick Institute and part of the University. Historic church documents are kept here.

Across the road is the ancient *Black Swan Inn,* which has been an inn for over 160 years. In the seventeenth century it was a private house held by the Thompson family, a female member of which was Henrietta Thompson who lived here in childhood and later became mother of General James Wolfe, the hero of Quebec.

The Minster Towers soar above York

Back along Goodramgate is **Holy Trinity Church** standing in its quiet churchyard garden. Holy Trinity is one of the oldest and quaintest of the city churches, dating from the thirteenth century. The chantry chapel of a century later has a squint and an old altar stone with crosses. There is fifteenth-century glass and eighteenth-century box pews.

At the city end of Goodramgate is **King's Square**(formerly Coney Garth) and the site in Roman times of the south-east gate. The paved area is the site of Christ Church demolished in 1937 and a model of which is displayed in the Chapel Gallery of the Castle Museum.

In Petergate the twin towers of the Minster are seen in the background. In the foreground to the right above a shop which until recently was still a tobacconist's, is the trade sign, a little Indian boy wearing a tiara and a kilt of tobacco leaves. This is one of the few remaining tobacco boy signs still *in situ* in the country.

South from King's Square runs the **Shambles,** formerly the Fleshammels, the butchers' street. Its tall timber-framed buildings with their over-hanging gables give it a truly medieval air. Some of the shops still have their front slabs where meat was displayed. No. 35, once the home of the Roman Catholic Martyr Margaret Clitherow (*d.* 1586), canonized by the Pope in 1969 as St. Margaret of York, is a chapel to her memory. Nearby in Newgate is an open-air market where wide varieties of goods are sold.

The Shambles lead on to **Pavement** once the site of a pillory and a place of execution. It was probably the first paved street in old York hence its name. An interesting building here is **Herbert House,** the lower part of which is used as a shop. This Elizabethan house was bought from the Merchants' Company by Christopher Herbert in 1557 and his great-grandson, Thomas, later knighted, was born here in 1606. Sir Thomas Herbert was a great traveller and a friend of Charles I, attending the latter at his execution. Notice at the side of Herbert House the narrow passage leading to **Lady Peckitts Yard** named after the wife of John Peckitt, Lord Mayor in 1702. The Yard leads into Fossgate at the northern end of which is the curiously named Whip-Ma-Whop-Ma Gate.

On the west side of Fossgate is the –

Merchant Adventurers' Hall *(weekdays, free)*, a fine example of a fifteenth-century guildhall. The Company of Merchant Adventurers of York was the wealthiest and most influential of the city guilds in medieval times. In the days when York was a Staples town for wool (then England's chief export) samples were weighed in the hall before shipment to Europe. Scales such as were then used may still be seen in the Hall. The Great Hall has an open-timbered roof, the Undercroft its original medieval oak pillars, the chapel the old rood screen.

Fossgate crosses the Foss by the attractive hump-backed Foss Bridge to **Walmgate** on the right of which is **St. Deny's Church** with a Norman porch and interesting twelfth-century glass. Further along on the left is **St. Margaret's Church** which also has a Norman entrance porch removed here from St. Nicholas Church destroyed in the Civil War. At the end of Walmgate is **Walmgate Bar** *(see page 111).*

Continuing through Walmgate Bar turn right and follow the line of the walls round into **Fishergate** and then fork left to re-cross the Foss by Castle Mills Bridge. Keeping to the right bear into Tower Street taking its name from nearby Clifford's Tower, York Castle.

Clifford's Tower *(daily, fee)* of white stone stands on its green artificial mound, one of two thrown up by the Conqueror in 1068 and 1069. The other mound is at Baile Hill across the Ouse. The present tower was built early in the thirteenth century and, save that at Pontefract, is unique in England in its design, being quatrefoil in shape, like a four-leaved clover. The tower was subsequently used as jail until in 1684 the roof was blown off by an explosion. From the top of its walls there are fine views of the city.

Castle Museum *(daily, fee)* is one of the most popular Folk Museums in Britain, and is unique in many ways. Housed in the former Female Prison, there are fascinating period rooms and galleries and three entire streets, composed of reconstructed old shops with their trade signs, coach house and inn, fire station, and tallow dip factory for candle manufacture. The shop windows are all filled with goods of the period and each is named after some appropriate merchant of the past.

An extension of the Museum is housed in the former **Debtors' Prison** nearby. Here the old felons' cells have been converted to craft workshops. Only the condemned cell remains virtually as it was, with cast-iron bedstead, crude fireplace and heavily barred window. Dick Turpin spent three months in this cell before being hanged on Knavesmire in 1739. The first floor is a pageant of costume, the second floor a military museum. There is a reconstructed Edwardian street with drinking fountain, inn, garage and gipsy caravan. By the River Foss is a reconstructed water-driven mill used for grinding corn a century and a half ago.

Facing the Castle Museum are the Assize Courts, now the Crown Courts, built in the late 1770s.

Following the curve from Tower Street we arrive in Castlegate where is **St. Mary's Church** one of the oldest churches in the city. Its graceful spire is 154 feet high, the tallest in York.

From the northern end of Castlegate, Low Ousegate gives on to Ouse Bridge to cross the river and then via Bridge Street to **Micklegate,** one of the oldest streets in York. At various times Roman remains have been found here. The street contains a number of Georgian houses and **Holy Trinity, Micklegate** part of an alien Benedictine priory attached to the abbey of Marmoutier in France. Some Norman work remains including the nave and part of the aisles. The present tower is from the church of St. Nicholas which once stood nearby.

In Queen Street to the right beyond Micklegate Bar, is the **Railway Museum** with a fascinating collection of old engines, carriages and other equipment.

Leading off to the right is Blossom Street which leads to Knavesmire and the racecourse. It was on the Knavesmire that the city's place of execution, the York Tyburn, formerly stood.

From the Railway War Memorial, Station Road leads to the graceful **Lendal Bridge** over the Ouse and so to Museum Street and **Lendal.** The name of this street is said to be derived from St. Leonard's Landing Hill, a road formerly leading up from the river. In time the name became Lendynge Hill and so corrupted to Lendal. A few yards down on the left is the **Judges' Lodging,** a large Georgian building standing back from the road. It was built about 1720 for a York doctor on the site of the old church of St. Wilfrid. Further down on the right-is the **Post Office** and, at the end of Lendal, **St. Helen's Square,** named after **St. Helen's Church** which stands on its northern side in Davygate.

The **Mansion House** is a fine eighteenth-century building, and the official residence of the Lord Mayor during his term of office. York's Lord Mayor has the style of "Right Honourable", and has the privilege of having his Sword of State carried point upwards in procession in the presence of any one except the Sovereign. The Mansion House was built in 1726. The Civic Plate and Regalia of York is of great antiquity.

The archway at the side of the Mansion House stands over the approach to the **Guildhall,** a restoration of a fifteenth-century Commonhall destroyed in 1942 in an air raid.

Off Museum Street are the **Public Library** and the **City Information Bureau.** Close at hand is the **Multangular Tower** which formed the western corner tower of the Roman fortress of *Eboracum* and is believed to date from the fourth century, about the time of Constantine's visit. It has several floors, and the late medieval upper structure with its large stones is clearly noticeable against the smaller Roman stones. The course of five red tiles is Roman.

The **Museum Gardens** *(free)* facing Lendal belong to the Corporation and have been laid out as botanical gardens. The dominating feature of the grounds is the ruin of the great Benedictine **Abbey of St. Mary** founded by a nephew of the Conqueror. The present remains are medieval and include church, guest house, wall, gatehouse, carvings and statuary, among which are five full-size figures. The ruins of the great church serve as the back-cloth for the medieval Mystery Plays which are the nucleus of York's Festival of Music and the Arts, held every three years for three weeks during June and July.

Also in the grounds is the **Yorkshire Museum** *(daily, fee)* housing important and extensive collections of archaeology, decorative arts, geology and natural history.

Lendal Bridge and the Minster from the Walls

The Circuit of the Walls

Micklegate Bar – Victoria Bar – Fishergate Bar – Walmgate Bar – Monk Bar – Bootham Bar.

The Minster apart, the city walls are perhaps historic York's greatest asset. The tall limestone defences, with their bars and bastions, are a striking architectural feature, and their beauty is enhanced by the green ramparts of the moats. This is especially the case in the spring, when the daffodils and tulips are in bloom. The walls, in their present form, date from the fourteenth century, and follow the plan of earlier fortifications. In 1829 the York Footpath Association, which had been formed some years earlier to protect public rights of way, opened a subscription. Enough money was forthcoming to defray the cost of restoration and, by the end of the century, the complete circuit of the walls had been made into a public walk.

From Lendal Bridge round to Bootham Bar, is a distance of some $2\frac{1}{2}$ to 3 miles.

Micklegate Bar is the principal of those remaining. It was the entrance to the city from the south, and almost all the nation's sovereigns since Edward IV have passed through it when on their various visits to the northern capital. There is some Norman work in its lower part while the upper part is of fourteenth-century date. From this date it contained three floors and became a massive defence position. It was extensively restored in 1727. The portcullis which formerly closed it was so decayed by 1820 that it was removed. The archways at the side were made in the nineteenth century to facilitate walking on the footpath and in 1826, the barbican which projected on the outer side was removed. Its position as the chief Bar gave it a rather grisly distinction, for it was here that the heads of those executed for treason, rebellion, or being enemies of the nation were set on spiked poles as a warning.

The next stretch of the wall runs to Baile Hill. At various points on the walk, from the wall, the visitor can see clearly individual buildings in the old medieval city, and also on the outer side, and appreciate how the city's growth has entailed expansion beyond the walls in recent years. This stretch of wall has an archway cut in it, made in 1838. Its purpose was to provide an easier way into the city from Nunnery Lane. It was built during the mayoralty of George Hudson, and named Victoria Bar.

At the end of this section of the wall is a tree-covered mound, all that remains of one of the two tower-topped mounds thrown up by William the Conqueror. The other was Clifford's Tower. The cost of maintaining the "Old Baile," as it was known, was later borne by successive Archbishops of York, who had property on this area of Bishophill. The tower at the corner was erected in 1878. The walls end here on this side of the river which provided a natural defence when they were built.

We cross Skeldergate Bridge, made in 1881 with a section which lifted to allow river traffic through, and Castle Mills Bridge and ascend the walls again at Fishergate Postern. When this postern was built the River Foss came right to the foot of it. The red roof was put on by the Corporation in 1740. Its original purpose was a look-out post. On this stretch we come to a break in the continuity of the wall, which means we have to descend to street level, cross the road and ascend the walls at the other side.

Fishergate Bar originally had a small barbican on its outer side. In 1489 the citizens of York rebelled against heavy taxes imposed by Henry VII to finance his French Wars. The rebellion was put down and, by royal order, the leaders were executed and the wall ordered to be bricked up at this point. It remained so until 1827 when it was cleared again to allow easier access from the Cattle Market to the city. Further along the wall, and on looking to the right, the visitor can see on the higher land "The Retreat," established in 1796 by the Society of Friends. This higher land was known as Lamel Hill, and here the Parliamentarians set their artillery in the Civil War.

At **Walmgate Bar** we descend to street level again. This is the only one of the four Bars to retain its Barbican, and this feature gives the gateway a broader, more squat appearance as well as one of massive strength. This is the entry to the city from the south-east, and the Bar stands near the old Roman road. It was the last of the Bars to be erected on account of the river defence at this side. At the inside of the Bar can be seen the heavy oak doors which when closed strengthened the portcullis defence. This gateway bore the brunt of the Parliamentary artillery in the Civil War, and was largely repaired from the stone of the church of St. Nicholas which formerly stood outside the city, on the Hull road. It was repaired again in 1713 and in 1840. The shallow dwelling-house built against the inside wall and supported by pillars is probably of Elizabethan date.

We now mount the steps at the opposite side of Walmgate and continue along the walls. Here they are rather lower than in other parts of the city as the natural river defences behind made them less vulnerable. This section of wall ends with the Red Tower, different from the usual terminal towers in that it is a small square building of dark red brick. Its walls are nearly four feet thick in places, and the structure dates from the sixteenth century.

To reach the next section of the walls we walk along Foss Islands, the name of which reminds us that the area was at one time marshland. Here too the king had a royal fishpool, the catches from which were for his use. At the corner we cross Layerthorpe Bridge which gets its name from the street to the right. The name is a very old one, being derived from the Old Scandinavian, "leir" – clay – the name meaning "clay village." This is borne out by the fact that there were several brickworks in the area until recent times.

We now ascend the walls again and walk towards Monk Bar. On the inner side of the wall can be clearly seen the Roman tower at the eastern corner of Eboracum, excavated in 1925–7. The immense strength of the structure can be seen from the bird's-eye view we have from the walls.

Monk Bar to which we now come, is the tallest of the four Bars and should be viewed from the outside. There are traces of Norman work in it, and the portcullis which is still in working order can be seen. Above the centre arch is a narrow balcony from which, it is said, proclamations were read to the people. The Bar was repaired in 1825 and has recently been again restored. To get back on to the walls we climb a narrow staircase which brings us to what is perhaps the finest stretch of the whole length of the walls. From here one obtains a fine view of the Minster from the north, as well of the old houses in the Minster Yard. Here too are the magnificent lawns at the back of Gray's Court and the other residences, and trees growing near the walls add to the charming effect. Again, this section follows exactly the line of the walls of Eboracum.

Bootham Bar – Here the walls walk ends. The Bar is probably the most photographed and therefore the best known of the gates. It is at the northern entrance to the city and stands on the site of an old Roman gateway. It contains some Roman stonework as well as some Norman masonry. In 1889 alterations were made to it so that it is now possible to walk through one of the chambers. One can look through the narrow windows into Bootham and so get some idea of its value as a vantage point. The figures now on top of the Bar represent a mason, a king and a knight. Originally perhaps they represented saints. This gateway figured prominently in the wars against the Scots. It was the city's chief defensive position against any attack they might make against it, and through it expeditions set out for the Border.

York to Teesside

Easingwold – Thirsk – Northallerton – Middlesbrough
Thirteen miles north of York on the main A19 road to Yarm and Teesside is –

Easingwold

Banks. – *Midland, Barclays, York County.*
Early Closing. – Wednesday.

Hotel. – *George.*
Population. – 3,000.

a charming small market town of irregular shape: the A19 passes through Long Street, a superior sort of back street of the town whose main centre is one spacious market square or green to the east; while further to the east again is the impressive street with wide grass verges which forms a distinct area of the town, Uppleby.

Drives from Easingwold

Between here and York lies the "Forest of Galtres", now no longer forested but formerly one of the royal hunting preserves. One can take a pleasant drive round this area from the south end of Easingwold through the picturesque village of **Stillington** to **Sheriff Hutton** where there is an imposing castle: it was built in the late-fourteenth century by John Lord Neville and was originally very similar to Bolton Castle, but it had a relatively short life, for little more than two centuries later it was in ruins. **Sutton on the Forest** is another picturesque village due south of Stillington on the York road, and a few miles further south on the same road is the turning off to the west to **Skelton** which has a little gem of a mid-thirteenth century church built, so it is thought, by masons from York minster, and well worth a visit. North up the A19 road, just before Shipton, is the turning off to the west to **Beningbrough Hall** *(National Trust, Wednesday and Saturday afternoon in the summer; fee)* a grand early eighteenth-century house whose greatest glory is its magnificent wood-carving and remarkable staircase. Beningbrough village is a small hamlet some distance away perched above the River Ouse which carves its way in deep meanders through the plain: here we are not far from the scene of a famous battle of the English Civil War, for Marston Moor lies only three or four miles away across the river. A few miles further north is the R.A.F. station of **Linton-on-Ouse,** one of a string of airfields by the Ouse and its tributary the Swale: several wartime airfields have been closed and returned to agriculture, but Topcliffe, Leeming and Catterick are still active further north, and the drone of their 'planes is a common feature of life in the vale. North of Linton one can cross the antiquated toll bridge at Aldwick, a favourite picnic spot, and proceed to Boroughbridge or meander through other villages on the east bank on the return to Easingwold.

A drive to the north and east of Easingwold will take one through completely different countryside. Due east is **Crayke,** an interesting little village on a "pimple" rising sharply out of the plain, from which there is a splendid view towards York. The Castle, now a private house, was once a palace of the bishops of Durham, and the whole parish until the nineteenth century was a little island of the county palatine of Durham in the middle of Yorkshire, for this land was a gift to St. Cuthbert of Durham in the seventh century.

To the north-east is **Brandsby** on the slopes of the Howardian Hills. The village is curiously divided, for until the middle of the eighteenth century it lay near the Hall and the Church, and was then removed about half a mile away to the west. The Church, erected about 1767, is a beautiful small building of unusual design. To the north the York-Helmsley road takes one over the wooded hills and down into Ryedale. **Gilling,** the next village, was for several centuries the home of the Fairfaxes, a prominent Yorkshire Roman Catholic family. The ancient castle, much modified over the centuries, is now a preparatory school to Ampleforth College and the home of the Abbot of Ampleforth, who opens the grounds to the public on certain days during the summer.

Across the little valley lies the Abbey and College of –

Ampleforth, which can be reached by turning left off the main road a little way north of Gilling, through the village of Oswaldkirk. The Benedictine community came here after fleeing from France during the Revolution in 1793, and established themselves in 1802 in a house provided by Miss Fairfax. Over many years the buildings have expanded to accommodate the celebrated boys' public school and the monastery. The Abbey Church was designed by Sir Giles Gilbert Scott, the architect of Liverpool Cathedral. Further along the road lies Ampleforth village, Wass and **Byland Abbey, Coxwold** and **Newburgh Priory.** This latter was a house of Augustinian Canons founded in 1145. At the Dissolution of the Monasteries by Henry VIII it was granted to the Bellasis family, later Lords Fauconberg, whose descendants hold it to this day. The house and gardens are occasionally open to visitors in the summer. Clearly this area has a long tradition of monastic occupation. One can return to Easingwold through Husthwaite and south down the A19.

Byland Abbey *(daily, fee)* is quite majestic. Founded by a small band of monks from Furness Abbey in 1171, it once boasted the biggest Cistercian church in England. The church is known for its unusual green and yellow glazed tiles, particularly in two of the transept chapels, the great wheel window in the west front, and some fine carved capitals which are preserved in a small museum on the site. Here in this Abbey was buried the great Roger de Mowbray, one-time Crusader and benefactor of the monks.

Coxwold is a charming village. The wide street bordered by pleasant buildings of warm stone, ascends boldly to the church, which, with its octagonal tower, is of exceptional interest. Externally the principal features are the pinnacles and gargoyles, inside, the fine monuments to members of the Belasyse family.

Kilburn, north-west of Coxwold, is famous for the workshops of Robert Thompson (*d.* 1953) whose carved woodwork is to be found in many parts of the world. Church furniture was his speciality and his sign-manual was a "mouse". There are examples of his work in the parish church.

Cut in the hillside near Kilburn is a well-known White Horse.

Ten miles north of Easingwold on the A19 is –

Thirsk

Banks. – *Barclays, Lloyds, National West-minster, Midland, York County, Yorkshire.*
Early Closing. – Wednesday.

Hotels. – *Golden Fleece, Royal Oak.*
Markets. – Monday and Saturday.
Population. – (with Sowerby) 2,880.

This is a very busy market town at the cross roads of several important routes: the main road from Scarborough and Ryedale in the east to Ripon and the Dales in the west crosses the main roads to Northallerton in the north and York in the south and the great North-South trunk road, the A19/A168, which carries all the heavy traffic of the steel and chemical works of Teesside. Until recently drivers of enormous lorries carrying steel girders and I.C.I. chemicals threaded their way night and day through the narrow streets and market place and round the sharpest corners, but now a great dual carriageway takes this traffic away to the east and south of the town which thus regains its old charm. The market square, its cobbles recently relaid, is always thronged with shoppers and visitors. The racecourse on the west side of the town on the Ripon road brings great crowds to meetings.

Nearby, on the way out of the town towards Northallerton, is **Thirsk Hall**, the residence of the Bell family, lords of the manor since the eighteenth century and landowners here for much longer: it is a mansion refronted by the celebrated architect John Carr of York in the 1770's. Next to the Hall and dominating this side of the town is the graceful and stately **Church of St. Mary,** the most splendid building in the Perpendicular style in the North Riding, almost entirely built in the fifteenth century. Through the town runs the tiny Cod Beck on its way from the Hambleton Hills to join the River Swale near Topcliffe: it is a little surprising to discover that this Beck was in the eighteenth century envisaged as one of the main trade routes and the waterways were made navigable from Thirsk to the sea. The little Beck separates "New" Thirsk (the Church and Market side) from "Old" Thirsk, the original area of settlement, which has its own Green, St. James', surrounded by small cottages.

To the south of the town, behind the cinema and swimming baths, there is a pleasant walk through the meadow land between the beck and the village of **Sowerby** which adjoins Thirsk. The wide main street of this village is a beautiful avenue of trees with fine rows of varied houses of a generally eighteenth and early nineteenth century flavour.

Nine miles north of Thirsk on the A168 lies –

Northallerton

Banks. – *Barclays, Lloyds, Midland, National Westminster, York, Yorkshire.*
Early Closing. – Thursday.
Hotels. – *Golden Lion, Railway, Buck.*

Market. – Wednesday (and a smaller one on Saturday).
Population. – 12,375 (with Romanby).

This is the county town of the North Riding: the handsome administrative headquarters of the county, designed by the York architect

Walter Brierley in 1906, are opposite the railway station at the south end of the town. The principal feature of the town is the long wide High Street which still retains a charming late eighteenth- and early nineteenth-century appearance in spite of extensive alteration to shop fronts and an increasing traffic problem. In the centre of the street is the ugly late-nineteenth-century Town Hall, but beyond it to the north one street opens out again to a view of the impressive parish church, and beyond that again, on the road towards Darlington, is what one might call the modern industrial quarter of the town, a few carefully designed small light industrial premises, such as a carpet factory. The town has expanded enormously in the past ten years and several new housing estates have mushroomed. There are few large open green spaces, but the town is proud of its little "Applegarth" behind the west side of the High Street: the Castle Hills nearby, remains of the motte and bailey castle and once the site of a palace of the bishops of Durham, are unfortunately rather spoilt by the railway lines and the cemetery. On the other side of the town are the Memorial Swimming Baths. To the south the village of **Romanby** has practically become part of the town, although it retains its rural green.

The Hambleton Hills

Both Thirsk and Northallerton lie in the Vale of Mowbray, a local name for the northern part of the Vale of York. Either of them is an ideal centre from which to explore the Hambleton Hills, the steep western slope of the North York Moors. From the plain these hills rise sharply like a dark wall, changing colours with the light and the seasons. At the foot of their slopes lie many small and picturesque villages built in a soft warm yellow sandstone contrasting with the dark brown brick of the villages in the plain. Due east of Thirsk on the main road to Scarborough is **Sutton under Whitestonecliffe,** and the cliff from which it takes its name rises precipitously little more than a mile along the road: the one-in-four gradient of **Sutton Bank** brings the motorist to a most magnificent view across the vale to the Pennine Dales, with Penhill standing out on a clear day at the entrance to Wensleydale. Just below the cliff is the small deep dark lake Gormire surrounded by trees. A gliding club makes use of the thermals of the cliffs here. This is really rambling country, and northwards from the top of Whitestone cliff along the ridge is the old drove road which brought the cattle from the highlands of the north to be food for the population of southern England and the metropolis in the days before railways and refrigerated transport made it redundant. Short sections are narrow metalled roads, but most of it is a wide grassy track ideal for a hike of five to ten miles. It passes above the Forestry Commission's plantations of Boltby Forest and Silton Forest – mazes of tracks and paths through timber at various stages of growth – and the beautiful woods of several private estates. All along here the views across the vale to the west and over the flat stepped plateaux of the moors to the east are magnificent. In the north is the appropriately named and somewhat forbidding "Black Hambleton", over 1,300 ft. Below this hill the track joins a narrow metalled road from the largest and best known of the Hambleton villages, **Osmotherley,** with its neat terraced cottages of all shapes and sizes, cobbled paths, colourful gardens, village square and market cross. (The less energetic motorist can arrive at the same spot by a pleasant drive from the top of Sutton Bank along the metalled part of the drove road for about three miles, turning right (east) to **Hawnby,** a small village in a most picturesque

116

setting in the heart of the moors, and following the road north along the upper valley of the Rye towards Osmotherley.)

The lane leading north up the hill out of the village takes one to the path to the Lady Chapel, well worth a visit not only as a place of pilgrimage recently revived and restored but also for its view across the plain. Below the chapel are the remains of **Mount Grace Priory,** but this has to be reached from the main dual carriageway A19 trunk road, either by going back through Osmotherley and proceeding about half a mile along the north-bound carriageway, or by continuing along the road from the Lady Chapel lane, past **Cod Beck reservoir,** a popular picnic spot, to **Swainby:** on the hill to the north-east of this village are the ruins of **Whorlton Castle.** A journey south and west along the main road from here for little more than two miles brings one to the fine **Cleveland Tontine Inn,** built in 1804 when a new turnpike road was made. A few hundred yards from here along the south-bound carriageway is the entrance to

Mount Grace Priory *(daily except Mondays, but open Bank Holidays, fee),* the best-preserved ruin in England of a house of Carthusian monks. The Carthusians were required to live for the greater part of their lives in silence and separation from each other, and the ways in which they achieved this curious mode of life can be examined here. It was founded in 1398. It is now in the care of the Department of the Environment, but the house adjoining which was the guest house of the monastery, converted into a private dwelling in 1654, is a National Trust property.

If one returns to Thirsk down the dual carriageway (from which there are splendid views of the Hambleton Hills), it is worthwhile stopping at **Leake** Church, with its Norman tower, set in the fields beside the main road, far away from the villages which it serves, about five miles south of Mount Grace. If, on the other hand, one returns to Northallerton on the A684 it is worth turning aside a mile or two before the town to visit the village of **Brompton,** where the church has a famous collection of Anglo-Danish hogback tombstones.

Some of the villages in the plain to the west and north of Northallerton are worth a visit. About six miles along the extraordinarily wiggly B6271 (which leads out of the town at the north end, off the Darlington road across the railway crossing) lies **Kiplin Hall** *(Sundays in summer),* the red-brick mansion built in the early seventeenth century for Lord Baltimore, the founder of Maryland. The churchyard in the next village, **Bolton-on-Swale,** contains the grave of Henry Jenkins who died in 1670 at the fabulous age of 169. The Old Hall nearby has the remains of a pele tower. This B class road, after passing near Scorton, joins the old Great North Road near **Catterick Bridge,** where there is a fine old hotel, and on the opposite side of the road, sandwiched between that and the new dual carriageway (A1) is the Catterick racecourse, now in close proximity to the encroaching gravel workings which are such a common feature of the meandering Swale in this area. **Catterick** village itself, now by-passed by the new road, and not to be confused with the sprawling mass of the military camp two or three miles away, is a pleasant place of rural appearance with a wide green. The church is of particular interest because the contract for building it in 1412, a most rare document, has survived. This area has another, and in its way much more important, interest for the Roman town of *Cataractonium* lay close by the bridge and the modern road cuts through the ancient citadel, now the site of Thornbrough Farm. North of the river beside the road lies a small modern industrial estate. One can return to Northallerton by travelling five miles down the A1 to Leeming Bar. The small town of **Bedale** lies a mile or so to the west of this point, something like a small version of Northallerton, with a wide main street flanked with newly set cobbles, a tall slender market cross, Georgian houses and shops, the Hall, a fine country gentleman's mansion now converted to council offices, at the north end, and, dominating the street on the opposite side, the imposing tower of the Church of St. Gregory. This is the way to Leyburn and Wensleydale (*see* page 180), but retracing one's way east along the A684 leads one back to Northallerton across the bridge at **Morton-on-Swale** which is a favourite place for anglers.

Teesside

The industrial area of North Yorkshire can be approached from Northallerton from two directions.

By the first route one can follow A684 and the A19 to **Yarm,** another typical town of the area with tall terraced houses on a wide cobbled street, a perfect little Town Hall built in 1710, all contained in a great loop of the River Tees whose crossing is dominated by the huge brick railway viaduct built in 1849. This town was the scene of the well known horse fairs, and even now the gypsies gather with shining, spotless, decorated caravans. The unobtrusive early eighteenth-century church is in the back street of the town. Across the bridge into County Durham the road leads to **Stockton,** an ancient borough with one of the longest and widest high streets in the country and a market famous in the North of England. It is now part of the recently created borough of **Teesside,** an amalgamation of several industrial towns on the North and South banks at the mouth of the River Tees. The largest single town in Teesside is **Middlesbrough** on the South bank of the river. It can be approached through Stockton and the rather uninviting area between the two towns (A67) or by a pleasanter route south of the river from Yarm (A1044).

[An interesting diversion can be made from this road about three miles from Yarm by turning left along the A1045 to **Thornaby.** Originally this was a small village which gave its name to South Stockton, the late nineteenth-century industrial development south of the river. Recently the old airfield has been converted into a miniature new town and industrial estate, a curious experiment in town planning similar to the better known Billingham but on a smaller scale.]

Back on the road to Middlesbrough, much development has taken place there and in the villages nearby. One of the largest and newest hotels, one of the well-known "Post Houses" is on this road. The best way to the town centre is to turn left at the first main roundabout, by the *Blue Bell Hotel.*

The second route by which to approach Teesside gives a more spectacular view of the area. Instead of following the A19 at the *Cleveland Tontine Inn* north of Osmotherley, take the fly-over to the A172 which leads north-east to Guisborough. This takes one round below the Cleveland Hills which form the northern edge of the North York Moors. The picturesque little market town of **Stokesley,** on the river Leven, is the centre of this district, and other attractive villages in the Leven valley are becoming increasingly popular as residential areas for Teesside. The A172 leads on to Marton and **Ormesby,** and from the brow of the hill overlooking the latter village on a fine day the traveller, by now immersed in rural scenes, meets an astonishing and unforgettable sight of miles upon miles of belching chimneys of blast furnaces and chemical works covering the plain below. Now being rapidly absorbed into Middlesbrough, Ormesby yet retains a little of its rural charm and the fine mid-eighteenth-century Hall is open to visitors on certain days. At **Marton,** the birthplace of Captain Cook, now also part of the outskirts of the larger town, were the country mansions of the two great iron-masters, Bolckow and Vaughan, who were largely responsible for the vast increase in the size of Middlesbrough in the latter part of the last century. They began the large scale mining of ironstone in the Cleveland Hills and smelting at the new town which had been founded a few years earlier as a coal port at the end of an extension of the Darlington and Stockton Railway.

Middlesbrough

At the beginning of the nineteenth century the population of the hamlet of Middlesbrough was 25, but by 1861 it was 19,000 and forty years later it had reached 91,000: this was the most spectacular growth England had seen, and in its progress the town engulfed and submerged rapidly several villages and hamlets in a somewhat formless sprawl of buildings. Although one of the main attractions of this town is that one can quickly escape from it to the beautiful countryside of Cleveland, it would be wrong to dismiss it as devoid of interest, for the very rapidity of its rise should make it an object lesson in the problems of industrial development and the achievements of the Victorians on a virgin site.

A little of the original town still stands, the parish **Church of St. Hilda** in the original Market Place laid out in the 1830's, the **Custom House** built close by in 1840 and the **Old Town Hall** of 1846, but much has been swept away for new blocks of flats, and some of the buildings of more interest to the visitor belong to the late Victorian and Edwardian eras. The **Transporter Bridge** here is the largest in the world and something of a tourist attraction. The Public Library is an impressive building overlooking an open square in the modern centre of the town, near the grand neo-Gothic "new" Town Hall, a delight for the enthusiast for Victorian architecture. Not far away is the **Dorman Museum** in Linthorpe Road. Very successful International Eisteddfods have been held on Teesside in recent years, bringing groups of folk singers and dancers from all over the world.

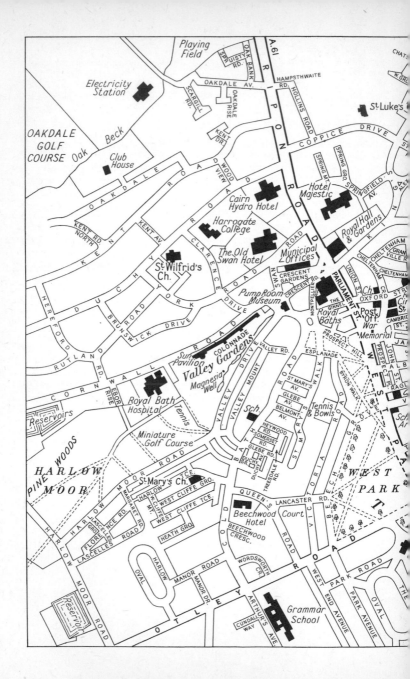

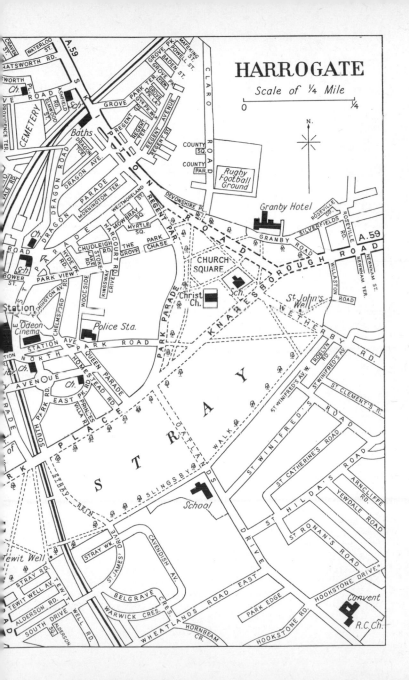

Harrogate

Harrogate, a healthful and cheerful holiday resort, is situated in the West Riding, on a tableland having a mean altitude of about 400 feet above sea-level. It is almost mid-way between the Irish Sea and the North Sea, and about equidistant (some 200 miles from each) from London, Edinburgh and Dublin.

The town is graced with healthful bracing air and is indeed a bright and well-ordered resort in which to stay, on its own account and as a centre from which to enjoy so much attractive and varied scenery. In recent years the town has become a popular conference and trade fair centre.

Harrogate itself has three golf courses and within a dozen miles there are a dozen more. Each Spring a competitive music festival, held in the Royal Hall, attracts large numbers of entries. The Spring Flower Show of the North of England Horticultural Society, held in April, is considered to be one of the finest in the North. The arrangements attract many home and overseas visitors. Other attractions include the Great Yorkshire Agricultural Show, the Harrogate Festival of Music and the Harrogate Drama Festival. There are theatre shows, cinemas and good concerts; and this wealth of entertainment within the town is surpassed by the extraordinary range and variety of scene in the neighbourhood. Harrogate has first-rate claims as a motoring centre, and these claims are equally strong if the excursions are made by rail, bus or coach, by cycle or on foot.

Its name is Harrogate's only link with the distant past. The name Harrogate is held to be simply a modification of *Haywragate, i.e.*, the road passing near Hayra, a spot a few miles west of Harrogate known today as Haverah. "*Hay* represents Anglo-Saxon *hege* and Anglo-French *haie*, and means enclosure or park; and *wra* is the Anglo-Saxon *wra*, a corner. That is to say, the road passed near the corner of an old enclosed park, a portion of the old Forest of Knaresborough" (*Skeat*). There are several other plausible derivations.

High Harrogate occupies a plateau commanding an extensive landscape; **Low Harrogate** is situated on the western slope of the hill and in the valley at its foot. The intervening area is occupied by the principal business thoroughfares and by the railway station. The chief public buildings are in Low Harrogate. The residential portion of Harrogate now extends over the high ground (the Duchy Estate) to the north and north-west of Low Harrogate, and, indeed, is spreading in every direction. Certain buildings in the modern town possess architectural interest. *Mansfield House*, in Church Square, was built as a theatre in 1788, and Edmund Kean played there. *Wedderburn House*, in Adam style, was built by Alexander Wedderburn, Lord Loughborough, in 1786. *Numbers 1-4 West Park* form a Regency terrace, and *Numbers 35-39 Swan Road* and 1 *Crescent Road* may be dated in the early eighteenth century. This building was an inn for two hundred years, with two sulphur springs in its wine-cellar. *Woodlands* is a well-preserved seventeenth-century farmhouse.

One of the most attractive features of the town consists of its open spaces. **The Stray** is a park-like common of 215 acres, extending from the Esplanade in Low Harrogate to the *Granby Hotel* in High Harrogate. It is open to everyone for riding or walking, and is universally a very popular resort.

The **Valley Gardens** form another popular resort, extending from the Pump Room Museum to Harlow Moor. A bronze plaque at the entrance commemorates American troops. The gardens are very attractively laid out and, as their name indicates, are sheltered from most of the breezes that blow. There is a fine display of colour in the borders and flower beds, well-kept lawns, intriguing rock gardens, magnificent trees, lily ponds, pools for children's paddling and boats, tennis courts, miniature golf course, putting-and bowling-green. Practically the whole of the northern edge of the Gardens is further sheltered by –

View from Prospect Gardens, Harrogate

The Sun Pavilion and Colonnade. The Pavilion comprises a tea lounge and ballroom, where dancing takes place during the year, and where there are also informal concerts. The glass-roofed Colonnade, facing south, is several hundred yards long, affording a delightful promenade or lounging place, and at intervals are glass-walled sun-lounges – large, pleasant rooms with flowering shrubs and plants – which can be warmed artificially if necessary. The views of the Gardens from the Colonnade are very pleasant. The large circular stones in the Gardens cover some of the 88 wells for which Harrogate is renowned, but no two of them (though they are only a few yards, and in some instances only a few feet, apart) are precisely alike. In the space of a quarter acre, more differing springs exist than in any other similar space in the world. The springs are chiefly sulphur, chalybeate, and magnesia. Towards the western end of the Gardens are public tennis courts and bowling-greens and a miniature golf course, and westward again is –

Harlow Moor, an expanse of firs, gorse and heather commanding extensive views, and intersected by broad paths. The pines, which form so agreeable a feature of the Moor, originated in the formation in 1769 of the King's Plantation, as it was named, covering some 65 acres.

The **Crescent Gardens** lie between the Old Pump Room, the **Municipal Offices** and the Royal Baths, and form an extension of the Valley Gardens, facing the Royal Hall. It will thus be seen that it is possible to walk for nearly a mile (with only two interruptions by roadways) through gardens

124

from the heart of Low Harrogate to the heights of Harlow Moor. At the western end are **Harlow Car Gardens,** the trial grounds of the Northern Horticultural Society. *(Open daily, charge.)*

Harrogate is well provided with facilities for indoor entertainment. The **Royal Hall** has a large and comfortable theatre, seating 1,350 persons, and is used also for conferences, orchestral concerts, lectures, etc. Here is held each Spring the annual Competitive Musical Festival, the annual Festival of Music featuring the Hallé Orchestra; in addition, it has been the venue of some of the largest and most important British conferences. A covered promenade practically encircles the building.

There are two **Cinemas,** while repertory is presented each week in the Opera House.

The **Public Library** in Victoria Avenue includes lending libraries, reading room and reference library. The building also contains an **Art Gallery.** The permanent collection contains 300 oil paintings, water colours, pastels and black-and-white drawings: a series of loan exhibitions is held each year.

At the junction of James Street, Cambridge Street, Parliament Street (the chief thoroughfare in Low Harrogate) and West Park is Harrogate's **War Memorial,** an obelisk of Portland stone with inscribed bronze panels.

The **Royal Pump Room Museum of Local Antiquities,** Low Harrogate, opposite the Valley Gardens, is housed in the building originally used as the Pump Room of the Harrogate Sulphur Well. This popular museum is maintained by the Corporation and attracts some 60,000 visitors a year. *(Open 11 a.m. to 7 p.m. in the summer and 11 a.m. to 5 p.m. in the winter. Admission free).*

The Harrogate Mineral Waters. The Mineral Waters which have long been famous possess in various degrees the curative qualities of nearly every known spring in Europe.

Geologically considered, Harrogate lies on the crest of an anticline or ridge pushed up by a volcanic upheaval which was not sufficiently powerful to make an active crater. The lowest strata of the Carboniferous Series are exposed. They are rocks which cannot be identified with any elsewhere in the neighbourhood and it is through them that the springs percolate to the surface. The waters are "juvenile" or "plutonic", *i.e.,* they are in no way dependent on rainfall, but rise direct from the underlying magma of igneous rock at a great depth and have never previously seen the light of day. As they rise to the surface they meet with the various minerals in vein formation, from which they obtain their saline content, and then emerge between the almost vertically situated strata.

Within an area of two miles there are eighty-eight wells, which may be divided into four classes:
Strong sulphur. Mild sulphur, containing alkaline salts. Saline chalybeate. Pure chalybeate.

A valuable constituent of some of the Harrogate waters is Barium. Barium Chloride has a great effect in raising the arterial blood pressure, and it is held that the compounds of the element contained in the waters have a definite therapeutic value, preventing the depression often caused by courses of sulphur waters not containing this element. Another important constituent of the waters is Manganese, which has a beneficial effect in accelerating the chemical processes in the body.

The Royal Baths. The Royal Baths building, where medicinal treatment and baths were formerly administered, is now a new complex of multi-purpose rooms, available for small functions as concerts, fashion shows,

Assembly Rooms and Royal Baths, Harrogate

conferences, trade fairs, film shows, art exhibitions, etc. The former Pump Room is now a popular restaurant where coffee concerts are held each morning.

On the Stray, opposite the Prince of Wales Mansions, is the **Tewit Well** the oldest of the Harrogate spas. It is of pure chalybeate water. Next in seniority is *John's* or **St. John's Well** on the Stray road leading to Wetherby Road. Its name is probably taken from its proximity to St. John's Chapel, the precursor of Christ Church.

There are two good **Swimming Baths,** one in Coppice Valley and the other at Starbeck.

The **Royal Bath Hospital and Rawson Convalescent Home** is in Cornwall Road.

Harrogate toffee, a sweetmeat peculiar to the town, has been enjoyed by many generations and is still available from local confectioners.

Walks from Harrogate

To Harlow Car. The direct route is by the footpath fronting the end of Cornwall Road; otherwise turn to the right presently crossing the Oak Beck by Oakdale Bridge. Beyond the ancient Irongate Bridge, a packhorse bridge of a single arch, turn left through Oakdale Farm and follow a ridge path, Long Crag, with Oakdale on the left and Birk Crag in full view on the other side. Turn left on to the Otley–Ripley road (B6161). At cross-roads the righthand turn is Penny Pot Lane, leading to Fewston.

Haverah Park. On the right further along the Otley road is Haverah Park, once one of the royal parks attached to the Honour of Knaresborough. Haverah is a corruption of *Haywra*, and according to the late Professor Skeat, Harrogate itself owes its name to the spot – *Haywragate (see* page 123).

On a hill at the western extremity of the park, some 5 miles in a bee-line from Harrogate, are the scanty remains of a strong tower or keepers' lodge, known as **John o' Gaunt's Castle.** Edward II is said to have been entertained in it for three days.

About a mile to the south-east of the ruins are a number of tumuli, known as **Pippin's Castle.** They are said to be the graves of the old inhabitants of John o' Gaunt's Castle.

Follow the high-road over the Oak Beck, which is crossed by **(Penny) Pot Bridge.** A short distance beyond the bridge turn to the left through a gate, passing a cottage on the left. A broad footpath leads along the brow of the slope and then through fields to the grounds of Harlow Car Hotel. Pass in front of the house, and then go straight on up the short hill into a road. Turn to the left, and in a few yards to the right, where follow a firm "public footpath" to the reservoirs passed on the outward journey. Continue down Cornwall Road or alternatively through the woods to Valley Gardens. For *Harlow Car Gardens, see* page 125.

To Pannal, returning by Pannal Ash. From the west end of the Stray, follow the Leeds Road for a mile and a quarter, and then turn out of it at the brow of Almsford (Humphrey) Bank by passing to the right along Stone Rings Lane, which runs just above the house called *Almsford Grange* and leads by an old stone quarry. At the foot of the lane cross the *Stone Rings Beck*, ascend the hill on the far side, and at the end of a quarter of a mile pass through a gate and along the terrace-like asphalt path in front of a block of private residences. From this point there is a fine view of the Crimple Valley. In a few yards the path joins Church Lane, where turn to the left, and less than half a mile brings you to **Pannal,** a pretty village standing on the side of a hill rising out of the Crimple Valley.

The **Church,** dedicated to St. Robert of Knaresborough, was made the headquarters of the Scottish troops who, in 1312, invaded the North of England. When they left they set it on fire. The oldest parts are the chancel and tower (thirteenth century). In the first window on the south side is a piece of old stained glass, representing the embattled gateway of some ancient building, supposed to be that of the priory to St. Robert of Knaresborough, to which house this church was given by Edmund, Earl of Cornwall, in the year 1348. In the chancel are many memorials to the Bentley family, who have been owners of the local estate for some three and a half centuries and have held the office of Lay Rector. The present owner, Mr. W. B. Bentley, is one of the very few Lay Rectors still in office in the Church of England, and the memorials owe their position to the fact that Lay Rectors have the privilege of burial in the chancel, in return for maintaining the chancel fabric "wind and weatherproof".

From Pannal the walk may be extended by **Burn Bridge** (*see* below) or Harrogate may be regained by Pannal Ash. The first portion of the route back to Harrogate is by Church Lane (by which we entered the village). At cross-roads, about a mile from Pannal, either turn to right down Leadhall Lane, with its pleasantly situated houses, to the Leeds Road, or keep ahead to Pannal Ash *via* Green Lane. From Pannal Ash, Harrogate is reached by Pannal Ash Road and Otley Road.

Up the Crimple Valley. From **Pannal,** follow the wooded bank of the Crimple *via* Mill Lane for half a mile to **Burn Bridge.** Here turn right opposite the *Black Swan*. Along this road Charles I was conducted on his way to London as a prisoner.

A quarter of a mile from Burn Bridge is Daw Cross, where turn to the left. In about a third of a mile is Hillfoot Lodge, at the junction of various routes (note tablet in wall on left marking site of Pannal's first Wesleyan Church, in which John Wesley himself preached). Turn to the right, up the hill, for a few yards and then climb the stone stile in the wall immediately on the right of the white gate of *Ardross*. Skirt the wall, ascend some stone steps and cross a wooden stile a dozen yards on. Hence the path bears round to the right below **Hilltop Hall,** once known as the *Half-way House*, owing to the ancient portion of it having been used as a rest-house for the monks passing to and from Fountains and Kirkstall Abbeys, between which it is approximately equidistant. Its architecture illustrates a mixture of styles from the fifteenth century. From here we have a complete view of the upper portion of the valley of the Crimple. At a fork, about a quarter of a mile from the lane, keep to the left, and then for half a mile the footpath runs parallel to the stream, at a distance of some two hundred yards from it. At the end of the half-mile the path crosses a brook, and immediately bears to the right of Hole House Farm. Pass Howe Quarry, on the opposite side of the brook. Thence, passing through a gate, take a footpath running in a north-easterly direction, and leading, in a third of a mile, to Beckwith Cottage. Here turn to the left, and pass over the cross-roads and into Otley Road, where turn to the right.

Montpellier Gardens, Harrogate

129

Excursions from Harrogate

To Ripley. This pretty village lies 4 miles north of Harrogate. Formerly a busy market town, its history can be traced to the days when the Danes invaded England. It consists principally of one broad street, prettily shaded with trees and a peaceful square with stocks and a market cross.

Ripley Church *(All Saints')* was erected in the fifteenth century. It contains tombs and monuments of many members of the Ingilby family, the most interesting being that on the south side of the chancel to "the right worthie and Illustrious Knight Sir William Inglebie." Follows a long inscription in the fulsome style of those times (1617), to which Cromwell caused to be added the terse footnote: "No pompe nor pride. Let God be honoured."

In the north-east corner is a tabard of black taffetas, decorated with a coat of arms: part of the funeral trappings customary in the days of chivalry.

In the churchyard is the pedestal of an ancient weeping cross. It is of circular form, and contains eight niches intended to receive the knees of worshippers. The cross is said to date from the second century.

The predecessor of the present church is said to have stood upon a round hill now covered with foliage and known as **Kirk Sink.** The Nidd in those days flowed past the base of the hill, and having in course of time undermined the site of the church, a portion of the building fell upon it, altering the course of the stream. The hill is said to have received its name in consequence.

Ripley Castle *(open Sundays and Bank Holidays, June to September. Gardens additionally on Saturdays, fee)* is the seat of the Ingilbys. It is a Tudor building on the site of a feudal fortress, of which the fifteenth-century gateway and sixteenth-century tower may yet be seen. After the battle of Marston Moor, Cromwell sent a relative of the Ingilbys to the castle to provide for the reception of himself and some of his officers. The head of the family was absent, but Lady Ingilby was at home, and as she and her husband were Royalists she only received the victorious general and his companions under compulsion. Tradition records how she met Cromwell at the gate with a brace of pistols in her apron-strings, and after expressing a hope that neither he nor his soldiers would misbehave themselves, conducted him to the great hall and watched him vigilantly the night through. When he left in the morning she bade him farewell rather unceremoniously. "It is well," said she, "that you have behaved in so peaceable a manner, for had it been otherwise, you would not have left this house with your life." James I stayed at the castle on his way from Scotland to take over the throne of England in 1603.

Ripley to Knaresborough

There is a direct road from **Ripley** to **Knaresborough** (4 miles), passing near the village of **Scotton,** where Guy Fawkes resided in early life. Part of the house in which he lived is still to be seen.

On **Gate's Hill,** overlooking the River Nidd, is a 300-bed Hospital built in 1937. The Woodlands are in the possession of the Forestry Commission and re-afforestation is in progress.

Ripley Castle

Away to the left is the **Scriven Park** portion of the Slingsby Estate. From the back entrance, by the keeper's lodge, are visible the trees and wall of Appleby Carr where fishing and skating are permitted in season, on payment of a small charge towards Scriven Village Children's Fund. Further on is the old main entrance and lodge, the gates reputed to have been designed by Inigo Jones.

Knaresborough is described on pp. 136–9.

Ripley to Hampsthwaite

The road between Ripley Castle and the Church descends to the river, and is continued as a bridle road to Clint and Hampsthwaite *(teas)* – a very pleasant walk.

Hampsthwaite stands beside the Nidd, its church and old bridge close neighbours. The Church *(St. Thomas à Becket)* stands close to the stream. Except for the tower, the church was almost entirely rebuilt in 1901, but it still contains some Norman and medieval relics.

The Roman road from Aldborough to Ilkley crossed the Nidd at Hampsthwaite by a ford. Traces of Roman work were found in the river-bank west of the present bridge.

Cote Syke Farm was the home of the Simpson family which could claim descent from one Archil, an Anglian thane. The house has an ancient salt-cupboard, a stone fireplace, and mullioned windows.

To Little Alms Cliff and Fewston. Half a mile beyond Beckwithshaw turn off on right and soon the stone wall which has borne us company for so long turns away to reveal a vast expanse of moorland scenery. A mile ahead and to the left is **Little Alms Cliff,** an outcrop of gritstone commanding fine views. The road drives on across the moors; and in about a mile meets another running right and left. Turn right and in about a quarter of a mile go down to the left, through the plantations, bearing right at the foot of the hill. Quite suddenly a most delightful view of the **Swinsty Reservoir** (Leeds Waterworks) opens up on either hand, the lake fringed with graceful trees beyond which are the green hills.

On the brink of the reservoir is **Swinsty Hall,** a fine old building dating from the sixteenth century. Tradition says that it was built by a poor weaver who visited London during a time of plague and there collected a wagon-load of gold, forsaken by its panic-stricken owners.

Continuing up the hill our road reaches –

Fewston, locally known as "the moving village", because at various times it has suffered subsidence.

The **Church** has been twice burnt down, a fact which accounts for the absence of ancient monuments. There has been a church on the site since 1234, and many of the Fairfaxes and other notables were buried within its walls. The present building is of late Jacobean architecture.

There are traditions of a Druidical altar and of the presence of a barguest, or demon-dog, at **Busky Dike.**

From Fewston the return to Harrogate may be made more or less directly by way of Penny Pot Lane; but it is worth while to follow the Timble road down the hill from the church to the embankment between the upper and lower reservoirs.

Spofforth Castle

The view of the lakes from this point is particularly good, and when the upper lake is full its waters overflow into the lower lake by way of a "stairway" down which they cascade very finely.

The trip can be enjoyably exciting by continuing through the hamlet of **Timble** to the Otley road, where turn right, descending steeply to the curiously-named hamlet of **Blubberhouses.** Hence the road is direct (9 m. – bus route to Harrogate).

To Alms Cliff. A pleasant drive through country lanes is by the Otley road to the gates of Moor Park, where turn left through Beckwithshaw. In about half-a-mile the road to North Rigton goes off on the left. In the village bear right at the stocks and to right again just beyond church.

Great Alms Cliff – there is some variety of spelling – is a striking outcrop of rock nearly 600 feet above sea level. It commands a splendid prospect. **Kirkby Overblow** is a pleasant village about a mile beyond the Harrogate–Leeds road. Return to Harrogate can be made by the edge of Pannal golf links and **Follifoot,** and so on to the Bilton road.

To Plumpton, Spofforth, Ribston. Plumpton Rocks *(admission fee to grounds; Refreshments available)* lie 3 miles from Harrogate along the Wetherby road. The rocks are huge blocks of millstone grit but most visitors are less interested in its geological aspect as in the large lake nearby and the pretty scenes.

Spofforth Castle *(daily, free)* is situated to the north of the village, not far from the Church. A fortified Manor House built on the site of a Saxon Hall *c.* 700; the Castle is usually referred to as a fourteenth-century building though the undercroft, in excellent state of preservation, probably dates from the twelfth or early thirteenth-century.

After the Norman Conquest it was given to William de Percy in 1067 whose family seat it then became for 300 years. It is reputably the birthplace of the re-nowned Harry Hotspur. In 1309 it was rebuilt and fortified, but after the death of "Proud Northumberland" at the battle of Towton, 1461, it was much damaged by the victorious Yorkists. It was finally dismantled in 1604.

The hall is 75 feet by 36 feet, and has fine arched windows. Interesting relics are kept in the custodian's care.

Spofforth village is dominated by the sturdy fourteenth-century tower of its **church,** a spacious building of Transitional Norman architecture. Within the church is a fragment of an ancient market cross, *c.* 850, an interesting effigy of Sir Robert Plumpton, *d.* 1323, in knightly armour, and some consecration crosses built into the walls. In the churchyard a few yards to the north of the chancel wall is the grave of John Metcalfe (Blind Jack of Knaresborough).

Ribston Hall, built in 1674, stands in beautiful grounds on the banks of the Nidd some 6 miles south-east of Harrogate. It was here in 1709 that the famous Ribston Pippin apple was first raised in England.

The return journey may be made (footpath only) by way of Goldsborough and Knaresborough. In **Goldsborough** some Saxon and Cufic coins of the ninth and tenth centuries were discovered during the construction of a drain in 1858. The chief features of the place are its Early English Church, restored by Sir Gilbert Scott, and its **Hall,** of the period of Elizabeth I.

To Harewood. Some 3 miles from Pannal is Harewood Bridge, just beyond which, by turning left along the main road, one reaches the ruins of **Harewood Castle,** which was built soon after the Conquest, but reconstructed in the reign of Edward III. The chief entrance is beneath a square turret, adorned by shields, one being that of Edward Baliol, King of Scotland, who found refuge here when he had been driven out of Scotland. *(Entry is prohibited as the ruins are unsafe.)*

Harewood. The name of the village has changed four times: Heraward, Whorewood, Harwood, and finally Harewood. The local people pronounce it "Harewood", whilst others pronounce it "Harwood". The village, on the eastern side of the Park, one time a considerable town, now consists of two streets, one running north and south, the other east and west. The latter leads into the Park, to the Church and the Hall. The **Church** *(All Saints')* is said to date from the time of Edward III, and to have replaced one erected when the Castle was founded. It is notable for its collection of alabaster tombs.

Harewood House. *(House and gardens open daily Easter to September. Sundays only in October. In winter Park and gardens only, on Sundays, fee.)* The seat of the Earls of Harewood, Harewood House was built in 1759–67, and is a good specimen of Corinthian architecture. From its elevated position in a park of great beauty (about 1,800 acres), designed by Capability Brown, the house commands a wide view. The pleasure grounds and gardens comprise nearly 150 acres. They are beautifully laid out with terraces, a lake and an exotic Bird Garden, containing over 200 different species of birds ranging from humming birds to flamingoes.

Harewood House

The main attraction of the house is the beautiful Adam-designed architecture and furniture. The entrance hall with its fluted columns and wonderful ceiling leads to the Music Room where the Chippendale furniture, superb carpet, Sèvres china and oil paintings are yet out-splendoured by the exquisite ceiling panels of Angelica Kauffmann. In the Dining Room is more Adam furniture, a fine chimney-piece and family portraits. The long Gallery is another Adam masterpiece, enhanced by contributions from Chippendale and Angelica Kauffmann and with family portraits by Gainsborough, Reynolds, etc. Two other state rooms shown to the public are the Green Drawing Room and the Rose Drawing Room. In these the chief interest is the collection of fine Italian paintings. Shown also are several private apartments containing pictures and other items of a more personal and family nature. In the Stable Block are three exhibition rooms displaying exhibits illustrating the history of the family, House and estate from 1759 to the present day.

To Wetherby and Boston Spa. From the east end of the Stray at Harrogate, Wetherby Road leads by Spofford (*p.* 133) to Wetherby.

Wetherby is a market town on the Great North Road. It was at one time held by the Knights Templars, and afterwards by the Hospitallers. A few Roman relics have been unearthed, and there are foundations and the lower part of a castle believed to date from the time of Henry I. A picturesque bridge spans the River Wharfe. There are several interesting inns including the *Swan and Talbot* and the *Angel* both being old coaching halts. Boating is popular on the river. There is also a golfcourse and a steeplechase course.

Five miles south of Wetherby is **Boston Spa,** a pretty place on the River Wharfe, which here falls gracefully over a weir. Boston became a spa by virtue of its saline spring. The water is said to alleviate rheumatism. There is some good fishing in the river.

To the south-east of Boston Spa is **Clifford** where the modern church has been built in Norman style. For **Tadcaster,** see p. 227.

Two miles north of Boston Spa and three miles west of Wetherby, near the village of Walton, is the **National Lending Library for Science and Technology.** Opened in 1962, the library houses the largest loan collection in the United Kingdom of the world's scientific literature, and provides a postal loan service to U.K. organisations. There is a small reading-room.

To Cowthorpe and Marston Moor. Reached by an eastward turning from the Great North Road about three miles north of Wetherby is **Cowthorpe** where the church is of great interest. Built from the materials of an earlier church, the tower projects on both sides of the west wall with an outside supporting arch. Only one similar construction is known – at Baginton, Warwickshire. There is an interesting brass to Brian Roucliff (*d.* 1494) on the north wall of the church.

East of Cowthorpe is **Tockwith** near which is **Marston Moor,** scene of the famous battle fought July 2, 1644. The topographical detail has changed very little and the scene can be envisaged. The present road runs along the battle line. A commemorative memorial stands on the moor.

Nun Monkton, to the north of the Knaresborough–York road, has a large village green with a Maypole. The beautiful little church is a gem of the Transitional and Early English periods and has a fine Norman porch.

Knaresborough

Angling (trout and grayling) – *Knaresborough Angling Club*: Day tickets. Applicant must be accompanied by member. *Knaresborough Piscatorials*: Day ticket from 1st May for non-members, from Mr. C. Nicholls, Sports Shop, High Street, Knaresborough.
Early Closing Day. – Thursday.
Population. – 11,700.
Golf (18 holes). – The links are 1 mile from Knaresborough on the Boroughbridge road; bus passes. Miniature Golf and putting at Conyngham Hall, putting-green also in Castle Grounds.
Hotels. – *Commercial, Board Inn, Crown*; all in High Street; *Dropping Well*, Low Bridge;

Mitre, Station Road; *World's End*, Bond End; *Station*, Kirkgate; *George and Dragon* and *Wellington* in Briggate; *Groves*, Market Place.
Car Parking Places. – Castle Yard, Fisher Street, Market Place, Waterside, Conyngham Hall, York Place, High Street. Free disc parking scheme.
Sports, etc. – Bowling Green in Castle grounds, and a club green at Elephant and Castle Hotel. Cricket ground at Crag Top; tennis in Conyngham Hall grounds; excellent facilities for boating and camping. Golf and Angling, *see* above.
Post Office. – 81 and 83 High Street.
Zoo. – Small zoo, Conyngham Hall Grounds.

Knaresborough is a royal borough, though not a municipal one, and was a parliamentary borough from 1553 till 1885. It is only $3\frac{1}{2}$ miles from Harrogate, and stands on the summit of a hill overlooking the river Nidd, which at this spot runs through a romantic glen and beneath precipitous rocks.

The town appears to great advantage when approached by the high-road *via* Starbeck, or by the footpath described on page 130. The luxuriant woods by which it is surrounded, the winding river at its foot, the venerable cottages, placed tier above tier on the face of the rock, the ruined castle and the old church, combine to make a beautiful picture.

The town is noted for its linen manufacture, but there is considerable other business activity, while visitors are attracted by the natural charms of the place and its historical associations. Coins of Roman emperors have been found within the borough. It is supposed that the Saxons had a fortress here; but it was not till after the Conquest that the place became important. William bestowed the manor on Serlo de Burgh, one of his followers, and that baron, or his immediate successor, built –

Knaresborough Castle *(open daily, Easter to October, charge)*. The Castle is now represented by a fragmentary keep and a number of isolated piles of weather-worn masonry among which are a putting-green and bowling-green.

After figuring in many sanguinary struggles, the Castle was demolished in Cromwell's days. It was to this castle that the knights fled after the slaying of Thomas à Becket in Canterbury Cathedral. The de Burgh of the reign of Henry III joined de Montfort in his rebellion, and his estates were forfeited to the Crown. They were subsequently conferred on the Earl of Cornwall, and later on John of Gaunt, from whose days they have been attached to the Duchy of Lancaster, the

Knaresborough

Sovereign being now the lord of the manor. The fortress was one of the prisons of Richard II, the apartment which he occupied being that now known as the **King's Chamber.**

During the early part of the Civil War the castle was an important post in the hands of the Cavaliers. Fairfax besieged and took it after the battle of Marston Moor; and only four years afterwards it was dismantled and reduced to ruins.

The walls, which were defended by eleven towers, encircled two acres and a half of land, on which were erected wards and other buildings, sufficient to accommodate a numerous garrison. The **Keep** is believed to have been built by John of Gaunt. It had three storeys, and was square – 54 feet on each side; below it was the dungeon, a gloomy vault, 23 feet long by 20 feet wide, reached by a descent of twelve steps. Near the keep are the ruins of the chief **Gateway.** A secret passage, discovered in 1890, leads from the castle yard to the moat. In more recent years, other underground passages have been opened up.

The site of the castle commands prospects of great beauty and extent, and "Knaresborough, from the Castle Hill", is a favourite subject with artists. The grounds have attractive gardens, bowling- and putting-greens and well-placed seats.

The **Parish Church** (Sunday services 8.30, 9.30, 11 a.m., 6.30 p.m.), dedicated to St. John the Baptist, is old and spacious, mainly Early English and Perpendicular. Mention is made of it as early as 1114, but the oldest parts now existing are the base of the chancel and part of the vestry, which probably date from the early twelfth century. The tower and portions of the adjoining chapels date from the latter part of the twelfth and the early part of the thirteenth century. The nave is entirely fifteenth-century work. The church was restored in 1869. The tower contains a peal of eight bells, placed there in the year 1774; and attached to the choir are the mortuary chapels of the Slingsby and Roundell families, the former containing some interesting monuments.

In the vestry are two full-length paintings on wood of Moses and Aaron. They formerly stood near the communion-table, and probably belong to the fifteenth century.

Between the High Bridge and the Railway Viaduct is the old **Manor House,** a many-gabled, half-timbered structure, nestling under the cliff on the banks of the Nidd. *The house is open to visitors. Lunch; Dinner available.* The house is reputed to be thirteenth-century. There is some beautiful oak panelling dating from 1400 to the time of the Commonwealth. The bed on which Oliver Cromwell slept here is still preserved.

One of the most curious natural attractions of the neighbourhood is **The Dropping Well** *(Admission fee)*. It is situated in the Long Walk, at the Low Bridge end of which is the Lovely Beech Avenue, part of the original "Forest of Knaresborough". The well can be approached through an iron gate near a Drinking Fountain close to the High Bridge, or through the Mother Shipton Inn, near the Low Bridge.

The water of the Dropping Well rises about 40 yards from the bank of the Nidd, and runs into an almost isolated block of limestone over the top of which it trickles. Below the projecting rock are suspended such articles as sponges, gloves, eggs, hats, stockings, etc., to be encrusted with the lime contained in the water. They become "petrified" in from four months to two years. A collection may be seen at the *Mother*

Knaresborough Castle

Shipton Inn. The deposit is of a brown colour, water-analysis revealing a predominance of lime, sulphates, chlorides and magnesia.

At the back of the rock is a **Wishing Well,** and the path to the right leads to **Mother Shipton's Cave,** of interest only on account of the tradition that it was the birthplace of that mysterious prophetess. She is said to have been born on July 6, 1488. A full account of her life is on sale in the town.

Across the river from the Mother Shipton Inn can be seen on the cliff-face a yellow-washed sculpture. This is beside the door of –

The Chapel of our Lady of the Crag, reached by steps from Abbey Road, at far end of Low Bridge. Though long attributed to St. Robert, this consecrated excavation in the cliffs post-dates the death of the saint by nearly two centuries. In fact, the licence to excavate the Chapel, granted by Henry IV in 1408, still exists. A graceful figure of the Blessed Virgin and Child was added when the Oratory was restored in 1916. The grotesque faces within have no significance, and the disproportioned armed figure outside (of which there is no mention before the eighteenth century) represents neither St. Robert nor a Templar. The Chapel is a very rare specimen of a medieval wayside shrine. Certainly there is nothing like it in England.

To the left of the chapel is **Fort Montagu,** a four-storey house hewn out of the rock by a weaver, who, after 16 years' hard work, left his task to his son to complete. The name is due to the Duchess of Buccleuch, who visited the place during its excavation (Montagu being her family name).

About a mile below Crag Chapel is the site of the *"House of St. Robert"* (1250), founded by Richard, Earl of Cornwall, to perpetuate the memory of the saint, and granted to the Trinitarians, significantly known in England as the Robertines, whose special work was to collect alms to redeem Christian captives from the Infidels.

Those who have climbed to the top of the house from the Chapel may be relieved to know that the town can be regained without descending the roughly-cut steps. It is, however, worth following the riverside road (motorists proceed with caution) for a mile to –

St. Robert's Cave. Permission to view to be obtained from Priest-in-charge, Roman Catholic Church, Knaresborough. The cave is situated on the right about 100 yards from the main road. Cars can return to Knaresborough by following road to main road, where turn left. This cave is named after a hermit who there spent nearly the whole of his life and who was buried in the tomb here hewn out of the rock. He gained great reputation for piety, and miracles are said to have been wrought at this spot. St. Robert, the son of a mayor of York, was born about 1160, and died 1218. In 1918 the spot was reconsecrated and from time to time Mass is celebrated here. Between five and six centuries after the death of St. Robert the cave was used by **Eugene Aram** as the burial-place of Daniel Clarke, whom he had murdered.

Conyngham Hall, near the High Bridge, was formerly the home of Sir John Coghill. The estate has been purchased by the town and the beautiful grounds laid out as a public park. In the grounds is the Knaresborough Zoo *(open).*

The conspicuous railway viaduct was first built in 1847, but collapsed and fell into the river before completion. It was rebuilt shortly after.

Ripon

Angling. – An excellent centre for angling. Trout, grayling and coarse fish. The *Ripon Angling Club* control water in the *Ure* from the Military Bridge to Sykes Wood, west side only, approx. ½ mile. In the *Laver* from Borrage Bridge (in Ripon) to Ings Bridge, approx. 4 miles – fly fishing only. Apply: Mr. Webster, 7 Gladstone Terrace, Ripon. The *Ripon Piscatorial Association* preserve 5 miles (with certain exceptions) from Military Bridge to junction of Ure and Ripon Canal. Day tickets obtainable from Mrs. Hodgson, Tackle Dealer, Queen Street. *Station Hotel, Studley Royal Hotel* and *Blackamoor Hotel*, no Sunday tickets. Below Hewick Bridge the water is inaccessible to visitors for a considerable distance. Fair coarse fishing on the Canal between Ripon and Bishop Monkton.

Baths. – The Spa Baths are in Park Street, close to the Market Place. Good open-air bathing can be had in the River Ure.

Bowls. – Public green in Spa Gardens.

Buses cross North Bridge to the Market Place, and also regularly to Bishop Monkton, Burton Leonard, and Harrogate; Thirsk; Studley, Aldfield and Pateley Bridge; Kirkby Malzeard and Grewelthorpe; Dishforth, Skelton, Boroughbridge and York; and Masham and Wensleydale. In the season there are motor-coach trips to various beauty spots.

Camping and Caravan Site. – Municipal site on Ure Bank. *Charge.* Modern facilities available. Further information from: The Site Warden, Ure Bank, Ripon.

Car Parking Facilities. – Market Place and a parking ground adjacent thereto.

Distances. – Fountains Abbey, 3 miles; Studley, 3; Newby Park, 4; Aldborough, 7; Ripley, 7; Brimham Rocks, 9.

Early Closing Day. – Wednesday.

Entertainment. – Cinema, dances and whist drives, etc.

Golf. – *Ripon City.* 9 holes.

Hotels. – *Spa*, Park Street; *Unicorn*, Market Place; *Black Bull*, Old Market Place; *Studley Royal*, Market Place; *Station*, North Road.

Hunting. – The district is hunted by the Bedale, West of York, York and Ainsty, Hurworth, and Bramham Moor Hounds. The Otter Hounds sometimes visit the neighbourhood.

Market Day. – Thursday.

Museum. – Wakeman's House, Market Place.

Population. – 11,110.

Post Office. – Head Office, Old Market Place.

Races. – Race course at York Road. Fixtures in May, June, July, August and September.

Tennis, bowls, miniature golf and other games are played in the Spa Gardens and at the Ripon Cricket, Tennis and Athletic Club,

Ripon is a pleasantly quiet and well-ordered city, occupying a beautiful site in the West Riding, 11 miles north of Harrogate, and 23 north-west of York. It stands 80–100 feet above sea-level close to the spot where the Skell and the Laver unite with the Ure, which henceforth becomes an important river.

Ripon resembles other ancient towns in having narrow streets. The oldest portions of the city are probably those forming **Stammergate** and **Allhallowgate,** both having been close to the monastery around which the city grew. A *gate* is a street. *Stammar* is probably a corruption of Santa Maria, commonly written *Sta. Ma.* Stammergate has now been renamed Stonebridgegate.

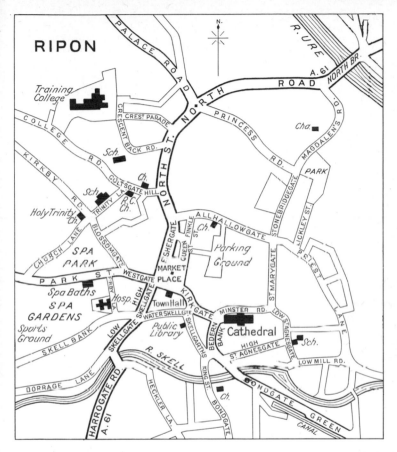

An Ancient Corporation

The government of the city is vested in a Corporation which now consists of a Mayor, four Aldermen, and twelve Councillors. The city, locally claimed to be the second oldest in England, was incorporated in the reign of Alfred the Great, 886. The still-existing Wakeman's horn was presented in token of the charter. The chief magistrate was styled "Wakeman," (Wakeman = Watchman) and associated with him were twelve Aldermen and thirty-six assistants. The last wakeman, Hugh Ripley, a certain "merchant and mercer," was nominated by the Crown as the first Mayor, who was appointed in 1604, in accordance with the terms of a charter granted by James I.

A link with earlier times is the –

Ancient Custom of Sounding a Horn

at nine o'clock in the evening. Four blasts are given at the Market Cross, and three in front of the Mayor's residence. The horn was originally blown at the setting of the watch. The practice was in existence long prior to 1598, for in that year an ordinance required the horn to be blown *according to ancient custom*, at the four corners of the Cross at nine o'clock. If any dwelling "in the gate side within the town" was robbed after the sounding of the horn, the wakeman had to compensate the loser if it could be proved that the wakeman and his servants were remiss in the performance of their duties at the time of the robbery. The expenses of the watch were met by an annual tax of twopence or fourpence, on every householder, according as he had only one door, or a "gate door and a back door," to his dwelling.

The original horn worn by the wakeman has been beautifully adorned at various times. Since 1607 it has been worn by the sergeant-at-mace on ceremonial occasions. The horn and other items of civic regalia may be seen at the Town Hall by prior arrangement, and permission of the Town Clerk.

The Wakeman's House, in the south-west corner of the Market Place, was the home of the last Wakeman and first Mayor of Ripon. It is a very interesting building (thirteenth-century) furnished in the sixteenth-century style. At the rear (entrance through the café) is a small *Folk Museum* containing some interesting relics of Ripon. *(Admission charge, open 10–6.)*

From the south-east corner of the spacious **Market Place** with its 90-ft. high obelisk as Market Cross, erected in 1780, it is only a short distance to the Cathedral.

Ripon Cathedral

Admission. – Admission to the Cathedral is free, but visitors are expected to put 2½p. in the box to see the Saxon Crypt. The nave, aisles and transepts are open to the public on weekdays from 7 a.m. until 5.45 p.m. (9 p.m. in summer). The tower, Chapter House and apse, Library and Saxon and Norman crypts may be seen on application to the vergers. The Dean and Chapter have to rely more and more upon the generosity of visitors for the maintenance of the Cathedral.

The Cathedral is dedicated to SS. Peter and Wilfrid, and is in various styles of architecture, from Saxon to Late Perpendicular. It is constructed of millstone grit, with magnesian limestone dressings, and consists of a nave and choir, with aisles, transepts, with an eastern aisle formerly divided into chantries, a square central tower (or lantern), and two others at the west end, all of the same height (121 feet). An apsidal building, on the south of the choir, serves as a Chapter House and Vestry, and over it is a Lady-loft. There is a Saxon Crypt, under the lantern, and an Undercroft below the Chapter House; the latter was for ages used as a charnel house, but the bones were re-interred in the graveyard in 1865. The Cathedral is 270 feet long internally. The nave is 87 feet wide and over 90 feet high, being exceeded in this direction by Liverpool Cathedral, Westminster Abbey, and York Minster alone.

Historical Note. – The Cathedral originated from the monastery founded by Eata, Abbot of Melrose, in 657. For only four years did the Scottish monks occupy the building erected. About the year 669 Bishop Wilfrid began to erect a new monastery, the foundations being laid some two hundred yards from the old building. Of this structure the crypt remains, but otherwise little is known of it except that it was of wrought stone, whereas Eata's was of wood.

A few years later, Wilfrid, having lost the Royal favour, was deposed, and his enormous diocese was divided into three sees of Hexham, York, and Lindsay. Subsequently another diocese was formed, and of this Ripon was made the cathedral

The Cathedral, Ripon

town. In 686 a new sovereign recombined the sees of York and Ripon, and made Wilfrid bishop of the reformed diocese. Eleven and a half centuries passed before there was again a Bishop of Ripon. The first was Eadhead (681 to 686), the next was Charles Thomas Longley (1836 to 1856), afterwards Bishop of Durham, then Archbishop of York, and finally Archbishop of Canterbury.

The monastery was destroyed by fire by King Eadred, Athelstan's brother and successor, during his devastation of the North, in consequence of a rebellion aided by the Archbishop of York. It is said to have been rebuilt a few years later either by the Archbishop of Canterbury or the Archbishop of York, and then, in the years that preceded the Norman Conquest, the monastery was converted into a college of secular canons.

Most probably ruin once more fell upon the minster when William laid desolate the land between the Humber and the Tees, for in Domesday Book "waste" is the description of the site of Ripon.

The facts respecting the earliest restoration of the minster are unknown, but south of the choir is Norman work, which is believed to be due either to the first Norman Archbishop, Thomas of Bayeux (1070–1100), or to Archbishop Thurstan (1114–1141). With the exception of the Saxon crypt and the Norman portion to which reference has just been made, the church was rebuilt by Archbishop Roger de Pont l'Evêque (1154–1181), and of his work there still remain the two transepts, half the central tower, and portions of the nave and choir.

Passing over the various alterations and additions made during a period of between six and seven centuries, we come to the year 1829, when restorative works were begun under the direction of Blore. From 1862 to 1870 a much more extensive restoration was entrusted to Sir G. Gilbert Scott. In 1956 a major restoration was begun and still continues. In 1836 the diocese of Ripon was re-created out of portions of the sees of York and Chester, and Ripon Minster became the new cathedral.

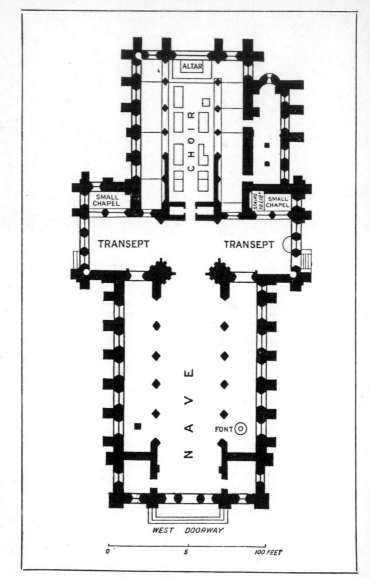

PLAN OF RIPON CATHEDRAL

The Exterior

The best general views of the exterior are obtained from the wooden bridge by Bondgate Green and from the south-eastern entrance to the Cathedral yard.

The **West Front** exhibits work of the best period of the Early English style. The height of the gable is 103 feet, while the towers rise to a height of 121 feet. The towers were formerly surmounted by spires. The central doors bear the date 1673, the figures being formed by nails. All the doors in the Cathedral are of considerable age. The south-west tower contains the bells, ten in number. All the bells were recast in 1933.

The **Central Tower** has the unique peculiarity of being vertically divided between two styles of architecture. The north and west sides are the Transition-Norman work of Archbishop Roger, while the other sides are Perpendicular, that being the style of the period in which they were rebuilt. The central spire was struck by lightning in 1593 and blown over in 1660. The two western spires were taken down soon after.

The Interior

The Nave is 133 feet long and 87 feet wide, and looks even wider by reason of the breadth of the western arch of the tower, through which the clustered columns of the narrow eastern arch are beautifully framed. The nave was originally built without aisles. The addition of these has made the Cathedral one of the widest in Britain, it being only surpassed in width by the naves of the cathedrals at York, Chichester and Winchester, and by the nave of St. Paul's. The western wall displays the Early English style at its best. The doorways are plainer than they are on the outer side, but the lancets above are much more elaborately ornamented. Together they occupy a space of 57 feet by 41 feet. The beautiful glass which fills them is by Burlison and Grylls, and was put up in memory of Bishops Longley and Bickersteth. The nave and its aisles are mainly in the Perpendicular style of architecture, but there are small portions of Transitional work at each end, and the west towers are Early English. At the base of the north-west pillar is the ring of the sanctus bell, and the worn stone shows where the foot of the ringer was placed. The triforium is elementary, consisting merely of a passage running along the base of the clerestory. The oaken vault was put up by Sir Gilbert Scott, who copied it from that of the transepts of York Minster.

In a window in the north aisle are a few fragments of glass dating from the seventeenth century. Near the font is an interesting altar tomb, bearing a representation in low relief of a man and a lion in a grove of trees. There is a tradition that it covers the body of an Irish prince, who brought with him from Palestine a lion as docile as a spaniel. An identical story is told of Roger de Mowbray, founder of Byland Abbey, in Yorkshire. It has been suggested that the scene commemorates delivery from a lion in answer to prayer. The tomb probably belongs to the fourteenth century.

In the south wall is a triangular piscina, believed to be one of the oldest in the country. In the pavement below is a trap-door concealing steps leading to the Saxon crypt. On the face of the north-west pier of the central tower is a figure of James I, which formerly stood in York Minster.

At the west end of the north aisle is the Consistory, or Ecclesiastical Court, over which the Chancellor of the diocese presides. The stone base of the railings is believed to consist of portions of St. Wilfrid's shrine. It was put together by Sir G. Gilbert Scott.

The **Saxon Crypt** is the most ancient portion of the cathedral. It is a barrel-vaulted chamber, 11 feet 5 inches long, 7 feet 7 inches wide, and 9 feet 10 inches high and is technically styled a *confessio*, built to serve as a local presence of the ultimate confession of faith of which man is capable, enduring torture and death rather than renounce his faith. It was later debased by removing back-stones from one niche and building steps under it for a trial by ordeal of women suspected of unchastity. Failure to pass through "the eye of St. Wilfrid's needle" was taken as a sign of guilt. This "threading the needle" was a source of revenue to the canons. The crypt was under St. Wilfrid's Church.

The **Transepts** have a total length (including the crossing) of 134 feet. The painted roof is of oak, originally of the Perpendicular period, but repaired and partially renewed by Sir G. Gilbert Scott.

The **North Transept,** almost in its original condition, is one of the best examples of the Transition-Norman period. The fifteenth-century stone pulpit placed here was formerly in the corner of the organ loft. Its aisle, often called the **Markenfield Chapel,** was originally the chapel of St. Andrew. After having been used as the burial-place of the Markenfields, of Markenfield, near Ripon, it became the place of interment of the Blackets, of Newby-on-Ure, near the city. Against the north wall of the transept is a fifteenth-century altar-tomb surmounted by the effigies of Sir Thomas and Lady (Eleanor) Markenfield. In the aisle is an altar-tomb with the figure of Sir Thomas Markenfield, of the time of Edward III. His collar of "Park palings" with hart clasps, denotes fealty to Richard II. The effigy of his wife has been destroyed.

Of the **South Transept** the south and west side are mainly the Transition-Norman work of Archbishop Roger. The east side is in the Perpendicular style. Against the south wall is a bust of William Weddell, of Newby, by Nollekens. The aisle is often called the **Mallorie Chapel.** It was long the burial-place of the owners of Studley Royal. Concealing a recess in the south wall is a monument to John Aislabie, sometime Chancellor of the Exchequer. Against the east wall is a monument to Sir John Mallorie, of Studley, in the time of Charles I. He defended Skipton Castle for the King, and delivered Ripon from the Parliamentarians. Other subjects of interest are a royal escutcheon bearing the motto of James I and two aumbries, one having modern doors with ornamental ironwork. From this transept a staircase leads to the library or Lady-loft.

The **Choir Screen** is of a date a little earlier than 1494.

The Choir measures 92 feet from the screen to the east end, and is 68 feet wide, including the aisles, but barely half that between the columns only. The first three bays on the north side are Transition-Norman, the three opposite them are Perpendicular, while the three easternmost on each side are mainly Decorated. As the Perpendicular work is of a very late character, it is believed to be the last important work done in the Minster before the Dissolution.

The great **East Window** is one of the finest examples of geometrical tracery in England. The glass (remodelled by Hemming of London) commemorates the revival of the See in the last century, and also the late Dean Fremantle.

The **Reredos** was erected as a Memorial to the men of Ripon who laid down their lives in the First World War (1914–1918). The **Sedilia** are remarkable for the carved ends of the cusps of the canopies. When looked at from beneath, these are seen to be the heads of grotesques, whose bodies are curled up against the under surface of the arch. The **Stalls** were restored by Sir G. Gilbert Scott, according to the design of the fifteenth century. Their arms and the misericords (original work) are most beautifully carved, by the Ripon Carvers, from 1489 to 1494. The Ripon Carvers were famous craftsmen of the Middle Ages, and their work has been traced in other Yorkshire churches and Manchester Cathedral.

Attached to the south aisle of the Choir is the **Chapter House.** This was restored in 1956 when the wall separating it from the old Norman Chapel beyond was replaced by an arch. This chapel contains an aumbry and a piscina which is probably one of the earliest in existence. The fine vaulting probably belongs to the time of Archbishop Roger.

From the Chapter House, a staircase, closed by a door in the west wall, leads to the **Norman Undercroft.** This is 68 feet long by 18 feet wide. It has been restored and is now in use as a mortuary Chapel, known as All Souls' Chapel. Much of it belongs to that Norman church which was replaced by the building erected by Archbishop Roger.

Above the chapel and Chapter House is the **Lady Chapel,** or lady-loft. It is reached by a flight of steps from the south transept.

It has been used as a **Library,** which originated in 1624 with the bequest of Dean Higgin of his books to the Chapter. Among several treasures is a MS. Psalter of 1418, containing the special lessons, hymns, etc., for the festivals of St. Wilfrid as observed at Ripon. This was presented to the library by a former Marquis of Ripon, who procured it at great cost. The library has many early printed books (incunabula) and contains one printed by Caxton. There is also a lovely thirteenth-century illuminated MS. Bible.

Minster House, immediately south-west of the Cathedral, serves as Deanery.

The former **Bishop's Palace** is in the township of North Stainley with Sleningford, about a mile north-west of the Cathedral. It is a spacious stone building in the Tudor style, and was erected during the years 1838–1841. It is now used by Dr. Barnardo's Home for children and the Bishop lives at Bishop Mount, a modern residence about 1½ miles north of the Cathedral.

From the south transept of the Cathedral descend the steps, pass through an archway in a wall and continue to the end of the short lane. To the left across the road is –

St. Agnes Lodge said to date from the time of Henry VII, but it has a wing added in the seventeenth century, and peculiar windows of comparatively modern date. The interior *(not shown)* contains many interesting features, including a panel on which is depicted the great Fire of London, two "powdering closets" (used during the powdering of ladies' hair and men's wigs), and a concrete floor in the attics. This house claims to have received Mary Queen of Scots, on her way from Bolton Castle to Tutbury.

Turning to the right past St. Agnes Lodge we reach –

St. Anne's Chapel dating from the early years of the fifteenth century, and believed to have been founded by one of the Nevilles. It originally provided homes for four poor men, four poor women, and temporary accommodation for two "casuals," and was under the charge of a priest. The domestic portion of the building, after having been divided into cottages, was pulled down in 1869, but the chapel, dating from 1100, though roofless, still exists and contains a stone altar, a piscina, and a font. The institution now provides for the wants of eight poor women.

Thorpe Prebend House adjoins. Built at the beginning of the seventeenth century it long formed several dwellings. The house contains some fine panelling and the main staircase is noteworthy. It is now let to the Ripon Old People's Welfare Association and is used as a club for old people.

The Hospital of St. Mary Magdalene situated in Magdalen's Road, was founded by Archbishop Thurstan (1114–1141) for secular brethren and sisters and a chaplain, who were to minister to the wants of lepers and blind priests born within the Liberty of Ripon. Provision was also made for the temporary relief of strangers. The dwellings were rebuilt in 1674, and again in 1875, and other cottages having been added, the institution now provides for the maintenance of twelve poor women.

From the south-west corner of the Market Place, by the Wakeman's House, Park Street leads in a few minutes to –

The Spa Gardens. In these gardens and in the **Spa Park** (on the opposite side of the roadway), tennis, bowls and miniature golf are all available to visitors. Adjoining the Spa Gardens are the **Spa Baths,** a modern swimming bath, with sauna baths, open daily.

St. Wilfrid's Roman Catholic Church, Coltsgate Hill, is remarkable for the height of its apsidal chancel, the pyramidal roof of which is unique in England.

Brimham Rocks

Excursions from Ripon

To **Brimham Rocks** *(daily, fee, Tea House)*, situated off the Pateley Bridge road 6½ miles from Ripon. The most interesting rocks are in the neighbourhood of Rocks House, and cars should follow the rough road round to this spot, where there is a parking place and where refreshments can be obtained. These Rocks appear on the skyline like a series of ruined walls and towers and occupy some sixty acres of a heath-clad table-land, 950 feet above sea-level. They form an ideal spot for picnics.

The rocks are huge masses 200, 300, 400 and even 500 tons in weight. They are of every conceivable shape, and are named according to their resemblance to objects, animate and inanimate. They were produced by a violent disruption in late Carboniferous times, during which heavy masses of millstone grit were upheaved to the ridge of the great Vale of Nidd. Exposed as they were to the action of desert winds and sandstorms in Permian times, they afford a magnificent example of wind-erosion in desert conditions. Millstone grit, or gritstone is one of the lower members of the Carboniferous formation. It differs from sandstone in that the particles are angular and not water-worn. These, by the action of heat, frost and moisture, fall apart. The eddying wind blows the splinters round and against the faces and bases of the masses, and wears them away. As the climate grew milder and wetter, moor-land and vegetation appeared, to clothe the barren wastes and give the Rocks their present appearance.

To **Boroughbridge and Aldborough. Boroughbridge** *(Three Arrows, Crown, Three Greyhounds)* prettily situated on the Ure, 6 miles south-east of Ripon, took its rise in the days of the Conqueror, when the main road to the north was diverted to cross the Ure at this point. Hence it became "Burgbridge" (the borough near the bridge"). There is good fishing in the Ure and its tributaries, and also boating.

The Devil's Arrows are three great monoliths in the fields to the west of the town. They are of similar dimensions, the central and largest being 30 feet in height (including 6 feet in the ground) and about 16 feet in girth. They are believed to have been set up about 2000 B.C., and are roughly contemporary with Avebury, with Stonehenge, and with that at Rudston in the East Riding.

Aldborough was once a town dating from the time of the Britons, who named it *Iseur*. Coins and jewels, as well as remains of baths, tessellated pavements, etc., of Roman origin have been discovered from time to time, and a course of the Roman wall may be distinctly traced. Portions of the wall are several feet above ground, and can be seen by visitors to the Museum. Aldborough is a quiet, charming village, with a maypole on a spacious green, pleasant houses and old church. Many excavations have been made disclosing foundations of walls and bastions.

The **Church** *(St. Andrew's)* is supposed to occupy the site of a temple of Mercury; a figure of that god which was formerly outside the church has been placed inside at

149

the west end, to preserve it, and is probably a unique instance of a heathen god in a Christian church.

Modern Aldborough stands within the walls which the Romans built around their stronghold, a portion of which, laid bare in 1846, shows that great pains were taken in defending the post from possible attack.

Seventy yards from the south-eastern angle of the "girdle of stone" is **Studforth Hill**, which Leland supposes to have been "the kepe of a castle," but which Drake considers to have been a theatre in which the Roman soldiers and gladiators engaged in the combats of the circus, or an "outwork, or fort, for the greater security of the town on this side." But gladiatorial displays were rare indeed in Roman Britain. The circus was probably used for bear-baiting and wolf-baiting.

Coins have been dug up within its area, and a Roman altar is preserved in the garden of Aldborough Manor.

Chapel Hill, or **Red Hills**, two fields between Studforth Hill and the walls of Aldborough, have always been considered a Roman burial-place; and the discovery on the spot of urns containing ashes of skeletons, etc., confirms this opinion.

Aldborough Hall stands a little to the east of the Church, near the site of a castle founded by William le Gros, Earl of Albemarle.

A little to the east of Boroughbridge and Aldborough, the Ure is joined by the Swale, and the two rivers henceforward become the Ouse.

To Newby Hall. The Hall is situated on the north bank of the Ure, about 4 miles south-east of Ripon. Almost immediately after the river along the Boroughbridge road, turn to the right and, in about a third of a mile take the right-hand fork. A little more than a mile from this is the entrance to the park.

Newby Hall *(Wednesdays, Thursdays, Saturdays, Sundays, and Bank Holiday Mondays and Tuesdays from Easter to early October, fee)* is one of the most famous Adam houses in England standing in 40 acres of grounds. The house contains a wealth of beautiful objects including fine classical statuary and Gobelin tapestries. The gardens are noted for their flowering shrubs and rock gardens. Refreshments in the old Orangery.

Skelton church near the principal park gates built as a memorial to a member of the Vyner family, contains an extremely beautiful altar cloth.

To Markenfield Hall. This fine fourteenth-century mansion *(Mondays, May to September, fee)* lies just off the Harrogate road 3 miles south of Ripon. It is reached by a lane on the right of the main road. The Hall is surrounded by a moat which is full of water, and there are also remains of a second moat. The principal features of the interior are the banqueting hall with some original windows, the kitchen (with an enormous fireplace), the chapel, and the dungeon. The undercroft is used as a farm. There is a fine view of the surrounding country from the roof.

To West Tanfield. From Ripon Market Place proceed along North Street and descend to the Clock Tower where bear left. Skirt the wall of Palace Park and the golf course and continue by North Leys (2 miles) and North Stainley (4½).

West Tanfield is a picturesque village beside the Ure, 6 miles by road (bus services) north-west of Ripon. Much interest attaches to the village by reason of its having contained the residence of the Marmions. For his services in the Scottish wars John, Lord Marmion, was allowed to castellate his mansion, but of that structure there remains only the fifteenth-century gateway tower or porter's lodge, containing several ancient fireplaces and a fine oriel window. The foundations of the Castle were discovered during excavations preparatory to the erection of the Old Rectory. The Castle well also was disclosed, and on being searched yielded several ancient dirks.

The Church, which stands near the scanty remains of the Castle, was originally a Norman structure, but its architectural features are of the Perpendicular style, from which we may conclude that it was rebuilt when the Castle was erected, as that has similar Perpendicular work. The Church is of great interest by reason of the splendour of its memorials of the dead. The **Marmion Tombs** are in the north aisle, which was rebuilt by Maude de Marmion in 1343. Unfortunately, during the so-called restoration of the Church in 1859–1860, some of the figures on the tombs were misplaced.

Just over the bridge at Tanfield – from which the river and the Church make a pretty scene – a path goes across the fields to **Mickley,** a neat village which can also be reached by a winding road from either Tanfield or Ripon, At the western end of Mickley the road rises to a beech wood, through which there are lovely views down to the river as it falls over a wide weir – an attractive place for a picnic.

Or, north of Tanfield, **Well** may most conveniently be visited. It is a most picturesque spot, a stream running down the main street. The church contains memorials of the great Latimer family, and hereabouts a former member of the family slew the great Dragon of Well. The village is also famous on account of its Roman bath – the biggest in Britain, excluding of course, those in the City of Bath itself.

From Well, return may be made by way of **Nosterfield,** the site of an ancient fortification, **Wath,** with waterfalls and beautiful woodlands, the former seat of the great Norton family, and **Sharow Cross,** the last of the eight sanctuary crosses, a mile from Ripon Minster.

To Masham, Jervaulx and Middleham. There is a choice of road *(bus service)* the prettier route being by Grewelthorpe.

Masham *(Kings Head)* 10 miles north-west of Ripon, is a pleasant little town. The large Market Place, even larger than that of Ripon, has a venerable cross in the centre.

Middleham Castle

The Church presents a very attractive picture with its graceful tower, Norman at the base, and rising to a symmetrical octagonal spire.

The picture above the chancel arch is said to be part of Reynolds' "Nativity," which was burnt at Belvoir Castle in 1816. There are monuments of the Harcourts and Danbys, which will repay examination.

There is an attractive 9-hole golf course at Masham, and coarse fishing can be enjoyed on the Ure. (Masham Angling Club, c/o Barclay's Bank, Masham.)

Some 5 miles along the Middleham road are the ruins of –

Jervaulx Abbey *(daily, fee)*. The name Jervaulx is pronounced in the French style. At the height of its power the abbey owned half the valley of the Ure from its site to the source of the river and the monks were renowned for horse breeding. After the Dissolution the Abbey fared badly, and the last abbot, Adam Sedburgh, was hanged at Tyburn in 1537 for complicity in the Pilgrimage of Grace. Until excavations were made in 1805 even the site of the church was unknown, and those parts which remained above ground were used as a quarry by local farmers and others. Apart from a few pillar-bases and the lower part of the walls the church is practically non-existent, but there are two altars, and the ground at the east end where stood the High Altar is raised. The remains of the Chapter House are entered by a doorway flanked by two round-headed windows. There are considerable remains of the domestic buildings.

The visitor may be interested in the various masons' marks clearly visible in the dressed stones. There are about fifteen different designs.

From Jervaulx the road continues past pretty **East Witton,** grouped round its village green, and so in 4 miles to **Middleham.**

Middleham Castle *(daily, fee)* was founded in the Norman period by Robert Fitzrandolph, but in the thirteenth century passed by marriage to the great Neville family. In 1469 Edward IV was held prisoner here by the "king-maker," whom he had offended by preferring to choose a wife from the Woodvilles rather than from the Nevilles. On the fall of Warwick, Edward gave Middleham to his brother, afterwards Richard III, whose only son was born and died in the castle. After the Battle of Bosworth, Middleham came to Henry VII, and it remained Crown property till James I gave it to Sir Henry Lindley in 1604. Its destruction was ordered in 1646 by a Parliamentary Committee sitting at York.

The extent of the Castle as represented by the ruins is small in view of its obvious strength, and there is ground for believing that at one time the fortress was much larger. There certainly existed an older castle of the motte and bailey type on higher ground to the left of the road leaving Middleham for Coverdale. Imposing as the ruins are when viewed from the road, it is only when one has passed through the Gatehouse and is confronted with the lofty walls of the Keep that one can fully appreciate the strength of the place. Projecting from the east side of the Keep (*i.e.,* to the left as seen from the Gatehouse) is the shell of the building, of which the Chapel occupied the third storey; in the corner of the Keep beyond this is a winding stairway. The Great Hall was over the cellars from which the stairway is entered; adjoining it, and partly over the Kitchen (in which was the well), were the Privy Chamber, and the Presence Chamber.

South of the Kitchen, and in the outer range of buildings, were a horse mill – the stone-lined channel remains – and adjoining it a great oven.

The **Church** (St. Mary and St. Alkelda). The earliest church of which a plan can be traced dates from about 1280. After 1340 the chancel was widened. The tower and the nave clerestory being added later. The windows of the present aisles are fifteenth century.

Studley and Fountains Abbey

Entrances. – There are two entrance gates to the Abbey and grounds.
West Gate, near Fountains hamlet, is the nearest to the Abbey and Fountains Hall.

Canal Gates is reached *via* Studley Roger village and Studley Park. There are car and coach parks at each entrance (*see* below).

The East Gates route is the more picturesque.

A very beautiful approach to the Abbey is by way of Studley Deer Park to the gates of the Abbey Grounds. From these the path continues *via* ornamental lakes, temples, statuary, lawns and trees to the Abbey itself.

The visitor is strongly recommended to allow *not less than four hours* for the full appreciation of the Abbey and grounds.

In Studley Park is a building known as *High Stables*, the residence of the owner of the estate. The former Studley Hall, of which this was part, was burned down in 1946.

From the lodge gates, around which cluster the few cottages forming the village of **Studley Roger,** the splendid avenue of beautiful limes leads to **Studley Church** about a mile distant and situated on the highest ground in the park.

The church, which is dedicated to *St. Mary the Virgin*, was built by the first Marchioness of Ripon in 1871, in memory of her brother, who met his death at the hands of brigands in Greece. The interior is even more beautiful than the outside and for richness is unsurpassed by any church of its size in England. Marble is the most conspicuous feature. The elegant detached shafts are of Purbeck marble; the three symbolic steps in the chancel, representing the fall of man, his redemption, and his purification, are of Belgian porphyry and Sicilian marble; the font is a single block of Tennessee marble; the credence table is of Californian marble; and the alabaster walls of the chancel are bordered with marble mosaics.

By branching off to the left from the **Long Avenue** we reach the **Lake,** of two acres. Adjacent is the restaurant at the entrance to the **Pleasure Grounds** around the remains of –

Fountains Abbey

Admission. – The Abbey and grounds are in the care of the Department of the Environment and an admission fee is payable. Open: June to August, 9.30 a.m. to 9 p.m. Sundays from 9.30 a.m. In May and September closes at 7.00 p.m. and in March, April and October at 5.30 p.m. Sundays from November to February from 2 to 4 p.m. only. Guide book obtainable at each entrance. Dogs admitted only if on lead.

Fountains Hall is privately owned and a separate admission fee is payable.

Parties: Special rates for coach parties (20 or more) on application. Special rate for organised parties of school-children on application to The Regional Director, Department of the Environment, Lawnswood, Leeds 16.

Catering: Refreshments, teas, etc., at the Lakeside Restaurant at north-east end of Grounds. Also a snack bar in the Ground – 50 yards from West Gate entrance.

Car Parks at each entrance.

Buses. – A half-hourly bus service operates between Harrogate and Ripon.

For five centuries the manor of Studley Royal was held in succession by the families of Aleman, Le Gras, Tempest, and Mallory. In the early part of the eighteenth

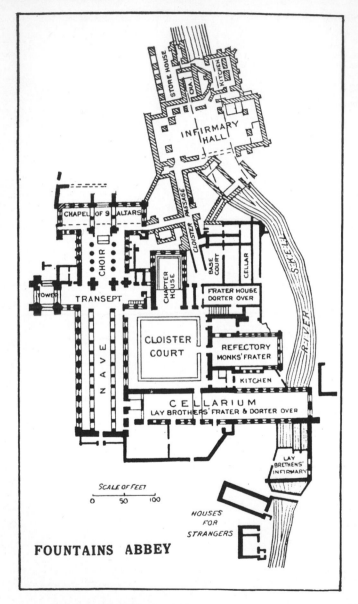

FOUNTAINS ABBEY

SCALE OF FEET
0   50   100

century it passed into the possession of John Aislabie (sometime Chancellor of the Exchequer) through his mother, the eldest daughter and co-heiress of Sir John Mallory. John Aislabie and his son employed their leisure in beautifying and improving the estate. On the death of the son the property passed into the hands of his eldest co-heir, Mrs. Allanson, whose niece, Mrs. Lawrence, was the next possessor, and by her it was bequeathed to the Right Hon. the Earl de Grey, one of whose ancestors married a sister of Aislabie, the Chancellor. The Earl was succeeded by his nephew, the Marquis of Ripon, K.G., the well-known statesman and ex-Viceroy of India who died in 1907, at the ripe age of 82. From him it descended to the late Marquis, on whose death in 1923 the title became extinct, and the estates passed into the possession of his nephew, Mr. Clare Vyner. They are now owned by the latter's son, Mr. Henry Vyner.

The natural beauty of the grounds has been enhanced by lily ponds, waterfalls, lakes and classic statues.

On passing through the lodge gates we have, on the right, a slope covered with laurels, shorn to a uniform height and shaded by forest and ornamental trees, while the left-hand side of the path is bounded by a matchless yew hedge of great height and thickness, and having apertures at favourable points of view. The first of these openings discloses the *Octagon Tower*, on the opposite side of the valley, and the figures of two *Roman wrestlers* on the border of the Canal which has been substituted for the natural channel of the Skell. Through the next opening are seen the *Temple of Piety*, set in the midst of trees, and the *Statue of Neptune* standing in the centre of the *Moon Pond*. A bas-relief on the "temple" represents a Roman daughter affording sustenance to her captive father. Then we come to the end of the yew wall, and the view before us includes a glimpse of the river issuing from a subterranean channel. Among the trees which here claim attention are a Norway spruce fir, 100 feet in height, and 14 feet in circumference at its base; a hemlock spruce, and a Wellingtonia Gigantea, planted nearly a century ago.

Presently we again have an evergreen wall on the left and through the first opening obtain an exquisite view of the *Moon* and *Crescent Ponds*, with their statues of *Neptune, Bacchus*, and *Galen*. The next break discloses a scene in which the foreground is occupied by statuary representing the *Conflict of Hercules and Antæus*, while in the background is the *Temple of Fame*.

Here the majority of visitors turn to the left for the sake of the *Surprise View*, but, in our opinion, Fountains is too noble a pile to be subjected to such theatrical artifices, albeit the "surprise" is admirable in its place, but that place is certainly not as an introduction.

We recommend the visitor to proceed straight on, passing the stately Abbey on his left, and allowing the while something of its majesty to impress itself on his mind.

Passing out of the gates at the west end of the grounds, a few yards bring us to –

Fountains Hall, a fine specimen of Jacobean domestic architecture. The interior of the Hall is well worth a visit, having in recent years been furnished for occupation. The chapel room is noteworthy for its magnificent stone fireplace (also from its Abbey), with a quaint sculpture of the Judgment of Solomon, and its oriel window with the original stained-glass armorial bearings.

There is also an interesting museum containing a beautiful scale model of the Abbey as it was in 1539 at the time of the surrender.

The Abbey. We enter the Abbey through the west doorway. Once within the **Nave,** a magnificent prospect delights the eye. On either side the massive pillars and arches (Transition-Norman) form a setting for the east window (Perpen-

Fountains Abbey

dicular) beyond which are the lights and shades of the Park woodlands. The clerestory is notably massive, but there is no triforium. The total length of the Church is 369 feet 6 inches. Proceeding up the **Nave,** turn into the North Transept, at the end of which is the great **Tower,** a majestic specimen of the Perpendicular style.

Leaving the Transept, we pass from beauty to beauty through the **Choir** to the glorious **Chapel of Nine Altars** (both Early English). There is no need to expatiate on the loveliness here. One may note, however, that the great East Window (Perpendicular) in no way mars the beauty of its surroundings, but seems rather to emphasize both theirs and its own.

We leave the chapel by an exit to the south, and, passing through the ruins of the Great Infirmary and other outbuildings (now no more than outcrops of masonry and referred to later), cross the *Skell.* Here we proceed along the Cloister passage, passing on our left the **Base Court** and *Dorter Subvault,* which had the Monks' Dorter (sleeping apartment) over.

The **Cloister Court** (125 feet square), is considered by some the gem of the building. On the east side is a row of four perfect Norman arches; on the north and west sides are massive walls against which was the gallery where the monks worked.

Three of the Norman arches referred to above lead into the **Chapter House.** Only the bases of the marble pillars remain. At the east end are the graves of several Abbots, notably the ridged marble tomb of John de Cancia.

Crossing to the south of the Cloister we enter the **Warming House,** one fireplace of which has been blocked up. Next we enter the **Refectory,** a building of singular grace and delicacy. The character of the architecture is Late Transitional, the Early English style predominating.

From the west side of the Cloister we enter the **Cellarium,** 300 feet long, divided down the middle by pillars from which spring stone vaults. It was originally divided into separate parts by cross walls, and was used as a refectory for the Lay Brothers, and as a buttery, cellar and store.

From the Cellarium the group of ruins to the left, and partly over the river, comprise the **Infirmary** of the Lay Brothers, and the **Guest House** for strangers, etc. A bridge over the river is well worth inspection.

Retracing our steps, if we leave by the east gate, we soon come to a **Wishing Well,** known by tradition as Robin Hood's Well, in memory of a conflict between the outlaw and the Curtal Fryer.

Soon we come to an open lake, on reaching which for a time we lose sight of the Abbey. By taking a turning uphill to the right, however, we come to **Anne Boleyn's Seat,** or **The Surprise,** which presents a most delightful farewell picture. This, we submit, is the artistic use of the Surprise. Beyond this a delightful round-about walk leads down by the Temple of Piety, from which we retrace our steps to the Lake, where we turn to the right, and soon rejoin the path by which the approach was made.

A mile south of the Abbey is **How Hill.** Here the monks had a watch tower and chapel.

Pateley Bridge and Upper Nidderdale

Road Route. – From Harrogate, *see* below.
Alternative route *via* Birstwith, Darley
and Dacre Banks to Summerbridge, 3–4

miles from Pateley Bridge.
From Ripon, *via* Studley Royal.
Buses serve either route.

From Harrogate follow the Ripon road to **Ripley,** at the far end of which bear off to the left and continue by the hamlet of **Burnt Yates,** the site of a Free School founded in 1760, and **Summerbridge,** at the foot of the long ascent to Brimham Rocks. The road, running along the eastern slope of Lower Nidderdale, gives splendid views and has much interest for cyclist and motorist alike. About 14 miles from Harrogate we reach –

Pateley Bridge

Hotels. – *Crown; Harefield Hall; Talbot.*   **Population.** – 2,000.

Of late years Pateley Bridge has become a very popular centre for walking and cycling holidays, and has much to offer to those interested in history, geology or botany. Deeply enfolded in the green hills, the surrounding countryside is of great beauty and interest. Pateley Bridge, Wath, Ramsgill and Middlesmoor are good centres from which to explore the upper portions of Nidderdale.

The bridge is not the first which has occupied the site. Some years ago workmen employed in cutting a drain near it discovered three causeways at different depths, one of which, three yards below the surface, was evidently the predecessor of the present bridge. The town consists of a steep and somewhat narrow main street, with two or three others branching from it.

A church, dedicated to St. Cuthbert, was built in 1827 to replace St. Mary's which dates from the middle of the thirteenth century, and stands, a roofless ruin, at the top of the road continuing upwards from the High Street. From the churchyard there is a fine view over the dale, through which the *Nidd* flows to join the Ouse.

The Kipling family were at one time resident here: Greenhow Hill, a name made familiar by Rudyard Kipling's Yorkshire soldier Learoyd, in *Soldiers Three* and other stories, rises on the opposite side of the dale.

Bishopside – that part of Pateley Bridge lying on the north-eastern side of the valley – derived its name from its connection with the Archbishops of York, on whom King Athelstane bestowed the manor in 939. It is surrounded by moorland 4,000 acres in extent, and is from 800 to 1,000 feet above sea-level.

Just over the bridge at Pateley is **Bridgehousegate,** a village forming part of Bewerley parish, Bewerley Hall, the manor-house (the seat of the

Pateley Bridge

Yorkes), was demolished in 1926 and the material sold. A round tower still stands.

The name "Pateley" derives from "pate", the local term for badger and "ley", a field, hence Badger's Field.

Pateley Bridge was constituted a market town by Charter of Edward II; an ancient "Feast" begun under the Charter still continues and is held on the Monday following 17th September.

We follow the Otley road for about $\frac{1}{2}$ mile or so from Pateley Bridge, and just past Bewerley Grange take a lane on the right. In a few hundred yards this arrives at a watersplash – or perhaps it would be more correct to say that it runs through the river at a series of little falls. The gate on the left is the entrance to –

Ravensgill

By courtesy of the owner the gates are opened from time to time to those who inquire at the neighbouring house. At times when the Gill is closed the moorland may be reached by the steep lane winding up from the watersplash. Strike up to left past quarries on reaching the top.

This beautiful gorge has few superiors.

The walk leads upwards through the woods till it emerges on open moorland. Crossing a wall, a sharp descent takes one to the bed of the Gill, which is crossed by a bridge.

A less steep ascent leads over the moor to the opposite summit of **Guy's Cliff,** a thousand feet above the sea and six hundred and fifty-three above the valley. On the top is a mock ruin (Yorke's Folly, or Two Stoops) from which there are extensive views.

The numerous outcrops and boulders of gritstone have assumed, as usual, fantastic shapes, and bear more or less appropriate names. One of these is the **Crocodile,** though the resemblance, except perhaps in respect of open jaws, is not easy to trace. At the foot of this rock is a singular hollow called the **Trough,** through which runs the road from Pateley Bridge to Otley. In the centre of the hollow is the site of a Baal hill. It was once believed that such hills were dedicated to the worship of Bel or Baal. It is now known that they were used for lead-smelting.

The walk may be continued over the moor, past Two Stoops and along the edge of Guy's Cliff, rejoining the road at Summerbridge; or Pateley Bridge may be regained by the upland road which divides the Cliff and runs through the Trough; or by following the first route to the end of Guy's Cliff, rounding the rocks, and returning through the wood, in which is **Guy's Cliff Tarn,** a beautiful little sheet of water.

This upland road leads by a fine high-level walk by **Padside** and **Thruscross** (interesting inn, built on a gateway of Knaresborough Forest) to the Washburn valley. By following the stream down, the Harrogate-Bolton Abbey road is joined at Blubberhouses. If the return journey to Harrogate is too long it may be shortened by taking bus from Summerbridge. In any case, the expedition is only one for good walkers.

Those who find the round too fatiguing are recommended to return after leaving the woods and before descending to the bridge over the Gill.

Amongst the most interesting sights of the district are –

The Stump Cross Stalactite Caverns

These are four and a half miles west of Pateley Bridge by the Grassington road (bus route, Sats.). The first 2 miles consist of a long, steep climb to Greenhow (1,400 feet above sea-level). The views are grand – first over Nidderdale and then, as we ascend, over a great expanse of moorland.

The entrance to the caverns is on the left soon after the descent begins. *Admission charge.* The caves are beautifully illuminated. A guide is in attendance during the season and refreshments are obtainable. The trip through Show Cave takes about 20 minutes.

The Caverns were found by two miners in 1860. The caves were surveyed in 1903; new findings discovered in 1921, and extensive discoveries have been made more recently, including the finding of five skeletons of reindeer. One of the skeletons may be seen on view at Stump Cross Caves. The caverns are reached by a sloping tunnel, and are of great extent. They vary in size and height, being in places very wide, in others so narrow that only one person at a time can walk along. The roof and sides are adorned with stalactites of all sizes.

There is a succession of caverns, named after peculiarities in appearance. One first enters the **Butcher's Shop,** the large red and brown formations reminding one of huge pieces of meat. The **Twins** provides a fine example of two stalactites sharing a single stalagmite. The **Jewel Box,** a cave within a cave, encrusted with sparkling crystal, is aptly named. The cave known as the **Chamber of Pillars** is so called from its snowy columns, which rise from floor to roof – about six and a half feet. The bulk of the stalactites are beautiful in form and colour. The **Snow Drift** is of dazzling whiteness; the **Sentinel,** a cylindrical shaft, rises in the centre of the cave from floor to roof. The Cathedral is a cavern some twelve feet high and forty feet wide, here are a number of stalactites arranged like the pipes of an organ; one can imagine the strange music they would produce. Other interesting features are the **Hawk,** the **Baby's Cradle** and the **Sand Castles.**

The road past the entrance to the caverns makes a long and steep descent to Hebden, where a lane on the right leads to **Hebden Ghyll.** From Hebden to Grassington is less than 2 miles.

To vary the return to Pateley Bridge take the by-lane on the right about a mile on the Pateley side of Greenhow. This winds over the moors for a couple of miles and then descends very effectively by **Ravensgill.**

Upper Nidderdale

Upper Nidderdale can be conveniently explored from Pateley Bridge. It consists of Stonebeck Down, Stonebeck Up, and Fountains Earth.

It is like no other of the Yorkshire Dales, for the silvery Yoredale limestones are here replaced by the tough, dark, craggy millstone grit, the fells rear themselves in grim contrast to the pastoral slopes of the dale, and the scenery, well wooded in places, is curiously reminiscent of Swiss valleys. The head of Nidderdale, shut in by mountains, is wild, lonely country.

Note: Throughout Nidderdale the adventurous explorer should avoid entering abandoned lead-workings. They are very dangerous.

Buses run from Pateley Bridge through Lofthouse to Middlesmoor, but the service is very infrequent.

The main road crosses the river at Pateley Bridge, but walkers are recommended to take the road on the north-east side of the valley. This joins the main road a few hundred yards beyond **Wath** *(Sportsman's Arms)*, with its pretty waterfall, on the left bank of the Nidd.

Wath stands near the foot of **Gouthwaite Reservoir** (Bradford City Waterworks); at its head is **Ramsgill** *(Yorke Arms)*, the most important village in Stonebeck Down. In the corner of the churchyard is the gate of an old chapel erected by the Abbot of Byland and pulled down when the present church was built in 1842. The village was the birthplace of the murderer Eugene Aram, whose crime Lytton and Hood have immortalized.

The reservoir at the head of *Riddings Gill* forms a pleasing foreground on our right as far as Ramsgill.

Near the hamlet of Stean, at the head of How Stean Gorge, are **Blayshaw Bents,** or **Crags,** on which are some pit holes extending for nearly a mile along the side of the hill, at one time thought to be evidence of a neolithic settlement; but this has since been disclaimed. The crags rise to an altitude of 1,100 feet above the sea – 600 above the bed of the river.

The **Calder Hills,** in the neighbourhood, are large heaps of slag, the refuse of ironworks which existed in medieval days.

Half a mile below the village of Lofthouse, in a field on the western side of the road, the Nidd issues from a subterranean channel by three mouths, two close together, the third about 200 yards east (*see* Goyden Pot, page 163).

Eight miles from Pateley Bridge we reach **Lofthouse** *(Crown)*, the only village in that division of Nidderdale known as Fountains Earth.

From Lofthouse a steep and narrow road leads over the fells to Masham and on through Wensleydale.

Just beyond Lofthouse a road on the left leads to –

How Stean

Admission, 2½*p.*; apply at cottage opposite gate.

How Stean separates the two divisions of Nidderdale. There is a parking ground just short of the bridge crossing the stream; the gorge is about two hundred yards above the bridge.

The gorge is very narrow, and in places the cliffs on either side attain a height of 70 feet. We cross the chasm by one rustic bridge and presently recross by a second, the view from both being very impressive. Part of the walk is at the water's edge; elsewhere it passes along narrow fenced galleries worn in the cliff-face by the waters in years long past. Care should be taken. The stones are apt to be slippery. Near the first bridge is a cave; and near the upper end of the explorable part of the gorge a stream rushes through another narrow cave. The whole course of How Stean is romantic.

Considerably beyond the head of the gorge "the **Stean Gill** flows in a crooked channel of its own formation, when suddenly an impassable barrier of rock rises in front, and it must either seek a new course, or accumulate and form a lake, until it runs over; when, as if to prevent such an occurrence, the accommodating rock opens a passage – at first by a double arch, but at the distance of a few yards, the dividing column disappears, and the waters pass along a single rugged passage . . . which bears the name of **Stean Gill Foot.**"

At High Riggs the stream throws itself over **Park Foss** a fall 16 feet high, and farther on is another called **Cliff Foss,** 6 feet high.

From Lofthouse a steep and twisting road leads in one mile to **Middlesmoor,** the principal village of Stonebeck Up. Car drivers should proceed with caution as the motor road ends here with a gradient of 1 in 3 at the top and a right-angled bend. It is one of the most picturesque moorland villages in Yorkshire. Perched high on a promontory, it commands wonderful views of Nidderdale. According to some, the best view of Nidderdale is to be obtained from Middlesmoor churchyard, and it would certainly be difficult to surpass it. The Church contains some interesting antiquities, including the Cross of St. Chad, Bishop of Lichfield, 664, and in the churchyard are curious epitaphs.

The head of the vale is well described as "Wild, grand, and desolate, surrounded on three sides by lofty, healthy mountains, the two most prominent being **Great and Little Whernside.**" The former, whale-backed, is at its highest point, 2,310 feet above the level of the sea. It is in a spring on its eastern slope, 2,000 feet in height, that the source of the Nidd is to be found.

The river will be found to sink in its bed above the right-angle turn it makes at the foot of Beggarmote Scar, about a quarter of a mile north of Limley Farm. A further land-mark is the old railway tunnel which lies to the west of the road near this point.

A short distance below the sink hole and only a few yards from the eastern bank of the stream, almost on the right-angle bend is the entrance to **Manchester Hole.** This is merely a hole in the roof of the cavern, but fallen boulders and a mud slope make it an easy scramble to the cave floor some twenty feet below. This is the first part of the underground course of the River Nidd and downstream leads into a spacious cave-passage where the water is rarely more than ankle deep. Some large cascade formations mark the place where it is possible to climb up a dry mudbank on the righthand side and view the main cavern from roof level. The further reaches are practicable, but wet; in any case adequate lighting is vital. The cave floods to the roof at times, although normally the sink above the cave limits the flow, and the surplus water bypasses the cave in the surface stream-bed.

Some three hundred yards down stream from Manchester Hole is **Goyden Pot,** the entrance to which is often dry and leads to a further stretch of the river. The entrance is an open cave mouth in the face of the scar where the surface stream bed ends abruptly. Inside the cave floor is cut into a miniature gorge and great care should be taken; this is especially important since the passage leads to the "Window", an opening into a large cavern with the floor some 15 feet below. The "Window" can be bypassed by taking a left turn on returning towards the entrance and taking care in the climb down the boulder slope to the stream. It is this water that has flowed from Manchester Hole, augmented in times of flood by water pouring through the Window from the Goyden Pot entrance. No ropes or ladders are needed to make the journey down the stream passage, but it involves scrambling over boulders and deep pools, and is not easy to find. The "Labyrinth", leads from the "Sump Chamber" but this and "Gaskells Passage", which leads beyond the sump, need a copy of the survey, and preferably someone who knows the cave, as a guide.

In 1955 the Craven Pothole Club of Skipton opened up a further section of this underground river between Goyden Pot and Lofthouse. Entry is difficult and enquiries should be made beforehand as to situation, permission, and tackle required. It cannot be too strongly emphasized that only experienced pot-holers should attempt to explore these most inviting caves. The danger of sudden severe flooding is always present as water from the reservoirs higher up the valley is periodically released and even a change of wind direction can cause sufficient water to go over the dams to cause a severe flood. A check should always be made with the Reservoir Keeper at Angram Reservoir who will advise as to whether there is any possibility of flooding. Permission to enter the caves should also be obtained from Bradford Corporation and owners on whose land the entrances are situated.

The underground waters of the river Nidd are not seen again until they appear in a field on the left-hand side of the road going up the dale, below Lofthouse, near the old Parsonage.

Barden Tower

Wharfedale

Wharfedale, and especially that part of it above Ilkley, is without doubt the finest of the Yorkshire Dales. It displays greater beauty and variety of scenery than any other, and its beauty is on an increasing scale almost throughout.

Otley

The "metropolis of Wharfedale" was of old the seat of manufacture of a famous woollen cloth. Today it is widely known for the important part it plays in the construction of printing and other machines connected with the production of books and newspapers. It is an ancient town with market rights which were granted in A.D. 1222. The **Parish Church,** founded in the seventh century, is dedicated to All Saints; the earliest part of the present building being the Norman chancel. There are several interesting tombs – notably that of the first Lord Fairfax and his wife and the remains of three Saxon crosses.

The most attractive feature of the place is the **Chevin,** a steep hill, overlooking the town. A path leads to its summit directly from the station. The view is fine and extensive.

Two miles from Otley, on the other side of the Wharfe, is **Farnley Hall,** with a valuable collection of Turners and other objects of interest. Immediately beyond Farnley village is the pretty **Lindley Wood Reservoir,** from which a choice of fine upland walks can be made to Harrogate.

From Otley the main road runs westward to Ilkley.

Ilkley

Angling. – Good fishing in the Wharfe – trout and grayling. *Ilkley and District Angling Association; Myddelton Angling Club.*

Archery. – Local headquarters: Ben Rhydding Sports Club.

Banks. – *Midland; Barclays; Lloyds; National Westminster; Yorkshire.*

Boating. – On the Wharfe. Boats on hire between the Old Bridge and the New.

Bowls on Middleton Sports Field, Ben Rhydding Sports Club and at Cunliffe Road.

Car Park (free) off Brook Street.

Early Closing. – Wednesday.

Entertainments. – Concerts, dramatic performances, etc., are given in the King's Hall, to which is attached a Winter Garden, used also for dances.

Golf – *Ilkley Golf Club*. On the banks of the Wharfe. 18 holes. *Ben Rhydding* (9 holes).

Hotels. – *Craiglands*, Cowpasture Road; *Stoney Lea*, Cowpasture Road; *Wheatley*, Wheat-ley Lane, Ben Rhydding; *Troutbeck*, Crossbeck Road; *The Star Inn*, Leeds Road; *Summerhill Guest House*, Crossbeck Road; *Lister's Arms*, Skipton Road; *Crescent*, Brook Street; *Crescent House*, West View; *Cow and Calf*, Moor Top.

Population. – 22,000.

Postal. – The Head Post Office is in Chantry Drive, near the Town Hall. Sub-offices: Skipton Road, Leeds Road and Wheatley Lane, Ben Rhydding.

Swimming pool (open-air) in Middleton Recreation Ground, on north side of river. Café, Car Park.

Tennis. – Public courts in Middleton Sports Field and elsewhere. The Ilkley Lawn Tennis Club grounds are on the south bank of the river; open to visitors – ticket obtainable from the groundsman.

Theatre. – *Playhouse*, New Brook Street.

Ilkley stands on wooded slopes on both sides of the River Wharfe. It is a prosperous holiday centre, and is also a favourite residential place. The air is bracing, and there are no factories to pollute it.

Ilkley first became known to the outer world as the "town of hydros." Hydropathy was introduced in 1843 by a Mr. Stansfeld who had experienced much benefit from the system in Germany. The first patients were accommodated in lodging-houses, but owing to the number desiring treatment, and the desirability of making special provision for their needs, the year 1844 saw the erection of the *Ben Rhydding Hydro*, now sadly demolished, the first institution of its kind in Great Britain. Ilkley is an elegant and pleasant town and a very good centre for walking or motoring in the Dales.

At the bottom of Brook Street, in Church Street, is the **Parish Church** *(All Saints')*. The ground on which the building stands was enclosed by a Roman fort. The original church is said to have been founded by the Saxons soon after the reintroduction of Christianity into Britain. The tower is supposed to be partly built of the material of the old fortress, an opinion supported by the fact that in the interior of the tower two Roman altars formed part of the wall, and it is supposed that a temple to Hercules once occupied the site. These altars are now exhibited at the west end of the church. At the west end of the north aisle is a carved high pew, dated 1633. In the churchyard are the shafts of some Anglican crosses.

Ilkley has another Anglican church, **St. Margaret's** (1879), considered to be one of the finest buildings in these parts. On the rocks in a public garden opposite the church, are three "cup and ring stones." They were found on Rombald's Moor, about a mile from the spot where they are now preserved. The largest measures 15 feet by 12 feet.

Similar stones have been found in other parts of the kingdom as well as in Madagascar, the United States, the Fiji Islands, and Palestine. Their origin and meaning are unknown. There is a monotonous repetition of the same figure on all, wherever found, and the same symbols are frequently found associated with sepulchral remains. The stones are associated with the heliolithic culture. The markings may be crude representations of the movements of the heavenly bodies. "The character of the localities where the stones are found is just such as would be chosen by a pagan people for what are called 'high places' in the Bible." A detailed description of the stones is given in *Ilkley Ancient and Modern*, by the Rev. Robert Collyer and J. Horsfall Turner and in *Rombald's Way*, by Eric Cowling.

The river at Ilkley is crossed by three bridges: the Old, described below; the New; and, lower down, a pedestrian bridge. At Ben Rhydding there is a further bridge.

Near the northern end of the New Bridge is the **Middleton Sports Field,** with tennis courts and bowling-greens and both indoor and open-air **Swimming Pools.** In Station Road the public library is open daily from 10 a.m. In Castle Yard, on the site of the Roman fort, stands **Manor House Museum and Art Gallery.** Restored in 1961 to its original Elizabethan period, it now houses local prehistoric and Roman material, and changing art and museum exhibitions.

From the Parish Church proceed along Church Street to the junction of four streets. That to the right leads to **Ilkley Bridge,** a substantial stone structure some three hundred years old. Originally a packhorse bridge, it is closed to motor traffic which now uses the modern bridge a little lower down the stream. Cross the bridge and follow the road to the left, uphill, to *Middleton Lodge,* erected in the time of Queen Elizabeth I to replace the former home of the Middleton family. Continue along the road until several branches are reached. Pass through the gate at the top of the broad path, take the first turning on the left, then pass through a wicket-gate on the right and follow this path to a small gate and a farm-house on the right. Pass through the gate, and the path will lead to a sequestered nook called *Mount Calvary* situated behind Middleton Lodge. Here, about the middle of the last century, the head of the Middleton family, a zealous Roman Catholic, erected an oratory and a number of sculptures representing scenes in the Passion of the Christ. The Retreat can be viewed on application at the cottage nearby (small gratuity).

From Mount Calvary continue along the road to a small gate opening into a field. From this a road, inclining to the left, leads to Ilkley Bridge. Cross the bridge, immediately use the steps on the left-hand side, and follow the walk from them by the riverside. Take the first opening you come to, and then by keeping right Brook Street is soon reached.

To Hebers Ghyll. It is an attractive walk. Follow the Grove, Ilkley's main thoroughfare, westwards up the valley, and in about a quarter of an hour Heber's Ghyll Road goes off on the left to the entrance to the Ghyll, which owes its name to the fact that it is on an estate which belonged to the ancestors of Bishop Heber, the author of several of our most popular hymns.

A path leads up the side of the Ghyll on to the moorland. Higher up and to the right is the **Swastika Stone.** The Swastika symbol is Indo-European in origin, and of vast antiquity. This stone possibly dates back to 800 B.C.

From the head of the Ghyll follow a path back towards Ilkley till a turning to the left leads to the **Panorama Rocks,** which command glorious views. The woods below are open to the public. Returning thence to the open moor, the **White Wells** and

Cow and Calf Rocks above Ilkley

the **Bath-house** are conspicuous on the right. The water is exceedingly pure and soft. The spring was the feeder of the beck which once ran down the main street to Ilkley.

A footpath leads upwards from White Wells to **Rocky Valley**. The walk can be extended by continuing along the path, crossing Backstone Beck by the stepping stones to the fine gritstone escarpment. Here are the **Cow** and **Calf Rocks.** The Rocks have not the slightest resemblance to the animals whose names they bear. The top of the Cow commands a grand and comprehensive view. A set of footholds have been made in the ribs of the Calf to enable people to reach the summit. Eastwards on the ridge is the **Pancake Rock,** a mile south of which is the **Greenbank Earthwork.** Half a mile long and about fifty feet wide, it is a survival of the Iron and Bronze Age.

Descend the Cow and Calf Rocks on the westward side, keep on the lower part of the Moor, and in an attractive setting is the **Tarn.** There is a promenade, and water fowl are seen. In winter it is popular with skaters.

Other attractive walks from Ilkley are to Burley-in-Wharfedale, two miles beyond the Cow and Calf Rocks; to Pancake Rock, returning *via* road and path near Cow and Calf Hotel to Ben Rhydding; to the **Doubler Stones** along the moor ridge towards Addington turning south at Wingate Nick, three miles to the west of Ilkley.

Ilkley to Bolton Abbey. Buses run between Ilkley and Bolton Abbey.
There is a road on either side of the Wharfe. That through Addingham is the busier, and between Addingham and Bolton Bridge there are lovely views across the river of well-wooded country rising to the moors. The road *via* Beamsley is prettier in itself and has some nice glimpses of the river through the trees; but motorists will find it narrow and winding. This is the preferable route for walkers.

167

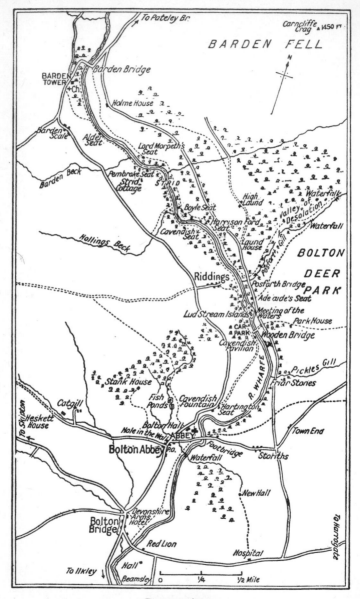

BOLTON ABBEY

The Addingham route leaves Ilkley *via* the Skipton road. For the Beamsley route, cross the river at Ilkley, turn to the left, past the golf links, and continue by Nessfield, where the stocks are still to be seen. Continue through Beamsley, below the **Beacon** (which commands a grand view), and so to **Bolton Bridge,** where take a footpath entered through a small iron gate in the parapet of the bridge.

In the field through which the footpath passes Prince Rupert and his troopers encamped in July 1644, on their way to defeat at Marston Moor. It was then waving with corn. As compensation for the destruction of the crop, the tenant was allowed £20 by his landlord.

Bolton Abbey and Woods

Note for Visitors. – It should be borne in mind that *Bolton Abbey* and the *Stepping Stones* are within a few hundred yards of the village and the Hole-in-the-Wall. The main entrance to the *Woods* is at the *Cavendish Pavilion*, about a mile from the village; the Strid is a further mile upstream, and *Barden Tower* another mile.

Good walkers will enjoy going to Barden on one side of the river and returning by the other; others may care to note that buses pass the road above Strid Cottage and Barden Tower *en route* between Ilkley and Grassington.

Immediately beyond the Post Office is the **Hole-in-the-Wall** passing through which we have a fine view down to the river, with the Stepping Stones, the neighbouring footbridge and the waterfall in front and the high moors to the left. The declivities on either side of the path from the Hole-in-the-Wall are the fish ponds in which were bred fish. It is believed that the canons introduced the grayling into the Wharfe.

As we descend the path the Abbey ruins appear, with the Rectory in front, and to the left is **Bolton Hall,** formerly the gateway of the Priory. The Earl of Cumberland, on whom Henry VIII bestowed the confiscated property in 1542 (for the sum of £2,490 1s. 1d.!), transformed the gateway into a shooting-box, and the present owner, the Duke of Devonshire, uses it for the same purpose. The outline of this, the main entrance to the Abbey, is familiar in many English households from its representation in Landseer's celebrated painting, "Bolton Abbey in the Olden Times." The original painting is at Chatsworth. The arch of the gateway spanning the road was built as an aqueduct to carry water to the corn mills.

The **Rectory** (*not shown*) occupies the site of the kitchens and other offices attached to the guest chamber and is constructed of fragments of the monastic buildings.

The Priory Church

Admission. – The church is open daily from 10 a.m. to dusk; no fee, but donations are gratefully accepted.
Services. – The church is in regular use as the parish church.
Principal Dimensions. – Outside length, 261 feet 7 inches; inside length of nave, 88 feet 6 inches; inside width of nave, 31 feet 3 inches; inside length of choir, 115 feet 8 inches; inside width of choir, 30 feet 9 inches; inside length of transept, 121 feet 5 inches; height of nave, 55 feet; width of nave and aisle, 47 feet 10 inches.

While the church as a whole is a ruin, much remains to evoke memories of its former glory. A model of the church in its hey-day stands in the nave. The nave as the normal place of worship for the people of the district, was preserved when at the Dissolution other portions of the church were allowed to fall into decay. The ruin of the conventual buildings is much more complete, yet their outlines can for the most part be clearly traced.

The original Early English west front is concealed by a Perpendicular tower, begun, as is recorded by an old English inscription, in the year 1520, by Richard Moone, the last of the priors. It was unfinished when Henry seized the monastery and is still without a roof. Had it been completed, the original west front would have been removed and the nave connected with the tower.

The **Nave** is Early English. On its western wall are four corbels, which were removed from their places when the roof was relaid in the latter half of the nineteenth century. The aisle was erected early in the thirteenth century, but the Decorated windows make it appear to belong to a much later date. On an ancient stone credence table near the organ is a finely-carved Agnus Dei, which was found in excavations. Its original position was probably over the high altar.

Near the vestry door is an ancient stone altar slab, one of the few sealed altar stones in England.

"It has the five crosses (signifying the five wounds of Christ), one at each corner of the upper side, partly obliterated, and a fifth on the front side in the middle. The cavity in the middle once contained a relic, and was covered with a very thin stone or brass slab, sealed. At a later period, however, the stone has been used as a memorial slab, and the cavity contained a brass bearing an inscription; the bits of lead at the corners show the means of fixing it."

However interesting the nave, it must be confessed that Bolton Abbey derives much of its charm from its situation.

The **Choir,** now in ruins, was originally a late Norman structure. It and the south transept were rebuilt in the fourteenth century.

Between the east end of the ruins and the river is a modern addition to the churchyard. By passing along the *outside* of this, we reach –

The Stepping Stones

Visitors are particularly requested not to approach these by crossing the middle of the graveyard and jumping the sunk fence.

These stones were fifty-seven in number. No one knows when they were placed, but the causeway was doubtless constructed in order that the dwellers on the hills on the opposite side of the river might more conveniently attend the services in the Abbey Church. The stones afford a safe passage when the water is low, but after heavy rain or a rapid thaw of snow the current sweeps over them in big waves. The footbridge has rendered the stones superfluous, and is a great boon to those who have occasion to cross the river.

Leaving the churchyard (noted as the scene of Wordsworth's "White Doe of Rylstone") at its north-west corner, we turn to the right along the Barden road for some 200 yards to the Cavendish Memorial Fountain, between which and the river runs a fence, in which is a small gate giving access to the **Hartington Seat,** a little to the left.

Near the fountain the road forks. The branch on the left is the road to Barden; that on the right is the road to Bolton Woods and Cavendish Pavilion (refreshments).

Soon we see, on the opposite side of the river, a high ridge of moorland, known as the **Hill of the Standard,** the legendary spot on which Francis Norton was assassinated, an incident familiar to readers of Wordsworth's "White Doe of Rylstone."

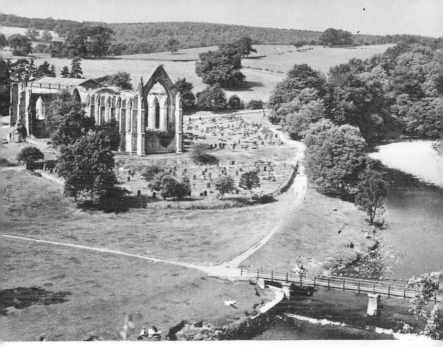

Bolton Abbey

Bolton Woods

Open to the public daily throughout the year *(small charge)*. Dogs must be kept on leash.

Cycles cannot be taken through the woods, but must be left either at the Post Office or at the Pavilion at the entrance to the woods *(small charge)*.

Cars are not allowed in the woods, but there are parking places beside the Cavendish Pavilion and Strid Cottage (and *see* page 169).

About three-quarters of a mile from the Abbey we come to a lodge and the **Cavendish Pavilion.** On the farther side of the river a rounded hill called the **Nab** rises above the trees. It is the centre of a former **Deer Park** of some seven hundred acres. Do not cross the bridge, however (except for one of the walks mentioned on pages 172–3), but follow the road past the Car Park and almost immediately turn down a path on the right which follows the riverside. It passes a sulphur spring running into a stone basin near the first seat on the left and soon leads to a group of pretty islets at a spot known as the **Meeting of the Waters.**

Beyond this point the broad path we left at the Car Park comes down on the left and provides level walking all the way to –

The Strid one mile from the Cavendish Pavilion. Tradition says that it is the supposed site of the death of the "Boy of Egremond," and of the legend of the "White Horse of Wharfedale," said to rise from the river before the occurrence of a fatal accident.

The Strid is a narrow chasm, from 4 to 5 feet across, and from 60 to 80 long, through which the Wharfe, which only a few yards higher up is 50 feet wide, rushes with great rapidity. At the entrance to the Strid there is a fall of about 10 feet, which gives additional impetus to the foaming flood. The water is usually about 12 feet below the top of the rocks which bound it, and is from 12 to 30 feet deep, the bed being uneven; but in times of flood the water covers the rocks on either side as far as the trees.

The name of the chasm is said to be a corruption of *Stryth*, Anglo-Saxon for tumult and turmoil, the corruption being due to the possibility of striding across the rift.

Turning up the hill-side from the Strid the track divides, the left-hand branch leading to the **Pembroke Seat,** a summer-house commanding lovely views, and a favourite spot for picnics. The path to the right at the fork runs high above the river and then past Strid Cottage to the Barden-Bolton Abbey road (bus route, 2 miles to Hole-in-the-Wall).

Continuing along the riverside and passing the aqueduct carrying water from Nidderdale to Bradford, we come, a mile above the Strid, to **Barden Bridge,** and turning to the left up the hill, quickly reach –

Barden Tower

(3¾ miles from the Abbey, through the woods; 2¾ by road.)

Barden Tower was originally one of six square towers or lodges occupied by the keepers of the once vast forest in this part of Wharfedale, and belonged to the Lords of Skipton Castle. The lodge at Barden was the occasional residence of "the stout Lord Clifford that did fight in France," who afterwards obtained the sobriquet of "the Butcher." on account of his barbarities during the Wars of the Roses. After his death at Dittondale on the eve of the battle of Towton, his estates were confiscated.

The tower is now a ruin; and the old **Chapel** attached to it is no longer used.

Part of the tower is used as a farm-house (refreshments).

(For return routes from Barden Tower, see below.)

The long steep climb from Barden Tower on the Skipton road is well worth while for the wonderful view obtained from the highest point (some 1,100 feet above the sea).

From Barden Tower a visit can conveniently be paid to –

Gill Beck Waterfall

Taking the road to Burnsall, we come, at the end of half a mile, to a bridge over the stream, and there passing through a little gate on the right, a few yards bring us to the fall. It is about 50 feet high. The spot is considered one of the prettiest of the many glens with which Wharfedale abounds, though the fall is of small account in dry weather.

The Return from Barden Tower can be made along the opposite side of the river, either by road or through the woods.

The better route is through the woods *(fee)*. Having crossed Barden Bridge, pass through the wicket gate beside the wall letter-box. Soon the path forks; take the lower branch, leaving a farm-house and a cottage on the left. Presently pass through a gate leading into the woods, and follow the high paths, for they afford the best views. At length we reach a **Moss Hut** and there have a choice of routes.

1. The shortest way to the Wooden Bridge. This route lies along a path on the right leading down to the river, then through a field to a bridge over **Posforth Gill,** beyond which it turns to the right, enters a field in front by a stile, and soon reaches the Wooden Bridge.

2. *Via* the Valley of Desolation. For this take the upper path, past the Moss Hut. Cross the road into which it leads, and follow a path up the hill-side. This leads to the lovely wooded ravine containing Posforth Gill. Walk up the stream, and in less than a mile is the **Parle Waterfall**, about 50 feet high. A quarter of a mile farther is a fall 30 feet high.

That part of the valley which lies along the northern base of the Nab Hill as far as the second waterfall is known as the **Valley of Desolation** *(see above)*, because the lightning in a great storm in 1826 played unexampled havoc with the trees, turning "the proud spreading oaks into blasted trunks and bare white branches." In the course of time Nature has made the damage less apparent.

Cross the stream at the Park Fall, and follow the road through the lodge gates to the road from Barden. Follow the Barden road to the left for rather more than a quarter of a mile; there turn to the right, and in a few yards is the Wooden Bridge.

The **Nab**, which rises 600 feet above the Wharfe, but 900 above sea-level, commands a wide prospect. It can be easily ascended after the stream is crossed at the Park Waterfall.

At the Wooden Bridge

also the visitor has a choice of routes. He may –

1. Cross bridge and retrace the course taken on outward journey.

2. Instead of crossing bridge, continue on road from Barden until about a quarter of a mile beyond Pickles Gill, and there take footpath which leads, in half a mile, to the Stepping Stones.

3. Proceed as in No. 2 until about a hundred yards from the stones, and then follow a grassy path between trees alongside, but some distance from, the river. In about a quarter of a mile the path reaches a waterfall, from the vicinity of which there is a fine view. Continue thence by the footpath through the fields. About three-quarters of a mile from the fall the path strikes the high-road to Harrogate. For the Devonshire Arms (a third of a mile) and the bus, turn to the right.

This is the ordinary route, namely, up the right bank of the Wharfe and down the left. But those who mean to walk all the way are recommended, on leaving the Abbey, to cross the bridge and reverse the route, taking a high-level path for the sake of the lovely views upstream. Seats indicate the finest view-points.

About 3 miles north from Barden Bridge *(see page 172)* by a pleasant hillside road skirting woods and with lovely views over the smiling dale, is –

Burnsall

a very popular centre for the exploration of this part of Wharfedale. (Hotels: *Red Lion; Fell.*) Among other noteworthy features of the church is an old Norse font with symbols of heathen mythology and beside it some Norse hogs-back gravestones with heathen emblems, and some Anglican crosses – but the building, like the village itself, has a charm that is quite independent of its archaeological interests. There is an attractive lych-gate with its stone weights, and in the churchyard are preserved the village stocks. Good facilities for angling. Boating above the bridge.

From Burnsall it is but a few miles to Grassington; or one can cross Burnsall bridge and return to Barden Bridge *via* **Appletreewick,** with lovely views of the dale; **Simon Seat** (1,592 feet), with its prominent outcrop known as the **Hen Stones** rising on the left, and Burnsall Fell to the right.

One of the best short excursions from Appletreewick is to **Troller's Gill,** near Skyreholme, a mile or so north-east of the village.

Grassington

Hotels. – *Wilsons Arms*, Threshfield; *Devonshire*, the Square; *Grassington House*; *Foresters Arms*; *Black Horse*.

Bus Services to Skipton, Buckden, Litton, Wensleydale, Ilkley, etc.

Grassington is a large village on the hill-side sloping down to the north-east bank of the Wharfe. With its main street, its diminutive market-place and its many quaint byways it is a place in which to linger. There are lovely seventeenth-century houses and farms, a fine sixteenth-century barn where Wesley is said to have preached, and an interesting bridge, bearing mason marks. It was once busy with lead-mining. Grassington is a good centre and although the surrounding hill-sides are somewhat bleak the river scenery is lovely.

Among the many walks from Grassington is that by the riverside to **Burnsall** continuing to Barden Bridge and through Bolton Woods to the Priory, about 14 miles of delightful walking through scenery that increases in charm as one proceeds. If Bolton Abbey is to be reached by car we recommend going *via* Hebden and Appletreewick and returning by the higher road from Barden Tower which passes Gill Beck and provides a lovely view of the valley as it approaches Burnsall.

Conistone and Kilnsey Crag

Another road which is worth doing is that from Barden Tower to Skipton over Easby Fell, especially on a clear day, for the summit is a wonderful view-point (*see* page 172).

Of the walks westward the best is that starting at a lane on the left a few hundred yards north of Threshfield cross-roads. A stile leads to a footpath. The path bears right round a wall to Skyrethorns where at the cross-roads Grisedale Lane continues to **Malham,** passing **Gordale Sear** (page 176) on the way. The return could be made by Mastiles Lane – the rough track connecting Malham and Kilnsey – which our outward route has joined above Gordale. No one, however, should leave Malham without seeing the Cove, which is just above the village.

Less than 2 miles from Grassington along the Pateley Bridge road is Hebden. A lane on the left leads to **Hebden Ghyll,** where the Hebden Beck comes down over the rocks in a very graceful fall known as Scala Force. This pretty spot is popular with picnic parties; cars may be parked and refreshments obtained at *Jerry and Ben Cottage* (*see* W. Riley's story), a little farther up the lane.

It is worth walking up the valley beyond the cottage, and in fine weather there is a grand walk over the moors to Great Whernside (the way becomes very wet after rain, however).

Two roads connect Grassington with Kettlewell, 6 miles up the valley; each has its own charm and it is worth while to go by one and return by the other. From Grassington go along Wood Lane into Grass Wood to Conistone. Here is an ancient church of Anglican foundation. Near the church Scot Gate Lane leads to Great Whernside. At **Conistone** a road crosses the river to link the two roads, giving a good view of the overhanging cliff of **Kilnsey Crag,** just north of which the Arncliffe road (*see* page 176) strikes off.

Kettlewell

Hotels. – *Race Horses*; *Blue Bell*; *King's Head*;   **Youth Hostel** – Whernside House.
    Chestnut Cottage.

Kettlewell is a grey, quiet, self-contained village situated in a fine part of Upper Wharfedale at the foot of **Great Whernside,** which rises to 2,310 feet almost from the village street. A new chapel has been built at Scargill House, a Church of England holiday and conference centre. Local limestone and disused stone walls provided much of the material for its construction.

The village is a splendid centre for walkers of the more energetic kind, for except towards Grassington the roads are quite hilly; and it has claims almost as strong on those who prefer a lazy holiday, for within a few hundred yards of the village are innumerable spots where one can lie and listen to the rushing waters and enjoy the beautiful scenery without exertion or interruption of any kind.

Excursions from Kettlewell

To **Middleham** or **Leyburn** (16 miles) by **Coverdale.** The best parts of this route are the ascent from Kettlewell to the top of the pass (1,620 feet) – Park Rash is very steep – and the descent into Wensleydale, though Coverdale is a curious little valley looking as if it had been carved out with a cheese-scoop. Those for whom the direct walk is insufficient may diverge to the right and take Great Whernside (2,310 feet) *en route.*

To **Aysgarth, Bainbridge** or **Hawes.** The views of Upper Wharfedale as one climbs from Buckden are very fine, while from points about Cray the panoramas are glorious. Routes are the same as far as **Buckden,** delightfully situated at a point where Wharfedale becomes Langstrothdale. From this point the road to Hawes (11 miles) goes off up the valley to the left – Langstrothdale. A mile from Buckden is Hubberholme Church, one of the quaintest in Britain; thence we follow the Wharfe past Deepdale to Oughtershaw, and continue to climb to the summit level (Fleet Moss, 1,900 feet). The views of Ingleborough are fine, and before one Wensleydale is spread. Except for the gradients, this is a good motor road, though narrow in parts.

For Aysgarth and Bainbridge, however, keep to the right at Buckden, passing through **Cray,** with gorgeous views of green hill-sides and luxuriant trees among which streams tumble down in series of cascades. Above Cray the rough track forming the worst part of *The Stake* route (*see* page 182) to Askrigg goes off on the left, but the motor road for Aysgarth continues level below the curiously terraced side of Buckden Pike. The summit of the pass is 1,376 feet above sea-level. Once over one descends to Bishopdale through the Kidstones Pass and on to Aysgarth (page 181).

To **Arncliffe** and **Litton** (5½ miles). A charming walk up the valley of the Skirfare, with lovely views of both Wharfedale and Littondale. Cross Kettlewell Bridge and go down the valley for about 2 miles. The Arncliffe road doubles back on the right just short of Kilnsey Crag. From **Arncliffe** *(Falcon Inn)* there is a wild and hilly route over the moors to **Malham** (page 178). Though rough in places, the road is motorable throughout (but use caution in descending to Darnbrook Farm, about 3 miles from Arncliffe) and as it runs for the most part over unenclosed moor it also provides a splendid walk. It may be well to caution strangers that the road starts in the corner *facing* the inn at Arncliffe (not beside it) and is that turning sharp to the left just over a hump-backed bridge.

A rougher route, for walkers only, is that starting beside the *Falcon Inn* at Arncliffe and continuing up above the Cowside Beck and over Great Close. With the Gordale Beck away to the left the path meets the Malham road about a mile south-east of **Malham Tarn.** At cross-roads go left for Mastiles Lane and Conistone or Grassington; straight ahead for Malham and **Gordale Scar.**

Or from Arncliffe one can continue by the road past **Litton,** opposite which a fine waterfall is seen bursting out of the hill-side. For Settle, motorists must continue a further 3 miles before crossing the river and climbing out of the dale, but walkers should leave the road half a mile beyond Litton and get on the broad green track climbing the hill-side on the other side of the river and meeting the road to Settle high up between Pen-y-Ghent (2,273 feet, on right) and Fountains Fell (2,191 feet, on the left).

Skipton and Airedale

For many people **Skipton** (*Sheeptown*, the ancient capital of Craven) is regarded as the gateway to the Dales and the first town in Airedale, although the Dale proper extends many miles farther downstream. It is a busy market town and the headquarters of many of the activities of the Dales, including the Craven Pot-holing Club.

Skipton Castle, on its rocky eminence, is a fine example of a fully-roofed massive medieval fortress, having an attractive fifteenth century courtyard and Tudor gatehouse. It has hardly a rival in England as regards completeness. The habitable part, which is private, dates from the time of Henry VIII, but the actual building can be traced back to the Conquest and its erection by William de Romillé (a member of this family founded Bolton Abbey), and to the early Plantagenets. The exterior is imposing, but the interior is devoid of contents. The yew-tree in the courtyard is reputed to be over 300 years old. Historically, the Castle is noteworthy for its defence against the Parliamentarian troops, and as having been the home of the Cliffords (*see also* under Barden, page 172). Their motto, *Desormais* (henceforth), forms the outer and inner parapets of the gateway tower. The Castle also sustained a futile siege at the hands of supporters of the Pilgrimage of Grace. In the seventeenth century portions were restored by Lady Anne Clifford, Countess of Pembroke. The Clifford coat of arms may be seen in the court yard and at the main entrance to the Old Castle. Admission 10p, children 5p. Open from 10 a.m. to sunset except on Good Friday, Christmas Day and Sunday mornings.

Skipton Church is famous for its roof, constructed in the time of Richard III, and also for the beautiful screen, which once bore the date of 1533, and which, up to 1802, supported a handsome roof-loft. The church is the burial-place of the Cliffords, Earls of Cumberland, whose emblazoned tombs will be found on either side of the sanctuary.

There is a 9-hole *Golf Course* at Skipton, and a modern indoor swimming bath at Aireville Park. The old Town Hall in Sheep Street has some ancient dungeons below the café, while the old stocks are built into the steps. There is an interesting museum at the public library.

The road from Skipton to Grassington passes the romantic village of **Rylstone** the scene of Wordsworth's "White Doe of Rylstone", thence continues through pretty **Cracoe** and **Linton** in Wharfedale. Near Linton Bridge the river is extremely beautiful, its banks being richly wooded.

Malham

Access. – By road (bus service) leaving the Skipton-Settle road at Gargrave; or the Skipton-Grassington road at Rylstone; by the wild road from Arncliffe; or by tracks from Grassington (page 174) or Settle.

Hotels. – *Buck*; *Lister Arms*; *Beck Hall*; *Sparta House*.
Youth Hostel. – Malham.

The upland village of Malham is the most popular centre for the exploration of Airedale, being set amid some of the most remarkable rock scenery in Yorkshire, with moorland walks to north, east and west and being yet in touch with the bustle of the outer world as represented by Skipton and Settle.

From the village two roads lead upward, enclosing the extraordinary **Malham Cove,** a great limestone amphitheatre of which the walls are 300 feet high. The full impressiveness of the Cove cannot be experienced from the road; it is necessary to stand at the foot of these huge cliffs, and to witness the infant Malham beck emerging from the rocks into the outer world.

Gordale Scar

Whether Gordale Scar is more impressive than Malham Cove is a delicate question which must be left to individual judgment. There is no doubt, however, that it is very well worth seeing. Turn to the right at the *Lister Arms* and keep straight on for about a mile (motorists should note that the narrow road winds between walls at a sharp bend where the road descends to cross the stream). From Gordale House across the stream, a path leads across the fields into the jaws of the great chasm which has been seen from the road. As one proceeds, the cliffs become steeper, the chasm more restricted, and then as one turns a corner the real wonder of the place is revealed in the fine waterfall by which the Gordale Beck plunges down from the heights above. At all times this is an impressive spot but never more than after heavy rain, when the water thunders down and its thundering is taken up and echoed and re-echoed by the cliffs.

Unless an unusual amount of water is coming down, the *really* sure-footed can scramble up the rocks dividing the falls, to be rewarded with the sight of a kind of miniature Malham Cove. Following the beck upward one reaches a rough track which to the right joins the Mastiles Lane route to Conistone and to the left leads to the road down to Malham village.

Malham Tarn, a large lake of 160 acres 1,250 feet above sea-level and about 3 miles north of the village, is best seen from one of the neighbouring heights, especially on a clear still day, when the reflection of sky and clouds mingles with that of the fringing trees. For **Victoria Cave,** off the Malham–Settle Road, and not easy to find, *see* below.

Settle

(*Golden Lion*, Duke Street; *Falcon*, Skipton Road; *Ashfield*, Duke Street; *Royal Oak*, Market Place. Population, 2,300) is very picturesquely placed on the Ribble and under a lofty limestone scar. The surroundings are all limestone and the town is of that quiet grey hue which harmonizes well

Malham Cove

with the scenery. It is a good centre for excursions – Ingleton (page 185), Ingleborough Cavern (*see* below), Malham Cove and Tarn and Gordale Scar, Pen-y-Ghent, and so on.

The curiously named town of **Giggleswick** adjoins Settle on the west. Here is a well-known School, and, to the west, the striking Giggleswick Scar.

Between two and three miles north-east of Settle, in the face of Langcliffe Scar, and nearly 1,500 feet above the sea, is **Victoria Cave,** "occupied by Neolithic settlers quite 3,000 years B.C. and by Romano-British refugees from the Anglo-Saxon invasions of *c.* 450 A.D." The excursion to the cave can be combined with that to Malham.

The Langcliffe road continues through **Horton-in-Ribblesdale,** from which visits can be paid to *Ling Gill* and *Hell's Pot (Helln Pot)* : the latter has with the aids of ropes and ladders been explored to a considerable depth, but it is emphatically not a place for the inexperienced in such matters.

Clapham, about midway between Ingleton and Settle, is a romantically placed village at the foot of **Ingleborough** (2,373 feet). It is an obvious starting point for the ascent of the mountain, but is probably more visited on account of Ingleborough Cave, with its magnificent stalactite formations. It is open 10.30 a.m.–6 p.m. daily. The walk is a mile through a wooded glen and up the lower slopes of the mountain.

For **Ingleton** *see* page 185.

Wensleydale

Access. – There are adequate bus services through the Dale.

Road Routes from Harrogate and Ripon *via* Masham past Jervaulx Abbey to Middleham and so into the Dale at Leyburn.

There are two parallel roads one each side of the River Ure. That on the south side is perhaps a preferable route to Hawes, at the western end.

To the minds of many, in captivating beauty Wensleydale is second only to Wharfedale of all the Yorkshire valleys. There is no attempt to grandeur or wilderness: the characteristics of the dale are verdure and gracefulness, and happily these features have been unaffected either by the railway or by the necessary improvements in the road running through the dale and forming part of a very attractive route between central and southern England and the Lake District and Scotland.

The valley is that of the *Ure* – that same river which flows past Ripon and unites with the Swale beyond Boroughbridge to form the Yorkshire Ouse. The dale takes its name from the little town of Wensley, which lies near the foot of the dale; farther up are Bainbridge and Aysgarth and at the head of the dale is Hawes. From Wensley to Hawes is a matter of about a dozen miles.

The mouth of the valley below Wensley is guarded on the south by **Middleham Castle** (*see* page 152); on the north side is –

Leyburn

(Hotels. *Bolton Arms; Golden Lion;* several private hotels.)

a small town spread out along a steep hill-side and with lovely views across Wensleydale, for the exploration of which it is a popular centre. The most noticeable feature is **The Shawl,** a lofty terrace behind the town, commanding a grand view of Wensleydale. Tradition has it that Mary Queen of Scots dropped her shawl here when attempting to escape from Bolton Castle. It is sad to have to question so romantic a derivation, but there is little doubt that the name is derived from the Scandinavian *skali* – huts – later modified to *schalls*, and so to *shawl*. Beside the river below Leyburn is –

Wensley

One of the prettiest villages in Yorkshire, it is of great antiquity, and was an important market town in pre-Norman times. The church has many interesting details, including a carved screen from Easby Abbey (page 188) and some well-carved stalls. The leading feature for ecclesiologists, however, is the very fine brass of Sir Simon de Wenslagh, Rector, 1390 (on Sanctuary floor).

From Wensley to Hawes there is a road on either side of the Dale: that on the south is the faster. **West Witton** is a favourite headquarters for walkers and cyclists: the hill behind it is **Penhill Beacon** (1,792 feet). The road turning away from the river at Wensley Bridge passes **Bolton Castle,** built in the days of Richard II by Lord Chancellor Scrope. The Royalists vainly endeavoured to hold it against a siege in the Civil Wars, and in 1645 it was dismantled. In 1568 Mary Queen of Scots was kept here for six months, and it was while endeavouring to escape (so says legend) that she dropped her shawl at Leyburn (*see* page 180). The ruins have been partly renovated by Lord Bolton, and in addition to Queen Mary's Bedroom and various other apartments (including a museum of curios ranging from fossils to Eton College birches) one can see the Chapel, the Dungeon and, most recently, a typical dales kitchen of a hundred years ago. (*Admission charge.*)

Aysgarth

Hotels. – *George and Dragon* in village; *Palmer Flatt* near Falls. **Youth Hostel.** – Aysgarth Falls.

is a handy centre for Wensleydale, but is principally visited on account of the river, which here falls in a series of picturesque cataracts, the best of which can be seen to advantage from the path starting at white gate beside the old bridge. (Car parking on both sides of river on approach to falls.) Three main falls and several cascades make up Aysgarth Force. The sight is a memorable one, espescially if there is a force of water. Aysgarth Church is near the waterfalls and half a mile from the village. It has an interesting rood-screen.

Among the most attractive excursions from Aysgarth is that to **Kettlewell,** in Upper Wharfedale, a matter of about 14 miles. The first part of the journey is a long climb up **Bishopdale.** A few yards past the summit (1,376 feet above sea-level) the track from Bainbridge by The Stake comes in (*see* below) and then Wharfedale appears in increasing veauty as we descend past **Cray.** The peculiar terrace-formation on the side of Buckden Pike is noteworthy and on the way down some pleasing falls are seen from the road. From Buckden to **Kettlewell** the scenery is delightful. **Wharfedale** is described on pages 164–76.

Askrigg (*King's Arms*), 5 miles west of Aysgarth, has an old cross and a bull ring. *Mill Gill Beck*, which here joins the Ure, has two pretty falls, and there is a splendid walk over to **Muker,** in Swaledale, about 6 miles.

Bainbridge (*Rose and Crown*), on the south side of the dale, is a very attractive village lying round a pleasant green on which the old stocks are preserved. Just above the bridge over the Bain the river falls over flat terraces of rock, making a pretty picture. From September 27 to Shrove-tide, according to an old custom, the horn is sounded at 9 p.m. at Bain-bridge for the benefit of benighted travellers crossing the fells.

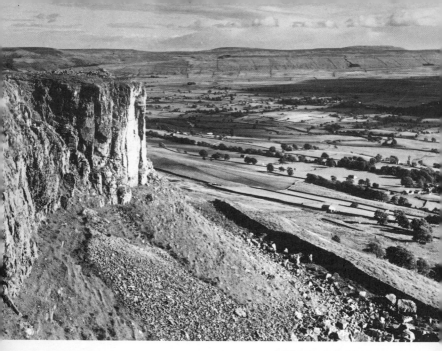

A Wensleydale View

From Bainbridge there is a grand fifteen-mile walk to Cray and Wharfedale by **The Stake.** The road passes Semerwater, about a mile beond which it strikes up to the left. (The road down leads to the hamlet of Stalling Busk, from which a short walk brings one to **Parker Gill Force,** a fine fall through a gap in a sheer wall of rock.) As far as the fork above Stalling Busk the road is quite good, but from that point to just above Cray it is little more than a moorland track. It is much used by cyclists as well as walkers, and for most of the way is possible for cars. (For Cray and route onward *see* above.) The views, especially during the latter part of the walk, are wonderful. Those who do not wish to cross into Wharfedale can return to Wensleydale by way of Bishopdale, by turning to the left on joining the Aysgarth-Buckden road above Cray.

Hawes

(Hotels. – *White Hart; Board; Fountain; Crown.*)

Hawes is a quiet, grey little town 850 feet above the sea, chiefly remarkable for being a market-town so far up at the head of a dale and set amidst the fells. It is an excellent centre for some good walks and motor tours. A mile along the Sedbergh road is Hardraw, where a path through the *Green Dragon Inn* (*fee* 2½p.) leads to **Hardraw Force,** the highest unbroken fall in Great Britain, the water leaping sheer from a height of 100 feet. The underlying rock has been so worn away that it is possible to pass behind the fall. From Hawes one of the best routes is by –

The Buttertubs Pass to Swaledale (7 miles). The "tubs" are deep holes, or "pots", in the fell-side – a formation characteristic of limestone uplands. The group of buttertubs – with depths varying from 50 to 100 feet – is at the side of the road about 4½ miles from Hawes and may easily be missed by the motorist. To get the best of the fell scenery and to see the holes, the walk from Hawes to Muker is recommended. The road surface is however, quite good for cars and the gradients not too steep.

The highest point is 1,726 feet above sea-level. Backwards there are magnificent views of the hills behind Hawes, but even finer is the view of the hills about Keld and Muker as the road emerges from the narrow gorge by which it and the Cliff Beck pass between the most aptly named **Lovely Seat** (2,213 feet) on the right and **Great Shunner Fell** (2,350 feet) on the left.

The road down is narrow and zigzags in places. Then we run alongside the river, with pleasant green slopes on either hand.

For **Swaledale**, *see* pages 187–90.

Hawes to Kettlewell. The walk or ride from Hawes to Kettlewell (17 miles), over Fleet Moss, is well worth taking. The first stage of the road is past **Gayle,** with its pretty falls, and then up the western flank of **Wether Fell** – a four-mile climb, almost incessant and finishing with a few stretches of 1 in 3 gradient. Near the top a track goes off on the right over the moors to Ingleton, joining the Widdale Road near Ribble Head. We bear left. Once over the top the views are indescribably grand. Flat-topped Ingleborough is prominent to the right, almost in front is Pen-y-Ghent, and all around are fells in which the infant Wharfe winds like a silver streak through Langstrothdale. Trees are few, but gradually become more plentiful and along by Buckden form an important part of the scene. To Kettlewell and Grassington as on page 181.

South-westward from Hawes there is a road excursion to **Ingleton** (page 185), and westward from Hawes the road continues very pleasantly down Garsdale to **Sedbergh**. Those who make this excursion should return by way of Dentdale.

Thornton Force

Ingleton

Hotels. – *Ingleborough; Bridge; Wheatsheaf.*
Youth Hostel. – Greta.
Angling. – The Ingleton Angling Association have seven miles of excellent trout fishing.

Swimming. – There is a fine open-air pool on bank of river 200 yards north of church.

Ingleton is known far and wide for its falls and caves. The falls are found in two dales – those of the river Twiss and the Doe or Dale Beck – which converge on Ingleton and unite to form the river Greta. The walk up the dale, across the intervening moorland and down the other – a distance of 4 miles – is very picturesque. Leaving the village at Broadwood (*café*) there is a pleasant walk alongside the river through Swilla Glen. The river is crossed by a wooden footbridge and **Pecca Falls** are soon reached, where a good view of the principal fall of the series can be best seen from a second footbridge. The way is now up a series of steps cut beside the stream in a picturesque gorge and a succession of falls follows quickly, notably those of Pecca Twin and Hollybush Spout. At the head of this section is **Thornton Force**; a fall characteristic of the limestone formation and dropping 40 feet into a pool surrounded by a natural amphitheatre. The way is now by a green walk past Scar End and Beezley Farms (refreshments) to **Beezley Falls.** Alternatively, there is a metalled road back to the village from this point.

Down the ravine formed by the river Twiss we see first the single fall and then the Triple Spout of Beezley followed soon by the pretty Rival Falls, seen by looking back upstream. The waters then plunge and roar through **Baxenghyll Gorge** and there is a delightful view of this wilderness from a bridge high above the stream. The continuation of this is known as Yew Tree Gorge and from here onward the scenery becomes less savage. **Snow Falls,** aptly named, completes the series, and the path, after recrossing the stream by a fourth bridge skirts a disused slate quarry and back to the village quite near to the point of leaving. A divergence from the path where it crosses the small stream, Skerwith Beck, as one leaves the walk brings one to Cat Leap Falls (30 feet). This is especially fine after heavy rain.

The Church of St. Mary overlooks the river. The tower is thirteenth century.

The road from Ingleton to Hawes passes **White Scar Cave** *(café)*. Here the visitor may penetrate ½ mile under Ingleborough Mountain. Discovered in 1923 the cave has two underground waterfalls, wonderful coloured stalagmites, stalactites and grottoes. The cave is electrically lighted and is open daily. Guides are provided. Admission charge. A cark park and picnic ground are available for visitors' use.

The limestone of this district is riddled with caves and potholes – caves containing vertical passages and accessible only from above – the preserve of those who specialize in such exploration. Weathercote Cave at Chapel-le-Dale further along the Hawes Road, is open to all and is well worth a visit. Here the river Twiss, after an extensive underground course issues from the rock face and plunges 70 feet into a rocky basin before disappearing underground once more. It is possible to descend by means of a flight of steps and stand at the foot of this fall. The water emerges again at God's Bridge, below the hamlet of Chapel-le-Dale. Nearby in the dry bed of the stream are two small potholes, Gingle and Hurtle Pots.

Whernside (2,414 feet) and Ingleborough (2,373 feet), two of the famous "Three Peaks" – Pen-y-Ghent (2,273 feet) completing the trio – can be climbed from (1) Ingleton (2) Chapel-le-Dale (3) Ribblehead.

Whernside. (1) From Ingleton by way of Scar End Farm and Scales Moor. A long ridge walk of 7½ miles.

(2) From Chapel-le-Dale. Leave main road at the School, down Philpin Lane to Bruntscar Farm and then straight forward. 3½ miles to summit.

(3) From Ribblehead. Under the viaduct to Winterscales Farm and straight up the Fell. It is quicker but steeper this way. 3 miles.

The summit can be seen most of the way up. There are some old coal pits on the S.E. slopes and the views of Lunesdale, Dentdale, Chapel-le-Dale and upper Ribblesdale are magnificent.

Ingleborough. (1) From Ingleton. A well-defined path leads from Storrs Common to the summit. Distance 3¾ miles.

(2) From Chapel-le-Dale. A path above Hill Inn leads to a point east of Meregill Hole. From here there is a steep climb to the summit. 3 miles.

(3) From Ribblehead. Climb Park Fell and follow the ridge over Simon Fell and on to Ingleborough. 4½ miles. A lovely ridge walk which can be extended to Ingleton following the reverse of (1) above.

The millstone grit cap is nearly 1 mile in circumference and horse races were held here at one time. It was a stronghold of the early Britons and there are many sites of horse-shoe shaped huts together with an enclosing wall. The views from the summit are unrivalled and can be easily identified with the help of the indicator on the shelter wall.

Swaledale

Access. – By road *via* Richmond or Leyburn (bus service) or by way of the Buttertubs Pass from Hawes.

Swaledale is the remotest and wildest of the Yorkshire Dales. The hills on both sides hem it in closely and woods abound.

The dale has become widely known in recent times by the establishment of great military Training Camps as at **Catterick,** which is in the Vale of Mowbray, but only 3 miles or so from –

Richmond

Amusements. – Angling, bowls, cricket, golf, tennis, concerts, operatic performances, cinema, etc.

Angling. – Excellent in the Swale from Richmond to Reeth. Trout in the river above Richmond. Grayling, chub, dace and barbel up to the falls near the Castle. Apply: Mrs. L. M. Small, Easby Abbey.

Early Closing Day. – Wednesday.

Golf. – 9-hole course on Blend Hagg Farm.

Hotels. – King's Head, Market Place; *Fleece, Richmond,* Market Place; *Terrace House; Black Lion,* Finkle Street, etc.

Market Day. – Saturday.

Population. – 7,500.

Road Route. – From Harrogate or Ripon; make for the Great North Road and follow to Catterick Bridge (a mile beyond Catterick village). Cross bridge and turn left.

Richmond is one of the most strikingly situated towns in Britain, being built on a rock around the base of which the Swale forms alternate pool and eddy. With its spacious cobbled Market Place, Norman church, Castle, Grey Friars Tower, remains of town walls, ancient wynds and alleys, it is a picturesque yet busy town. The original **Castle** *(open daily admission charge)* was built in 1017 by Alan Rufus, on whom the Conqueror bestowed the title "Earl of Richmond," together with "a jurisdiction over all Richmondshire, about a third of the North Riding." As in many other cases, the town grew around the Castle and rapidly assumed importance. Succeeding earls added to the building, and the fifth earl, about 1146, raised the great Keep, placing it at the weakest point of the *enceinte* – that which is on a level with the town. On the south side the rock rises abruptly 100 feet above the river. The Keep is 109 feet high, and the walls are 11 feet thick. There is a very fine view from the top.

Trinity Church. in the Market Place, is notable from the fact that a shop is let into the exterior of the sacred building itself. The curfew and the 'Prentice Bell are tolled at 8 p.m. and 8 a.m. respectively on the larger of the two bells in the tower

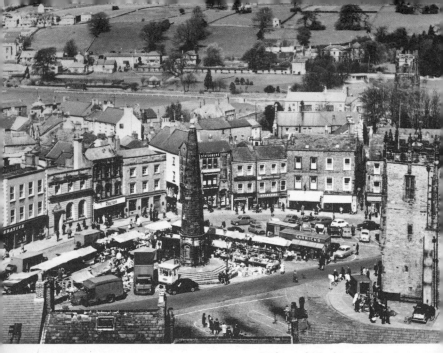

Richmond Market Place

of this church. The smaller bell is rung at 11 a.m. on Shrove Tuesday to "bid the housewives tend the fire to cook the pancakes well."

The **Parish Church,** St. Mary's, extensively restored by Sir Gilbert Scott in 1860, is off Station Road. The carved choir stalls were brought here from Easby Abbey (*see* below) – note the grotesque *misericords*. There are two Norman pillars at the west end – one square, the other round. The Green Howards have a regimental chapel here. Near the Market Place is a very graceful Perpendicular Tower, which is the only remnant of a new church begun for the Grey Friars (who settled here in 1258) at the time of the Dissolution of the monasteries, but never completed.

In Friars' Wynd is the old and unique Georgian Theatre, dating from 1788. On its stage have appeared Edmund Kean, Macready, Kemble and Mrs. Siddons. It is the only small eighteenth-century theatre surviving in Britain in practically its original state.

A pleasant walk of about half a mile down the river from Richmond brings one to the straggling ruins of –

Easby Abbey

Admission: 5*p*. Open March, April, Oct. Weekdays: 9.30–5.30. Sundays: 2–5.30. May–Sept., 9.30–7, 2–7; Nov.–Feb., 10–4, 2–4.

founded in 1155 by Roald, Constable of Richmond Castle, for Praemonstratensian canons, and most picturesquely placed beside the river. As a whole, the ruins are more beautiful in their situation than in themselves. There seems not to be a single angle of 90 degrees in the whole structure, but the Ministry of Public Building and Works supply a plan, from which, with little trouble, the lay-out of the Abbey may be understood. The principal remains are those of the Refectory and adjacent buildings at the south side and parts of the Infirmary at the north. Between the two and running east and west was the church, of which little is to be seen except the east end of the choir, parts of the transepts and pillars of the nave. Adjoining the Abbey is the Parish Church, dating some seven years earlier, and famous for its medieval mural paintings and Norman font.

Swaledale

Following the Reeth road westward from Richmond we immediately have a foretaste of the beauties of Swaledale. (A bus service operates as far as **Keld**.) Well-wooded hills rise steeply on either hand – trees cling to even the most precipitous rocks – and from the road there are glimpses of the river as it alternately brawls over its rocky bed or reflects the over-hanging foliage in its mirror-like surface. In a few miles the hills fall back and instead of trees we look up to heathery slopes falling to fields of that vivid green peculiar to the Dales. On by Marske, Ellerton and Marrick Priory the dale gradually opens out. So by the bridge over the Swale at **Grinton** (Grinton church is worth seeing) and another at the entrance to the village we come to **Reeth** (*Buck, Arkleside,* etc.). The village is set around a large scree at the foot of **Arkengarthdale** and with views of the Dale up which we have come from Richmond. The hills around are no longer the closely-wooded cliffs by which we have passed, but bare slopes and shelves which are themselves an incitement to walkers: it is possible, too, to make a way by the riverside to Muker and Keld.

Rising out of Reeth there is a grand view ahead of the Dale as it narrows along by Gunnerside, with the massive Great Shunner Fell (2,340 feet) beyond. Between Healaugh and Feetham on the left is the beginning of a fine walk over to Aysgarth and Bainbridge, in Wensleydale. **Feetham** *(Punch Bowle)* overlooks the valley at a point where a road comes over from Arkengarthdale and Barnard Castle. Two miles farther is **Gunnerside** *(inn)*, a stone-built village at the foot of a narrow gorge up which there is a fine walk to Keld, bearing left near the source of the stream and then south-ward over **Rogan's Seat.**

At Gunnerside we follow the brawling stream down to the Swale, which is crossed by a picturesque bridge. Then on the right are glimpses of the beck tumbling down its narrow gorge from the moors in a series of falls, followed by a sight of the steep-sided **Kisdon,** at the foot of which the Swale comes down from Keld. **Muker** *(Farmer's Arms)* is an endearing little stone-built village in the angle formed by the junction of the Cliff Beck with the Swale, which makes some very pretty falls on its way down from Lovely Seat, beside the Buttertubs Pass. There are walks in every direction – the best is that alongside the river to Keld, passing Kisdon Force on the way, returning maybe over Kisdon itself. Muker is near the northern end of the Buttertubs Pass (*see* page 183), and so has ready access to Wensleydale – but there is enough in this corner of Swaledale to occupy most people for a week or more.

Keld

Most motorists, intent on their "circular tour," turn up the Hawes road a mile or so above Muker, but for a final glimpse of Upper Swaledale it is worth turning off through Thwaite to **Keld,** a handful of houses dropped as it were in a pocket in the hill-side at the meeting-point of Great Sleddale with Swaledale, where the Swale begins to rush the gorge between Kisdon and Rogan's Seat. Though small, it is a splendid centre for walks – by the riverside or over Kisdon to Muker; across the river and over **Rogan's Seat** to Gunnerside; up the southern flank of Great Shunner and down by the Heanne Beck to Hawes, up Whitsundale, and many others.

Those with little time to spare should pass beside *Birk Hill View* and follow the path round to the right behind *Park Lodge* to where stone steps afford a view of the series of falls which the river takes as a preliminary to the gorge below the village. Opposite *Birk Hill View* another path leads to another series of falls, where the beck hurls itself down from Rogan's Seat to join the Swale. Just below the falls the conjoined waters rush between steep wooded cliffs – a beautiful spot whether it is seen from either of the paths above the river or from the water's edge. If at first acquaintance Keld seems unattractive, it certainly grows on one very rapidly. There is a Youth Hostel at Keld Lodge.

Four miles from Keld on the Brough road is **Tan Hill,** which to many is memorable as the site of one of the highest inns in England.

The **Buttertubs Pass** to Hawes provides a glorious view of the head of Swaledale. The road mounts steeply, and in a very short while we are looking down on Kisdon, Rogan's Seat and other hills which a moment ago seemed quite formidable heights. For notes on the Pass, see page 183.

Barnard Castle and Upper Teesdale

From a few miles above Middleton to the sea, the Tees forms the northern boundary of Yorkshire. In its lower reaches it passes through such industrial areas as are centred around Darlington, Stockton-on-Tees and Middlesbrough, but at Barnard Castle the scenery is more characteristic of a Yorkshire Dale.

Barnard Castle

Access. – Road *via* the Great North Road and Scotch Corner.
Hotels. – *King's Head*, Market Place; *Station*, Harmire; *Mount*, Park Terrace; *Montalbo*, Montalbo Road.

Picturesquely situated on a steep hill-side running down to the river 16 miles above Darlington, Barnard Castle (though actually on the Durham side of the Tees) is an excellent centre for the exploration of this northernmost part of Yorkshire, which includes not only the valley of the Tees but that of the Greta, which joins the bigger river a few miles below the town.

The. **Castle** (admission 5*p.*) was founded in the twelfth century by Bernard Baliol, who uncle had come over with the Conqueror and taken his share of the royal gifts distributed after the raid on the North. "Castle Barnard" it is called by Leland, who adds, "It standeth stately upon Teese." Set high on the rocky cliff the ruins cover 6¼ acres, the most notable being the great round tower, traces of the moat and the inner ditches. It is now in the care of the Department of the Environment.

Near the *King's Head Hotel* (where Dickens stayed while at work on *Nicholas Nickleby*) was a watchmaker's shop, "Humphrey's," hence the title of *Master Humphrey's Clock*.

Beyond Newgate is the **Bowes Museum,** a magnificent building set in a park of 20 acres. In the Collection are masterpieces of painting of the European Schools, including the famous *St. Peter* by El Greco, porcelain, tapestries, embroideries, furniture, historical relics, and a children's room with toys. A section illustrates Teesdale Rural Life and Work. The Museum is open May to September 10-5.30; Oct., March, April 10-5; Nov. to Feb. 10-4; Sundays in summer 2-5, in winter

High Force, Teesdale

2-4. Admission 10*p*. children 2½*p*. There are tennis courts and a bowling green. A tea-room is attached to the Museum.

Among the most popular short excursions from Barnard Castle is that to **Greta Bridge,** at the meeting of the Greta and the Tees. The bridge is four miles from Barnard Castle by road and the sight of the Greta flinging its bright clear-flowing waters down a wooded glen into the larger stream of the Tees is a delight, though the view has been somewhat spoiled by the steel bridge on the north side.

The excursion may be extended by an exploration of **Rokeby Park,** beautiful grounds in a beautiful situation, though those who come full of expectations induced by reading Scott's poem must be prepared for a possible disappointment.

Another extension of the Greta Bridge excursion is to return to Barnard Castle by the Roman road running westward from Rokeby to **Bowes,** a Roman station which retains the ruins of a Norman keep, in the care of the Department of the Environment. In many minds, however, the most interesting fact about Bowes is that it is the scene of Squeers' Academy – Dotheboys Hall – in *Nicholas Nickleby*.

Another route between Greta Bridge and Bowes is by **Brignall Banks,** a walk of 7 to 8 miles of which the greater part is very delightful going through a lovely glen. In the heart of the glen, some 2½ miles from Greta Bridge, is Gill Beck, and a little farther west the hamlet of Scargill is passed. Beyond this point the walk is over open ground with wide views of the bare moorland.

Another very attractive short walk from Barnard Castle is along the riverside *via* Gray Lane to the Abbey Bridge and **Egglestone Abbey** 1¼ miles to the south-east. The attractive bridge was opened in 1773 and from it are pretty river views. On the right are picturesque remains of a Praemonstratensian Abbey, comprising a thirteenth-century chancel and much of the twelfth- to fourteenth-century nave. (Admission 2½*p*.) There is a choice of several return routes to the town.

Middleton *(Cleveland Arms)* is about ten miles west of Barnard Castle, in High Teesdale. Its principal interest to tourists is as a centre, notably for visits to High Force, which is undoubtedly one of the finest waterfalls in England. The Alston road is followed from Middleton, with some good views of the Tees making its turbulent way over its rocky course. Five miles from Middleton a path opposite the *High Force Hotel* takes us down to **High Force** itself. There are actually three falls. The first and shortest is split into two by a pinnacle of rock; the last and greatest has a sheer drop of about 40 feet. Round the basin the rock has been hollowed out by the rush of water and the stones in flood-time, and higher up trees and grass grow out of the crevices.

Some 6 miles farther upstream is **Cauldron Snout,** another fine cascade, though here the fall spreads itself over a distance of 150 yards in which the stream rushes through a deepening chasm only a few yards wide, in places less.

Egglestone Abbey

Sheffield

Banks. – *Barclays*, 2 High Street, Fitzalan Square, 175 Eyre Street, 2 West Street; *Lloyds*, 14 Church Street and The Moor; *Midland*, 17 Church Street and Market Place; *National Westminster*, 42 High Street, 16 George Street.

Cinemas. – *ABC*, Angel Street; *Classic*, Fitzalan Square; *Gaumonts One and Two*, Barker's Pool; *Studio* 7, The Wicker; *Cineplex*, Charter Square; *Cinecenta*, off Pond Street; *Sheffield Film Theatre*, Tudor Place. (This is a regional Film Theatre; performances are given one week in each month beginning on the Sunday. Details from public library.)

Concerts. – *Oval Hall*, City Hall, Barker's Pool, on alternate Fridays and Saturdays from September to May. Details from the Philharmonic Offices, City Hall.

Cricket. – Bramall Lane.

Car Parking. – Meters in central area, also off-street metered and other car parks; multi-storey car parks in *Bank Street, Burgess Street, Eyre Street, Norfolk Street, Wellington Street* and *Pond Street*.

Dancing. – *City Hall*, Barker's Pool; *Tiffany's*, London Road; *Top Rank Suite*, Arundel Gate. Also at dance halls in the suburbs.

Football (Association). – Sheffield United, Bramall Lane; Sheffield Wednesday, Hillsborough.

Golf. – *Abbeydale Golf Club*, Twentywell Lane; *Beauchief Golf Course*, Abbey Lane; *Dore and Totley Golf Club*, Bradway; *Hallamshire Golf Club*, Sandygate; *Hillsborough Golf Club*, Loxley Chase, Wadsley; *Lees Hall Golf Club*, Hemsworth Road, Norton; *Tinsley Park Golf Course*, Tinsley Park; *Driving Range*, Bradway Road, Bradway.

Greyhound Racing. – Owlerton Sports Stadium, Penistone Road.

Hotels. – *Grosvenor House*, Charter Square; *Hallam Tower*, Manchester Road, Broomhill; *Harley Hotel*, Glossop Road; *Kenwood*, Kenwood Road, Sharrow; *Montgomery*, Montgomery Road, Sharrow; *Roslyn Court*, Psalter Lane, Sharrow; *Royal Victoria*, Victoria Station Road; *Rutland*, Glossop Road; *St. Andrews*, Kenwood Road, Sharrow, and many others of all grades.

Information Bureau. – Civic Information Service, Central Library.

Library. – Central Library, Surrey Street.

Museum. – City Museum, Weston Park.

Population. – 519,700.

Post Office. – Fitzalan Square.

Swimming (indoor). – Attercliffe Baths, Attercliffe Road; Glossop Road Baths, Convent Walk; Heeley Baths, Broadfield Road; Hillsborough Baths, Langsett Road; Park Baths, Samson Street; Sutherland Road Baths; Upperthorpe Baths, Daniel Hill. In the following schools swimming baths are available to the public each evening and on Saturdays and Sundays. Hurlfield Comprehensive, East Bank Road; King Edward VII, Clarkehouse Road; Woodthorpe High, Chadwick Road.

Swimming (Open-air). – Longley Park, Milhouses Park.

Sailing. – Dam Flask, Underbank and Ewden Reservoirs.

Speedway Racing. – Owlerton Sports Stadium, Penistone Road.

Ten Pin Bowling. – Firth Park Bowl, Sicey Avenue.

Theatres. – *Crucible*, Arundel Gate; *Library Theatre*, Tudor Place; *Merlin Theatre*, Meadow Bank Road.

Sheffield is the phoenix of Yorkshire. Heavily bombed during the Second World War it has transformed itself from the oft-quoted "dark picture in a golden frame", into the showplace among Yorkshire cities, of which it is the largest, as well as being the fifth largest city in England.

Far from being the grim and grimy place many strangers imagine, Sheffield is considered today to be an outstanding example of smoke control and is probably the cleanest industrial city in Europe, regularly visited by clean-air experts from all over the world.

Sub-standard pre-war houses have been replaced, most strikingly by the Park Hill/Hyde Park flats, the biggest development of its type in Western Europe. High on a hill overlooking the city centre, this houses some 2,000 families on a site once occupied by 800. A contrasting picture of modern housing is presented in the Gleadless Valley, where houses in wooded settings terrace the hillside. Indeed, Sheffield now has perhaps the widest variety of post-war housing in this country, well suited to the dramatic rises and falls of its hilly landscape.

The city has always taken pride in its craftsmanship in the production of steel, silverware and cutlery; now it has found a new prestige as perhaps the finest shopping centre in the North, with more department stores, it is claimed, than any other city north of London.

Everyone on his first visit to Sheffield is impressed by **Castle Square** – a subterranean shopping area familiarly known among Sheffielders as "the hole in the road". This award-winning engineering feat combines a round-about, pedestrian underpass and shopping precinct, resulting in safer shopping and a better traffic flow in the city centre. Escalators connect the subways with street level.

Despite such modernity, the city is by no means of recent growth. It began as a mere cluster of houses by the side of the River Sheaf, and few of its early inhabitants dreamed that their apparently pastoral surroundings held the seeds of industrial greatness. Water, wood, stone and iron ore – all were here as if awaiting their cue – the water for power; the wood for fuel; the stone for grindstones. As early as the fourteenth century, Chaucer mentioned a Sheffield "thwitel", or knife, in his *Canterbury Tales* and by the time of the first Elizabeth, Sheffield cutlery was renowned throughout the land.

Long before Elizabeth's reign, another monarch had visited the area. At **Dore** *(south-west of the city off the A625)*, there is an inscribed stone erected to commemorate the proclamation of King Ecgbert of Mercia as King of England in the year 829. The inscription reads: King Ecgbert of Wessex led his army to Dore in the year A.D. 829, against King Eanred of Northumbria, by whose submission King Ecgbert became first overlord of all England.

Early in the twelfth century William de Lovetot, a Norman, held the manor of Sheffield. He founded the parish church and also built the second Sheffield castle, now destroyed.

The year 1297 was important for the people of Sheffield, for then it was that Thomas de Furnival granted a charter creating a Burgery of Sheffield, thus giving the townsfolk some say in the running of their own affairs. In 1530 Cardinal Wolsey spent eighteen days in Sheffield after his arrest on a charge of high treason, near York.

The tragic Mary, Queen of Scots, spent fourteen years in captivity in Sheffield Castle. The castle is gone now, but still standing beside the Manor Lodge is the **Turret House,** which is believed to have been built to accommodate the royal prisoner during her visits to the Lodge.

It was the invention by Benjamin Huntsman, a Lincolnshire clockmaker, of the crucible process of making steel (*see* Abbeydale Works, page 199) that laid the foundation of Sheffield's future industrial eminence.

Not that steel and cutlery represent the whole of Sheffield's industrial activity, which includes fashion, confectionery, brewing, food canning – and even snuff manufacture, for Sheffield is claimed to be the largest producer of snuff in Great Britain.

The Cathedral, Sheffield

Notable Buildings

Cathedral. The cruciform **Church of St. Peter and St. Paul** in Church Street, Sheffield's cathedral since 1913, when the bishopric was founded, originated in the twelfth century and was rebuilt in the fifteenth. As a result of bomb damage, part of the church had to be rebuilt again. There is now a wonderful coloured lantern soaring through the roof to a height of sixty-two feet. Throughout the Cathedral the stained glass is a fascinating feature: in the Chapter House there are scenes from the early history of the city, and, surmounting all else, a picture of the Sheffield Cross, the shaft of which is now in the British Museum.

Cutlers' Hall. Among the most impressive of Sheffield's city centre buildings is the Cutlers Hall (1832), also in Church Street, which was built as an administrative centre for the Cutlers' Company in Hallamshire. Among its many fine rooms, the marbled main hall and the Regency-style banqueting hall are outstanding.

The Company of Cutlers was formed by Act of Parliament in 1624 by Sheffield cutlers and North Derbyshire scythe and sickle makers. At one time the company held unique powers in Hallamshire, which was virtually an industrial kingdom. The Cutlers' Company, which since 1860 has admitted all manufacturers of steel articles with a cutting edge, is the registered proprietor of the trade mark "Sheffield". The office of Master Cutler, who is spokesman during his term of office for the industry of Sheffield, is second only to that of Lord Mayor. One of the most splendid occasions in the North is the annual Cutlers' Feast, attended by Cabinet Ministers, ambassadors and other high-ranking personages.

The **Central Library,** in Surrey Street, nearby, home for a valuable collection of manuscripts (including the Arundel Castle manuscripts), as well as over a million volumes, is a fine building in Portland stone. The **Library Theatre** here, used by the city's many amateur dramatic societies, is considered one of the best small theatres in the country. Here also is the **Graves Art Gallery,** containing important oriental pictures as well as an extensive collection of European art. One of the leading galleries in this country, it includes among its most treasured possessions the Grice Ivories.

The Town Hall. Also in Surrey Street is the Town Hall, whose tower, 193 feet high, is surmounted by a seven-foot bronze of Vulcan, symbolising the trades by which Sheffield lives. Other statuary includes a figure of Thor and representations of Steam and Electricity, as well as Queen Victoria, during whose reign Sheffield was established as a great industrial city. The Town Hall has a magnificent staircase and a series of very fine rooms. With its rich carving, its splendid ceilings, its marble, oak and alabaster, this is a grand example of Victorian architecture.

Eventually the Town Hall, along with the Central Library and Graves Art Gallery will form part of a new Civic Centre which will include new Law Courts and an Arts Centre.

City Hall. At Barker's Pool nearby is the City Hall built of Darley Dale stone in 1932. It contains the fine Oval Hall which can seat 2,800 and the organ is considered one of the best in England. Regular choral and orchestral concerts are given here.

The Crucible Theatre. Sheffield has what has been claimed to be the most revolutionary theatre in Britain. This is the Crucible, situated near the junction of Arundel Gate and Norfolk Street in the city centre. Immediately impressive by reason of its extremely modern design, the Crucible continues Sheffield's fifty-year-old repertory tradition, replacing the former Playhouse. Regarded as unique in Britain for its splendid audience facilities, the Crucible's main auditorium seats 1,000 in steeply-rising seats around three sides of a stage which thrusts 28 feet forward into the audience. Even more intimate is the small octagonal experimental theatre, which will house 250.

The University. The University of Sheffield was established by Royal Charter in 1905 and provides courses in Arts, Pure Science, Medicine, Law, Engineering, Social Sciences and Architectural Studies, among many others. The main buildings are less than a mile from the Town Hall.

Sheffield Polytechnic, in its spectacular buildings on the Pond Street site, offers a wide variety of courses and is also closely linked with industry, to which some of its departments act in an advisory capacity. The Polytechnic provides a home for the regional Centre for Science and Technology.

Forty-eight parks

In fine weather Sheffield's forty-eight parks offer an immediate attraction. They range from the small but attractive gardens at **Beauchief** to **Ecclesall Woods,** only three miles from the city centre, offering 305 acres of natural woodland with bridle paths for horse riding; or **Graves Park,** with 206 acres, where the facilities include a café, tennis, bowls, miniature golf and boating.

Well worth a visit are the delightful **Botanical Gardens,** which include an aviary and aquarium.

At **Hillsborough Park** there is an athletics arena, besides tennis and bowls. Here the Sheffield Show is held each September.

Sheep-dog trials are held, usually in early September, at **Longshaw,** near Hathersage, on the city's western boundary.

Other parks and open spaces include **Millhouses,** with its lido, boating lake and children's paddling stream charmingly placed beside the River Sheaf, and **Weston Park** containing the **City Museum and Mappin Art Gallery.** Not surprisingly the museum has a unique collection of cutlery as well as the world's finest collection of old Sheffield plate, together with general and natural history sections. The **Mappin Art Gallery** is known for its fine examples of British Art. There is another park at **Whiteley Woods** and **Forge Dam,** where the *Shepherd Wheel* may be seen. On the banks of the River Porter, this comprises a waterwheel and two grinding hulls. Mentioned in records since 1584 this very ancient wheel has been restored and may be seen by the public, with its machinery working, on summer Bank Holiday Monday afternoons. Educational parties may also see the wheel working at other times during the summer by arrangement.

Whirlow Brook Park contains one of the most beautiful water gardens in the North of England. Rose gardens and a restaurant add to the visitor's enjoyment.

Pleasant Walks

There is an abundance of walking country. Reminiscent of a miniature Switzerland are places like **Lodge Moor, Wyming Brook** and **Hollow Meadows,** with their dams and conifer trees. You may follow field and river paths through the peaceful **Mayfield Valley** to **Ringinglow,** from there following the **Limb Brook** through **Bole Hill Plantation, Whirlow Brook Park** and **Ecclesall Woods** to **Beauchief,** with its eleventh century Premonstatensian Abbey tower. Another walk from **Ringinglow** takes you by paths across **Dore Moor** to **Redcar Brook** near Dore.

Natural history enthusiasts may wish to follow one of the nature trails being developed by Sheffield City Council. The first to be devised covers a two-mile stretch of the **Rivelin Valley** and offers a comprehensive study dealing not only with the flora and fauna of the area but covering interesting historical remains, such as water wheels. A descriptive guide to the trail may be obtained at a small charge from the Civic Information Service, Surrey Street, or from the Recreation Department, Meersbrook Park.

There is splendid walking country, too, in the Peak District National Park, part of which, along with a grouse moor, lies within Sheffield's western boundary.

The most famous walk of all, however, where Sheffield is concerned, is the **Round Walk** of ten miles from **Hunter's Bar** (a mile and a half from the city centre) to **Graves Park** and **Bunting Nook.** The scenery is delightfully varied and there are some enchanting views. Those who lack the time or the energy to make the entire walk on foot can follow the route in easy stages by taking buses to and from various points. The Civic Information Service at the Central Library or the Corporation Transport Department would be pleased to offer advice on this or other excursions.

Then there is the Town and Country Tour, a three-hour trip visiting the Hope Valley and Hathersage, the "Morton" of *Jane Eyre*, and according to tradition the burial place of Little John.

Abbeydale Industrial Hamlet *(daily, fee)* is situated on Abbeydale Road South, the main Bakewell road, 3½ miles south-west of the city centre.

It was the invention by Benjamin Huntsman, a Lincolnshire clockmaker, of the crucible process that laid the foundation of Sheffield's industrial eminence.

Huntsman's achievement is finely commemorated at the Abbeydale Works. Restored only a few years ago, this old scythe works is now open to the public as an industrial museum. Preserved on this site is an early furnace of the type developed by Huntsman in 1742 for producing steel in crucibles. From the crucibles the molten steel was teemed into moulds to produce ingots, which were then re-heated and forged into rough shape by means of tilt hammers, finally being tempered and shaped by craftsmen to produce the finished object.

Water was the chief source of power – for the tilt hammers, for the hafting and boring shop, for air-blowing machinery for the fires, and for the grinding machinery; though during the nineteenth century, water power was supplemented during times of drought by a horizontal steam engine.

Sheffield to Huddersfield

The trunk road A616 crosses moorland dotted with reservoirs. Nine miles from Sheffield is **Stocksbridge,** a mainly rural area occupied by small farms and rolling country which at its southern end runs into the Peak District National Park. A few miles before Stocksbridge is the village of **Wharncliffe Side,** and, on the right, the impressive **Wharncliffe Crags,** from the summit of which extensive views may be enjoyed. Many querns (stone-age implements used in grinding corn) have been found at the base of the Crags and it has been suggested that the name of Wharncliffe is derived from the word quern.

There are delightful walks in **Wharncliffe Park** (owned by the Earl of Wharncliffe), which is open to visitors on Mondays, Thursdays and Saturdays and throughout the week at Bank Holidays. Entrance from Wortley. Turn right at **Deepcarr,** two miles from Wharncliffe Side. Access to Crags from park. No admission fee.

On the left of the road, is the Ewden Valley, through which runs the Ewden Beck. Here Sheffield Corporation has made reservoirs. On the edge of the moors beyond can be seen the site of early medieval ironworks, now largely overgrown by heather and bracken.

Stocksbridge Urban District includes **Deepcar** and **Bolsterstone,** the last being much the oldest of the three. At one time it was well known for glass production. Standing on the highest point of the area, it is the scene of some remains of an old manor house and a Saxon chieftain is said to lie buried on **Walderslow** nearby.

The presence of clay, coal and water for power ensured the development of Stocksbridge and Deepcar. The district has one of the foremost steelworks in the country.

After passing the long, attractive Underbank reservoir set amid conifer trees and used both for sailing and fishing, turn right at **Langsett** (yet another reservoir here) and so to Penistone.

Penistone, once a small market town, was specially noted for the moorland sheep sold at its markets and fairs. Penistone existed before the Norman Conquest as a small village. In course of time it became a cottage industry centre for the cloth trade. Then, in the nineteenth century, an overspill from Sheffield's industry turned it virtually into a steel town.

Beyond Penistone the A629 road continues north-westward to Huddersfield passing **Kirkburton** near which is the huge **Emley Moor Television mast** towering to a height of 1,000 feet. Ahead is **Almondbury** with the Victoria Tower conspicuous upon Castle Hill. For **Huddersfield,** *see* page 229.

Rotherham Church

Sheffield to Doncaster

Rotherham

Six miles from Sheffield, Rotherham is a busy industrial town relying chiefly on steel, coal and iron-founding.

The magnificent **Parish Church** of All Saints in the town centre, is one of the most interesting buildings in the town and is claimed to be one of the finest examples of Perpendicular architecture in Yorkshire. The present church, the third to stand on the site, is mostly fifteenth century.

In 1875, when Sir Gilbert Scott restored the church, he preserved many features of interest. Particularly notable are the fifteenth-century choir stalls, a brass of Robert Swyfte in the North Chapel and a mutilated altar tomb near the South Door. The Jacobean pulpit dates from 1604. Also of interest is the organ, the original of which was built in 1777 by the great John Snetzler, whose console may be seen in a glass case in the North Transept.

On Rotherham Bridge is the **Chantry Chapel of Our Lady,** one of only three such chapels to be found in England. The others are at Wakefield and St. Ives (Hunts.). The chantry, dating from 1483, has had a somewhat chequered career, having been used as an almshouse, town prison, and in the nineteenth century as a tobacconist's shop. In 1924 it was rededicated and scheduled as an ancient monument. The bridge, widened in 1805, was returned to its original width of 15 feet and was also scheduled as an ancient monument after the completion of the present Chantry Bridge (alongside Rotherham Bridge) in 1930.

In 1643, during the Civil War, the old bridge was the scene of a battle between Royalist troops, under the Earl of Newcastle, and the townspeople including boys of the local Grammar School. Not surprisingly, the Earl, who had 8,000 men at his command, captured the town.

A mile and a half south-west of Rotherham is **Templeborough,** once the site of a Roman fort. Finds from here can be seen in the museum, an eighteenth-century mansion, at **Clifton Park.** Re-erected on the museum lawn are the colonnade and columns from some of the large buildings which were discovered.

Four miles north of Rotherham town centre is **Wentworth Woodhouse,** which has the longest frontage (600 ft.) of any English country house. The seat of the Earl Fitzwilliam, it is now a teachers' training college, though the present Earl still occupies a few rooms there. The house is not open to the public but visitors are admitted to the splendid wooded park which contains some remarkable monuments. The house was built in the eighteenth century by Flitcroft for the first Marquis of Rockingham.

Seven miles east of Rotherham and reached by the A631 road is –

Maltby

Although Maltby (pop. 15,100) has been inhabited since about 1500 B.C., when the area was peopled by the Brigantes, it remained a very small place, until the Maltby Main Colliery to the east of the town was sunk in 1908. This mine, which employs about 2,000, has been modernised and reconstructed.

Despite the town's antiquity, it has few buildings of historic interest, an outstanding exception being **Roche Abbey** (*see* page 204), about 1½ miles to the south-east.

St. Bartholomew's Church, which stands on a bank above the stream can be reached via Church Lane from the junction of High Street and Low Blyth Road. The tower contains masonry said to be even older than Roche Abbey (founded 1147), although with the exception of the western tower, the church was rebuilt in 1859. There are a number of interesting inscriptions in the church, giving the names of benefactors, and a beautiful stained glass window in the Hoyle Chapel.

The site of the old *Maltby Hall,* off the Rotherham Road (A631) close to the beginning of the High Street, is now occupied by the Grammar School. While in Rotherham Road close to the market place is to be seen the remains of an old medieval cross.

Perhaps the most notable modern building is the **Civic Centre** at the junction of High Street and Braithwell Road which accommodates the administrative offices in a pleasant landscaped setting.

There are many acres of easily accessible open spaces and recreation areas and a first-class open-air swimming pool in Meadow Lane.

A few miles east of Maltby is **Tickhill** with a ruined castle and ancient church.

Roche Abbey *(daily, fee)* lies 1½ miles south-east of Maltby, just south of the A634. The remains of this twelfth-century Cistercian foundation are set in a thickly wooded valley where a fast-flowing stream enlivens the scene. Surrounding the ruins and enhancing their medieval dignity are green lawns.

Founded in 1147 by Richard de Buslei and Richard Fitzturgis, the abbey was built over the water because the two men owned land on opposite sides of the stream; some of the buildings span the stream by means of bridges.

Much of the ruin is only fragmentary, but the eastern part of the church still stands and a good deal of the vaulted gatehouse with its narrow arch for pedestrians and a broad archway for waggons is well preserved.

The monks of the Rock, as they were to be known, came from Newminster to found their abbey in the shade of a cliff of magnesium limestone. At one time the apparent outline of a cross could be discerned on the face of the crags and to the devout brothers this seemed an unmistakable sign of divine approval. It became a place of pilgrimage. The "cross" is no longer to be seen, but one can still make out the marks left in the rock by the monks as they hewed the stone for the labour of beauty and piety which was to survive their own brief lives by so many centuries.

Only feet away from the native rock, the transepts of the abbey church rise in loveliness. South of the church are the remains of the walls of the cloister walk, where the monks once read and meditated.

At the Dissolution under Henry VIII, the abbey was sacked and much of its stone pillaged for building cottages.

In the eighteenth century the famous landscape gardener "Capability" Brown "improved" the valley on the instructions of the 4th Earl of Scarborough. Today the abbey's remains are in the care of the Department of the Environment.

The Keep, Conisbrough Castle

Beyond Rotherham the A630 Doncaster road passes through **Thrybergh,** once the home of Sir John Revesby (born 1634), a friend of Queen Henrietta Maria. His memoirs are highly valued by historians. The fourteenth/ fifteenth-century church is worth a visit, as is the church at **Hooton Roberts,** the next village along the road, which stands on a hillside above the River Don. The countryside is scarred with industry in this region, but the road nevertheless provides many surprise views as it loses and regains contact with the winding course of the Don.

Five miles south-west of Doncaster is ——

Conisbrough, a township of steep streets and intriguing corners dominated by its Norman castle.

The twelfth-century **castle** *(daily, fee)* was made famous by Sir Walter Scott in *Ivanhoe* as the home of Athelstane. Now scheduled as an ancient monument, it stands beside the River Don on a steep, man-made bank. Approached by a flight of steps, the cylindrical keep, which soars almost 90 feet, and measures 52 ft. across, is supported by six buttresses, tapering towards the top, which were once surmounted with turrets. The keep, considered to be unique in England in design, has been called the finest in the country. The walls are 15 feet thick and there is a deep moat.

One may admire the Norman fireplace in the main apartment and then visit the floor above where there is an hexagonal oratory described in *Ivanhoe*, set in one of the buttresses. In another buttress there is an oven, in another a pigeon loft, while yet another contains two cisterns which at one time held water drawn from a well beneath the central tower. From the battlements is an excellent view of the surrounding country, the four counties of Yorkshire, Lincolnshire, Nottinghamshire and Derbyshire being visible.

The castle was probably built by Hameline (or Hamelin) Warrenne, sometimes called Plantaganet, reputedly a half-brother to Henry II; he was at the coronation of Richard I and was treasurer for the Lionheart's ransom.

Warrenne probably built Conisbrough's **church,** too, which contains a great deal of Norman work, as well as some Saxon stone, a fifteenth-century clerestory and font, a medieval stone altar and a chalice dating back to before the first Elizabeth. A Norman gravestone has a fascinating set of carvings including Adam and Eve, a dragon and two knights on horseback taking part in a tournament.

For **Doncaster,** *see* page 242.

Sheffield to Barnsley

Barnsley is about $13\frac{1}{2}$ miles north of Sheffield via the A61 (or more speedily by the M1). East of the motorway, roughly seven miles north of Sheffield, is **Wentworth** (on the B6090), setting for the magnificent **Wentworth Woodhouse** (*see* page 202). Further along, to the west of the motorway, stands **Wentworth Castle,** near Stainborough, built by Thomas Wentworth and his son in the eighteenth century. This splendid house in a beautiful park is now, like Wentworth Woodhouse, a college of education. Horace Walpole called Wentworth Castle one of the most beautiful homes in England. It contains a gallery 180 ft. long and 30 ft. high. In the grounds are a "temple" and a mock castle, a mile or two from which are some remains of Rockley Abbey.

Barnsley

Banks. – *Barclays*, Church Street and Queen Street; *Lloyds*, Market Hill; *Midland*, Market Hill; *National Westminster*, Church Street, Market Hill and Peel Square; *Trustee Savings Bank*, Peel Square; *Yorkshire*, Market Hill.

Car Parks. – Baker Street/Park Row: Churchfield; Court House Station; Grahams Orchard; Lancaster Gate; Mark Street; Peel Parade; Piper's Cottage; Silver Street Area; Taylor Row, Town End, Westgate Area. Street parking in St. Mary's Place; Churchfield; Falcon Street; Eastgate; Silver Street; Sadler Gate.

Cinemas. – *Odeon*, Eldon Street; *ABC*, Peel Street.

Dancing. – *Civic Hall*, Eldon Street; *New Arcadian Hall*, Market Street; *Portcullis Club*, Pitt Street; *Regent Court*, Regent Street.

Early Closing Day. – Thursday.

Golf. – *Barnsley and District Golf Club* Course, Dodworth; *Barnsley Golf Club*, Wakefield Road, Staincross.

Hotels. – *Queen's*, Regent Street; *Royal*, Church Street; *Waverley* (unlicensed), Victoria Road; *White Hart*, Peel Square; *King George*, Peel Street.

Libraries. – Central Public Library, Eldon Street. Branch libraries at Athersley, Kendray and Monk Bretton.

Market Days. – Wednesday, Friday and Saturday.

Museum. – *Cannon Hall Museum*, Cawthorne.

Population. – 75,315.

Post Office. – Pitt Street.

Swimming. – At *Corporation Baths*, Race Street.

Barnsley, 14 miles north of Sheffield, was mentioned in Domesday Book as Berneslai – "the field of Bern". Coal mining, on which the town's fortunes have been built, began very early in the town's history. Glass blowing, the other principal industry, began in the early part of the seventeenth century. Both industries are represented on the county borough coat of arms, where the supporters are, on the left, a miner with his lamp and pick and on the right a glassblower complete with blowpipe and glass bottle. (There is a memorial at **Silkstone Church** to 26 mineworkers drowned in a flooded pit in 1838, while a monument on **Kendray Hill** records 361 deaths in the Old Oaks colliery disaster of 1866). Today there is a variety of other manufacturing industries, including textiles, paper, plastics, steel and toys. Barnsley market, one of the biggest in the country, which dates from 1249, is still held three times a week on a site at the centre of the town and attracts visitors from a vast area.

Barnsley's first railway station was opened in 1850, a date of special importance in Barnsley since Joseph Locke, who worked with George and Robert Stephenson, was a Barnsley man. He is commemorated in one or two street names and by the 46-acre **Locke Park** at the southern end of the town, opened in 1862.

The **Town Hall,** in Church Street, is easily the most striking modern building in Barnsley at present, though it is proposed to build a large new civic centre. Opened in 1933, the Town Hall is impressively massive, occupying nearly 34,000 square feet and containing 140 rooms. Its four storeys are surmounted by a fine clock tower, 145 ft. high. Faced with Portland stone, it stands out strikingly against the predominantly dark colours inevitable in a town at the very heart of the country's largest coalfield.

In contrast with this comparatively modern building is the parish **Church of St. Mary,** whose embattled and pinnacled tower dates from the fifteenth century. The rest of the church is later, but many of the fittings from the fifteenth-century building are preserved within.

The **Cooper Art Gallery,** in the old grammar school in Church Street, contains a good selection of English paintings and drawings.

Cannon Hall, Cawthorne

Locke Park, in the south-western quarter of Barnsley, was given to the town by the widow of Joseph Locke. Its tower, a local landmark, was presented in memory of Joseph's widow by her sister. It affords a commanding view of the rest of Barnsley. Locke Park includes a fountain and the very popular quarry gardens.

North-east of Barnsley, at **Monk Bretton** are the remains of a Cluniac priory of 1153 *(open daily; admission fee)*.

Cawthorne is a charming village 5 miles west of Barnsley, off the A635 famous for its **Cannon Hall Park,** a favourite picnic spot.

Cannon Hall *(daily, free)* stands in a former deer park. Designed by John Carr, the hall is now an excellent museum of the decorative arts containing fine collections of furniture, paintings, silver, glass and Victoriana. Since 1969 it has also been the home of the Regimental Museum of the 13/18 Royal Hussars (Queen Mary's Own).

In bygone days Cannon Hall was the home of the Squire of Cawthorne, Sir Walter Spencer-Stanhope, who had the delightful habit of giving a great feast annually for his poorest tenants. Quite possibly William Wilberforce, the slave emancipator, of Hull, was a guest at some of these parties for he was a great friend of the squire. At one time joints of beef were presented to tenants at Christmas, a custom which won for Cannon Hall the nickname of "Roast Beef Hall". As the squire and his wife produced fifteen children, the hall had to be enlarged by the addition of an extra room or two to each wing. All things considered it must have been a lively place. Cannon Hall is seen at its best in May and June when the rhododendrons are in flower.

The ancient village **church** contains memories of the warm-hearted squire. There are some pre-Raphaelite paintings on the pulpit panels by Roddam Stanhope. Also in the village is a small museum with pieces presented by John Ruskin.

Pontefract

One of the oldest boroughs in England, Pontefract, 14 miles north-east of Barnsley, was settled from a very early date. It was once a Brigantian settlement; later the Romans had a camp there. The Danes, too, saw the strategic value of the site.

The Castle. Today the castle is merely an empty shell set in an ornamental pleasure garden. Its once awesome proportions are now difficult to imagine, though its site high above the town on a craggy hill is still unquestionably impressive. In the days of its strength it covered about seven acres, was surrounded by a ditch and a wall and had a drawbridge and a barbican. Today, the most complete remains are of part of the *Round Tower,* though the steps to a dungeon may be seen, as well as a sunken room among the shattered walls.

These apart, little remains but foundations, from which may be traced (on the west side) the site of the *Piper Tower* and the base of the *Gascoigne Tower.* There are traces of *King Richard's Chamber* and the *Treasurer's Tower,* bakehouses, kitchens and stables. On the north side were the *Queen's* and the *King's Towers* and on the east, the *Constable Tower.*

The remains of two chapels lie close together. One of these, *St. Clement's Chapel,* dates from the fourteenth century. Soldiers who fought in the Civil War are said to lie buried in its nave beneath the flowers which now bloom there.

A small **museum** in the porter's lodge contains numerous objects found not only at the castle but at other ancient sites in the town.

Undoubtedly it was Pontefract's geographical situation that largely determined its destiny. When he saw it after the battle of Senlac Hill in 1066, William the Conqueror was much impressed by the rock on which the castle now stands. Not only did it afford a commanding position; it overlooked the meeting point of what in those days were the main roads north to south and from the Mersey to the Humber. Therefore

Buttercross and St. Giles, Pontefract

William gave the site and its surroundings to Ilbert De Lacy, making the condition that De Lacy must erect a castle there. Thus Pontefract Castle developed during the next 250 years into one of England's most formidable Norman fortresses.

As a result of its military importance, Pontefract was spared when William ravaged Yorkshire as retribution for the Yorkshire rebellion in 1069. Now only a ruin, the castle is steeped in memories of historical intrigue and the many dark deeds perpetrated within its massive walls. Here Richard II, deposed by Parliament, was imprisoned and died, probably murdered on the orders of Henry IV. Here, Archbishop Scrope of York was executed for treason – the first archbishop to be executed by the civil power. James I of Scotland was imprisoned here and Charles, Duke of Orleans, who was captured at the Battle of Agincourt. Yet more executions took place here during the Wars of the Roses.

It was at Pontefract Castle, too, that Henry VIII first learned of the guilty romance between Katherine Howard and Thomas Culpepper, who ultimately died for their love. Henry's illustrious daughter Elizabeth also visited Pontefract and presented the town with the pump in the market place.

During the Civil War, Pontefract Castle was besieged three times and was the last Royalist stronghold to hold out against the Parliamentarians. King Charles I was executed during the third siege but the defenders refused to surrender, saying that they were now holding the castle for the King's son. They struck coins bearing the name of the new King and the inscription, "Poste mortem patris pro filio". To this day those words appear in the borough's coat of arms beneath a castle with four towers. On orders from Cromwell, who not surprisingly may have borne something of a grudge against the castle that had caused him so much trouble, the Town Council petitioned Parliament for its demolition, which was begun in March 1649.

All Saints Church, the oldest church in Pontefract, stands in South Baileygate in the shadow of the castle ruins. The original church is a ruin but the central portion was restored in 1967 (the 700th anniversary of the first incumbent in 1267), and is in use. All Saints, no doubt splendid in its day, was probably built during the reign of Henry III, but there has been a church on this site since before the Norman Conquest. The church was the scene of fierce fighting during the Civil War because of its strategic position, and in the course of the three sieges of Pontefract Castle it repeatedly changed hands. The roof was damaged, the interior destroyed and the lantern beaten down. Today the fifteenth-century nave and aisles are empty and roofless, like the fourteenth-century chancel and chapel.

Facing the market place is the **Old Town Hall** (1785) which contains, rather surprisingly, the original plaster cast for one of the Trafalgar Square panels, depicting the death of Nelson. In the market place is the **Butter Cross,** an arcaded stone shelter, first erected in 1734, altered in 1763 and renovated yet again in 1967.

In the triangle formed by Southgate and Mill Hill Road are **Friarwood Valley Gardens.** Here settled the Black or Preaching Friars after their Order was introduced to England in 1221.

Adjoining the gardens is the Pontefract Hospital beneath which is a hermitage, founded in 1368.

Pontefract's parish church, **St. Giles's,** in the Market Place, became the parish church after the Civil War, when All Saints was in too ruinous a state to be used. It is first mentioned in a charter dating from the reign of Henry I, but is believed to have existed long before that. Over the centuries it has frequently been enlarged and altered. St. Giles's, until recently a garrison church, is perhaps best known today for its square tower, its octagon lantern and its peal of ten bells. The tower was built in 1795. There is an arcade of five bays, dating (like the tracery of the windows) from the fourteenth century, which has survived the seventeenth-century refashioning of the church; the chancel was renewed in the nineteenth century. The altar plate of St. Giles's includes an Elizabethan chalice and paten.

Perhaps even more widely known than Pontefract's castle and its ancient churches are *Pontefract cakes*, those delicious discs of liquorice which are probably as much loved by children of today as ever they were. And even these sweets are closely linked with the history of the town.

It has been said that the liquorice plant was introduced to the district by the Romans, but the majority verdict would seem to be that liquorice-growing came to Pontefract with the Black Friars in the 13th century, who apparently found its soil congenial to the cultivation of what to them was less a sweetmeat than a medicinal herb. In years gone by, locally-grown liquorice was used in the manufacture of sweets by local factories. In later years, however, it has proved cheaper to import the root than to use the locally-grown variety and little, if any, liquorice is grown in Pontefract today.

North of the town is **Pontefract Park,** covering about 300 acres, which contains the racecourse, with its modern stands and totalisaters.

Around Pontefract

About three miles south-east of Pontefract, just off the A1 is the village of **Darrington** with its white church built of magnesian limestone. Bridging the north aisle of the church is a small arcaded gallery the purpose of which is something of a mystery. The churchyard contains an eighteenth-century dovecote.

About three miles west of Darrington is **Womersley.** Mentioned in Domesday Book, this very English village has a hall dating back to Elizabethan days, a beautiful Early English church and an old moated farm.

Ackworth, $2\frac{1}{4}$ miles south of Pontefract, is the home of the famous Quaker public school founded by Dr. John Fothergill in 1779 as a foundling hospital.

The church at High Ackworth is said to have been the resting place of the body of St. Cuthbert before it found its final home in Durham Cathedral, and twice a year a sheaf of corn is tied to the saint's staff in connection with an ancient custom of giving a sheaf of corn to the birds. Largely modern, but with a fifteenth-century tower, the church has two fonts, one bearing the name of a chaplain to Charles I. An inscription in the church records the murder of Robert Gully by Chinese in 1842, after being shipwrecked off Formosa. He was the son of John Gully, who, during an adventurous life, made a fortune from horse-racing and bought *Ackworth Park*.

Near the church is Mary Lowther's Hospital, founded in 1741.

About two miles north-east of Pontefract is **Ferrybridge,** where the huge cooling towers of the nearby power station command the industrial landscape.

Wakefield

Angling. – At lake at Newmillerdam. Permits from Parks Superintendent, City Cemetery, Doncaster Road; Wakefield Tradesmen's Angling Club has facilities at several other places.

Banks. – *Barclays,* Wood Street, Westgate and Kirkgate; *National Westminster,* Westgate and Bull Ring; *Lloyds,* Westgate and Kirkgate; *Midland,* Westgate and Lower Kirkgate; *Trustee Savings, York County, Yorkshire Bank,* Westgate; *Co-operative Bank,* Northgate.

Bowls. – Greens at Thornes Park and Holmfield Park.

Car Parks. – Almshouse Lane, (multi-storey behind Upper Kirkgate); Crown Court, Wood Street; Drury Lane (behind Central Library); at rear of Little Westgate. In addition there are temporary car parks near the city centre.

Cinemas. – *Playhouse,* Westgate; *ABC,* Kirkgate.

Cricket. – At ground of *Wakefield Cricket Club* in College Grove. There are also other teams in the city.

Dancing. – *Tiffany's,* Southgate.

Early Closing Day. – Wednesday.

Football (Association). – Numerous local clubs. Rugby League at ground of *Wakefield Trinity* at Belle Vue; Rugby Union at grounds of *Wakefield R.F.C.* at College Grove and of *Sandal R.F.C.* at Standbridge Lane, Milnthorpe Green.

Golf. – *City of Wakefield (Municipal) Golf Course,* Lupset Park; *Wakefield Golf Course,* Woodthorpe; *Low Laithes Golf Course,* Flushdyke.

Greyhound Racing. – Denby Dale Road Stadium.

Hotels. – *Cesars Wakefield Hotel,* Westgate; *Cornhill Commercial Hotel,* Westgate; *Grove House,* 108 Barnsley Road, Sandal; *West House Commercial Hotel,* Drury Lane; *White Horse Hotel* and *Woolpacks Hotel,* Westgate; *Parkland,* 143 Horbury Road.

Libraries. *Central Library,* Drury Lane. Branches at Sandal, Flanshaw and Kettlethorpe.

Market Days. – Mondays, Fridays and Saturdays.

Museums and Art Gallery. *City Museum,* Wood Street; *Lakeside Museum,* East Lodge, Newmillerdam; Wakefield City Art Gallery, Wentworth Terrace.

Population. – 59,650.

Putting. – Green at Thornes Park.

Post Office. – Head Office, Trend House, Providence Street; Sub-offices throughout the area.

Swimming. – At *City Baths,* Sun Lane and Almshouse Lane.

Tennis. – Courts at Thornes Park; *Wakefield Sports Club* (College Grove) Ltd.; *Sandal Lawn Tennis Club.*

Wakefield, the county town of the West Riding, stands on the River Calder. It has a large number of Georgian buildings, an impressive cathedral and one of the two or three chantry chapels remaining in England (the other one in Yorkshire is not far away at Rotherham).

Wachefeld is mentioned in Domesday Book, though it was probably little more than a hamlet then. In 1204 King John granted the local earl the right to hold an annual fair.

Records show that cloth weaving, still an important industry, though secondary now to engineering, was practised at least as early as the thirteenth century and before the year 1400, Wakefield was the biggest cloth town in the West Riding with its own cloth market.

Tragedy came to the town in 1460, when, on the 30th December, the Battle of Wakefield Green was fought in which 2,000 men were killed in an hour and the town suffered grievously. But more settled times were to come and by 1500, Wakefield was the biggest and richest town in the area, said to have been fully twice as large as

Leeds or Bradford. It did not retain its superiority for long, however, and today it occupies only a moderate position in the list of West Riding towns and cities.

Wakefield had further experience of warfare in 1643 when Sir Thomas Fairfax, the Parliamentary general, attacked and entered the town, though *Sandal Castle*, south-east of the city (*see* page 215) held out for the Royalists for a further two years.

In 1704, the Aire and Calder canal was completed to Wakefield and this gave a great boost to the town's economy.

The Cathedral. The parish church of All Saints was raised to cathedral status with the creation of the See of Wakefield in 1888. Its lofty spire, 247 feet high, rebuilt in 1861 is one of the highest in the county.

Begun in Norman times, the church was originally a simple building with transepts and a central tower. It was rebuilt in 1329 and a clerestory was added in 1470. The west tower was added early in the fifteenth century. The most recent addition in the twentieth century, has been the extension of the eastern end beyond the high altar, thus restoring to the church its cruciform style.

The cathedral contains a replica of the Saxon cross which once stood on the site of the Cathedral.

Upper Kirkgate is the centre of the shopping area. Close at hand in Wood Street is –

The City Museum (*daily except Bank Holidays*) containing a natural history display and a costume gallery. There is also a room devoted to Charles Waterton (1782–1865), naturalist, eccentric and practical joker. There are some interesting reconstructions of period shops, with a bar of an old public house.

Next door to the museum in Wood Street is the **Town Hall** with its impressive clock tower nearly 200 feet tall. It was built in 1880.

Close by is **County Hall,** the imposing administrative headquarters of the West Riding County Council, which has a dome rising to 130 feet above street level.

Well worth seeing is Wakefield's nineteenth-century **Court House,** with its splendid columns and statue of Justice.

Wood Street leads via Bond Street to Wentworth Terrace and the **City Art Gallery,** originally built as a vicarage. The gallery (*open weekdays, 11–5; Sundays 2–5)* contains sculptures by Yorkshire-born artists Henry Moore and Barbara Hepworth, among others, as well as modern and eighteenth- and nineteenth-century paintings.

Northwards, Wood Street is continued by Margaret Street, where **Wakefield Girls' High School** has buildings on both sides of the street; Margaret Street leads to St. John's Square, in the centre of which, set in a garden, is the fine Georgian **Church of St. John,** designed in 1791. The church has a tower surmounted by a cupola and a parapet decorated with vases. The ceilings are very fine and there is some beautiful carving.

Traffic crosses the River Calder by a wide concrete bridge built beside the Old Bridge, a graceful nine-arched structure, some 600 years old. On this bridge stands the fine medieval **Chantry Chapel of St. Mary** (*open Saturdays 2–3; Sunday service at 3)*. Dating from the fourteenth century the chapel retains much of its original detail in spite of restoration. It is adorned with pinnacled buttresses, a turret with battlements and seven traceried windows.

St. Mary's Chapel, Wakefield Bridge

Around Wakefield

To Sandal Magna. The A61 Barnsley road leads to Sandal Magna, within the city's eastern boundary. Only a few fragments remain here today of what in the thirteenth century was a great fortress much favoured for residence by Richard III. Recent excavations on the site have revealed the great drum bases of the huge towers which stood at each side of the drawbridge.

At the foot of the hill in Sandal, is the impressively arched **St. Helen's Church,** mostly fourteenth century, though part of the central tower is Norman. Among a number of interesting relics, the church has two very fine Jacobean chairs, two excellent linenfold screens as well as beautiful coloured glass.

At Kettlethorpe off the Barnsley road is **Kettlethorpe Hall,** now a residential centre for the elderly. The hall displays the original frontage of the chantry chapel on Wakefield's Calder Bridge, which was removed to Kettlethorpe Hall last century and used as a boathouse.

A favourite spot for walks on fine days is **Newmillerdam** a village about four miles south of Wakefield, on the Barnsley road. Here a delightful lake, with an abundance of water fowl, makes it difficult to believe that one is still on the Wakefield city boundary. A small **museum** *(open from 2–5.30 at weekends and Bank Holidays from May to September)* in the lodge near the gates of the park contains numerous specimens of wild life from the area and articles of local archaeological interest.

Nostell Priory *(Easter to early October, Wednesdays, Saturdays, Sundays and Bank Holiday Tuesdays. Additionally daily in August and early September, fee)*, on the Doncaster road 6½ miles south-east of Wakefield, is one of the most splendid houses in Yorkshire; especially famous for its collection of Chippendale furniture. The mansion stands on the site of a priory of Augustinian canons founded in 1110, and was built in 1733, Robert Adam adding a new wing at a later date. Besides furniture there are many fine pictures. A modern attraction is an interesting motor-cycle collection. The grounds comprise a large park with lake.

Adjoining the park is **Wragby Church** noted for its Swiss glass and some fine woodwork.

Walton Hall, set in a pleasant village three miles south-east of Wakefield, is the former home of Charles Waterton, the eccentric naturalist and traveller, who created a sanctuary here for birds and other creatures. It is said to have been the first bird sanctuary in this country. On the front door are two knockers, each surmounting a face. One of the faces is smiling because the knocker is a dummy. The expression on the face beneath the real knocker can perhaps be imagined! The house, set on an island in a 21-acre lake, is reached by an iron bridge. Walton Hall is said to occupy the site of a fortified house dating from a much earlier date. The present hall was for some years a maternity home.

Heath Hall, two miles east of the city on the Normanton Road (A655) was built in 1707 and extended by John Carr, the locally-born Georgian architect who became Lord Mayor of York. This agreeable house, the home of Mr. and Mrs. Muir M. Oddie, which is open to the public *(Wednesdays 2–5, May to September, or by appointment, fee)*, is well worth a visit for the charm of its woodwork and ceilings.

Woolley, seven miles south of Wakefield, between the M1 and the A61 is a charming unspoilt agricultural village with pine trees, vivid gardens and a fifteenth-century church. **Woolley Hall,** in its park, once a home of the Wentworth family, is now a teachers' college.

A similar fate has befallen **Bretton Hall**, at West Bretton, five miles south-west of the city and a few miles west of Woolley. Once the home of Viscount Allendale, it is now a college for teachers of drama, music and arts, owned by the West Riding County Council.

Leeds

Banks. – *Bank of England*, King Street; *Bank of India*, Devereux House, East Parade; *Barclays, Leeds, Skyrack and Morley Trustee Savings Bank*, and *National Westminster*, all in Park Row; *Williams and Glyn's*, East Parade; *Yorkshire*, Infirmary Street.

Cricket. – Yorkshire County Cricket Club, St. Michael's Lane.

Cinemas. = *ABC*, Vicar Lane; *Odeon*, Merrion Centre; *Odeons* 1 *and* 2, The Headrow; *Plaza*, New Briggate; *Tower*, New Briggate.

Car Parking. – (Undercover) City Parking, Merrion Centre; Commercial Garage, Tenter Lane, Swinegate; Greek Street multi-storey; Queen's Hall Car Park, Sovereign Street; Woodhouse Lane multi-storey. There is meter parking in the central area. A plan showing central open-air parking places is obtainable from the Information Bureau at the Central Library.

Dancing. – *Mecca*, Merrion Centre.

Early Closing Day. – Wednesday, although a few shops close on Saturday or Monday. Some larger shops are closed only on Sundays.

Football (Association). – *Leeds United*, Elland Road; **(Rugby League)** *Leeds*, St. Michael's Lane; *Hunslet*, Parkside Ground; *Bramley*, McLaren's Field. **(Rugby Union)** *Headingley*, Bridge Road, Kirkstall.

Greyhound Racing. – Leeds Stadium, Elland Road.

Golf. – Municipal: Temple Newsam; Gotts Park; Middleton Park; Roundhay Park. Private courses: Alwoodley; Headingley; Leeds Cobble Hall; Moor Allerton; Moortown; Sand Moor; South Leeds; Brandon, Holywell Lane.

Hotels. – *Faversham*, Springfield Mount; *Golden Lion*, Lower Briggate; *Great Northern*, Wellington Street; *Griffin*, Boar Lane; *Guildford*, The Headrow; *Manston*, Austhorpe Road; *Merrion*, Merrion Centre; *Metropole*, King Street; *Parkway*, Otley Road; *Post House*, Bramhope; *Queen's*, City Square; *Victoria*, Great George Street; *West Riding*, Wellington Street; *Mount*, Clarendon Road (unlicensed); *Parker's*, New Briggate (unlicensed). There are also many private hotels and guest houses.

Library. – Central Library, Calverley Street.

Market Days. – Tuesday, Friday and Saturday.

Museums and Art Galleries. – *City Museum*, Calverley Street; *Kirkstall Abbey House Museum*, Abbey Road; *Thoresby Society Museum*, 23 Clarendon Road; *City Art Gallery*, The Headrow; *Temple Newsam House*, Halton; *Lotherton Hall*, Aberford.

Putting. – The Hollies, Weetwood Lane; Kirkstall Abbey; Meanwood Recreation Ground; Middleton Park; New Farnley Recreation Ground; Stanningley Recreation Ground, Intake Lane.

Post Offices. – Head Post Office, City Square; Victoria Square P.O. and The Headrow P.O. both in The Headrow; Markets P.O., New York Street.

Population. – 501,080.

Swimming. – *Leeds International Pool*, Westgate; *Armley*, Carr Crofts; *Bramley*, Broad Lane; *Holbeck Lane*; *Hunslet*, Joseph Street; *Kirkstall Road*; *Meanwood Road*; *John Smeaton Pool*, Barwick Road. Open-air pool is open in Roundhay Park from May to September.

Ten Pin Bowling. – Merrion Centre.

Theatres. – *City Varieties*, The Headrow; *Civic Theatre*, Cookridge Street; *Grand Theatre*, New Briggate; *Leeds Playhouse*, Calverley Street.

Leeds, for long the great commercial centre of the West Riding, probably began in Roman times as a point at which to ford the River Aire. With a population of over half a million it is now England's sixth largest city in population and the second largest in Yorkshire, Sheffield being the largest.

Leeds is continually changing and expanding. It has an abundance of shops and recently the provision of traffic-free precincts in the centre has made shopping easier and pleasanter.

A city of many trades, Leeds produces not only clothing and wool textiles, but also furniture and leather goods. It is a centre for printing, engineering and concrete manufacture.

Leeds is said to contain the oldest railway line in the world, instituted in 1758 to take coal to the River Aire from mines at Middleton. At first its trucks were pulled by horses, then in 1812, the horses were replaced by two steam locomotives designed by Matthew Murray to use the Blenkinsop rack-rail system. Murray, a brilliant and many-sided engineer and inventor, to whom Leeds as an engineering centre owes an incalculable debt, is commemorated by an obelisk in St. Matthew's Church, Holbeck. A rather more lively memorial is a comprehensive school bearing his name.

Murray's memory and the age of steam he helped to inaugurate are also commemorated by the existence of the **Middleton Railway Trust,** formed in 1959, who have a collection of old locomotives which the public are sometimes allowed to inspect. They may also (at weekends from March to October) take a ride on the track for which Murray once provided the engines.

What a contrast to those early days is **Leeds City Station,** which faces on to City Square!

City Square presents a striking mixture of periods and styles. Contrasting oddly with **Mill Hill Chapel** (rebuilt in 1847) where Dr. Joseph Priestley ministered for eleven years from 1767, are great tower blocks of offices.

The heart of City Square is Brock's mounted bronze of the *Black Prince*, whose companions are *James Watt*, *Joseph Priestley*, *John Harrison* and *Dean Hook*, as well as the eight so-called "nymphs", the bronze "flambeaux" figures of *Morn* and *Even*.

From City Square **Park Row** leads to **The Headrow,** a fine broad thoroughfare on which stands the large and immediately impressive **Town Hall,** designed by Cuthbert Brodrick. Notable for its graceful Gothic style with a clock tower supported on columns, and for the stone lions guarding its steps, this is a building of which any city might well be proud. Until recently it soared above the skyline like a sooty colossus; now its stone has been cleaned at considerable expense, though in some eyes the act is almost a sacrilege!

At the Town Hall's entrance there is yet another memorial – a tablet in bronze commemorating Joseph Aspdin, a bricklayer who was one of the inventors of Portland cement.

The **Civic Hall,** behind the Town Hall, is a striking building with twin towers on which perch the owls (eight feet tall) which figure in the Leeds coat of arms. The Civic Hall, opened in 1933, contains memorials in its various rooms to many notable Yorkshire citizens, from both ancient and more recent times: in the splendid banqueting hall you are reminded of Phil May, the famous Leeds cartoonist, John Green, the inventor of Leeds pottery, Congreve, the dramatist, who was born not far away at Bardsey, and others. The council chamber recalls Ralph Thoresby, the Leeds historian and Joseph Priestley, the discoverer of oxygen, who was the minister at Mill Hill Chapel.

The **City Art Gallery** *(daily)* next door to the Town Hall contains a notable collection of sculpture, including works by Jacob Epstein and

Henry Moore. Moore was trained at *Leeds School of Art* not far away in Cookridge Street and the City Art Gallery was one of his earliest patrons. In addition to sculpture, the gallery has an excellent and varied collection of oil paintings and water colours from many periods.

Also on the Headrow is the **City Varieties,** said to be the oldest music hall in England and the setting for the popular television series of Edwardian music hall, "The Good Old Days". Many great stars of days gone by, including Charlie Chaplin as a small boy, have trodden this beautiful old theatre's boards.

Leeds is a city of arcades. Just off the Headrow, two of them, side by side, span Lands Lane (next to the City Varieties) and Briggate. These are **Thornton's** and **Queen's Arcades.** Across Briggate from Thornton's Arcade is the **County Arcade,** while the northward continuation of Briggate, **New Briggate,** is linked with **Vicar Lane** by the **Grand Arcade.** Lower down, off Briggate itself, is the **Market Arcade.** Both Thornton's and the Grand Arcade contain remarkable clocks with moving figures.

Leading north from the Headrow, **Cookridge Street** contains the **Leeds Civic Theatre.** The setting for some excellent amateur theatrical performances, the "Civic" was designed as a Civic institute by Brodrick, the creator of the design for the Town Hall.

In Cookridge Street is **St. Anne's Roman Catholic Cathedral.**

North-west of the Civic Theatre, just off the Inner Ring Road is the newest Leeds theatre, the **Playhouse.** The shell of this building was provided by Leeds University, on a site within the University purlieus, on a ten-year lease. The Playhouse has quickly earned a reputation for lively and inventive productions of all forms of drama.

The other Leeds theatre is the **Grand** in New Briggate, with its fine large auditorium. It is often the setting for prior-to-West End productions and performances by large touring companies.

From New Briggate, **Merrion Street** leads to the **Merrion Centre,** a shopping complex which includes a covered market, offices, an hotel, two discotheques, a dance hall and a bowling alley.

On the Wade Lane side of the Merrion Centre are the studios of *Radio Leeds* which provides broadcast services of local news and entertainment.

The University, reached by Woodhouse Lane, is strong in science and technology. Magnificently housed and surmounted by an impressive tower, it contains the **Brotherton Library** with its priceless collection of rare and valuable books, as well as many valuable letters, some written by members of the Brontë family. The library, which has space for a million books, is set in a domed, circular building bigger than the Reading Room of the British Museum.

Leeds University grew from the Yorkshire College of Science, which was founded in 1874. The School of Medicine, which began in 1831 and won international renown, especially for its surgical training, was incorporated in 1884 and the University was granted its Royal Charter in 1904. Today it is one of the largest and best equipped provincial universities in the country.

City Square, Leeds

Not far from the University is **Leeds Grammar School,** which moved to its present site in Moorland Road in 1858. Founded in 1552 by William Sheafield, it is a public school which has produced a long list of distinguished Old Boys, including John Smeaton, who built the Eddystone Lighthouse, and Sir John Hawkshaw, who helped to plan the Suez Canal. The city's other public school is the **Leeds Girls' High School,** in Headingley Lane.

Leeds Polytechnic, based principally in Calverley Street, has faculties in many fields including the arts and sciences, education, business and environmental studies and social sciences. There are many Colleges of Further Education in the Leeds area.

Leeds contains the country's oldest independent adult education centre in the form of the **Swarthmore Centre** in Woodhouse Square.

There are many interesting churches in Leeds. **St. Peter's** the parish church, rebuilt in 1841, is said to be the fourth church on its site in Kirkgate since Domesday Book recorded the first. A notable feature is the alabaster reredos which depicts Christ against a background showing the Apostles in mosaics. There are many interesting and some curious brass inscriptions and portraits and a great deal of carved wood. There is a fine east window in the chancel.

Among the local worthies commemorated here is the seventeenth-century traveller, antiquary and diarist, Ralph Thoresby, whose name and fame are perpetuated by the world-renowned Thoresby Society, whose library in Clarendon Road is open Tuesday and Thursday, 10–2.

Another name of hallowed memory in Leeds is John Harrison, who founded and endowed **St. John's Church** in New Briggate in 1634. An alderman and merchant of the city, Harrison was a great benefactor, some of whose good deeds are illustrated in a memorial window which depicts him presenting a tankard, ostensibly of ale, to Charles I, who was imprisoned in Leeds at the time. In fact, the tankard contained golden guineas, the idea being that the king could use them as a bribe to win his freedom. However, the plot failed. St. John's is a fine example of seventeenth-century Gothic architecture. It contains Caroline box pews and a splendid Renaissance-style chancel screen.

St. Aidan's Church in Roundhay Road, consecrated in 1894, is notable for the mosaics by Frank Brangwyn showing scenes from the life of St. Aidan.

Holy Trinity Church in Boar Lane was built in the 1720's in the style of Christopher Wren. Containing some fine woodcarving and interesting monuments, it is regarded as the only important early Georgian building surviving in Leeds.

The **Leeds Library** in Commercial Street has an interesting history. A private subscription library, founded in 1768, it is the oldest of its kind in England, and the great Dr. Joseph Priestley was its first secretary. Among its inaugurators was a bookseller named Binns, whose shop has been described as almost a forerunner to Leeds University. Binns, incidentally, founded the printing firm which was later to buy the *Leeds Mercury,* one of the oldest of English newspapers, which survives as part of the *Yorkshire Post,* now housed in huge, modern offices in Wellington Street.

Roundhay Park. There are a number of open spaces in the city but none rivals the 616 acre Roundhay Park beautifully laid out with two lakes (boating) and a fine open-air pool. John of Gaunt is said to have once used the area as a hunting ground. The park was bought by the city in 1872 for £139,000 and though eyebrows were doubtless raised at what must have seemed extravagance a century ago, Leeds citizens have good cause to be thankful for what is undoubtedly one of their pleasantest amenities.

Woodhouse Moor, a fine open space, next to the University, **Woodhouse Ridge, Holbeck Moor, Potternewton Park, Harehills** and **East End** Parks, **Gotts Park** off

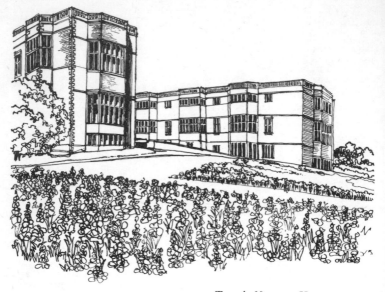

Temple Newsam House

Stanningley Road and **The Hollies,** off Weetwood Lane, are others of Leeds's abundant and often delightful open spaces. North Leeds contains the **Headingley Cricket Ground,** setting for Test Matches and a hallowed name to cricket-lovers the world over.

Five miles south-east of Leeds is –

Temple Newsam House *(daily, fee)*, a large brick mansion known as the "Hampton Court of the North". Temple Newsam was owned by the Knights Templars from 1155 to 1308. The present house, set around three sides of a great court amid beautiful grounds planted with many thousands of rose trees, is in its oldest portions partly Elizabethan. In 1622 Sir Arthur Ingram made certain additions. Originally built for Thomas, Lord Darcy, the house is said to have been the birthplace of Darnley, husband of Mary, Queen of Scots. It was acquired by Leeds Corporation in 1922 from Lord Halifax, whose family had owned it since Jacobean times. Temple Newsam is now an art gallery and museum of domestic and decorative art.

Treasures from many ages are to be seen here. There is a great Victorian staircase in oak, its posts richly carved, splendid oak panelling, wonderful ceilings, furniture by Chippendale, as well as gorgeous tapestry, fine pottery and paintings by many of the great masters.

Each room has its peculiar splendour; in the New Library there is eighteenth-century furnishing; the Blue Drawing Room is noted for its Chinese wallpaper, while a collection of snuff boxes is to be seen in the Terrace Room. In the Staircase Hall there is a sedan chair and there are Georgian furnishings and damask wall coverings in the Blue Damask Room; while the Green Damask Room and the Boudoir contain more furnishings and paintings. The Long Gallery is of special interest for the series of portraits it contains.

222

Quarry Hill Flats. To follow a description of Temple Newsam with a reference to Quarry Hill Flats (at the eastern end of Eastgate) seems a strange juxtaposition, but at least it indicates what extremes are to be found in a city the size of Leeds.

When the estate was first designed in 1935 during the city's onslaught on the thousands of slums it then contained, it was revolutionary. The largest municipal housing project in England at that time, it provided homes for more than 3,000. Ranging in height from four to eight storeys, the development contains 938 separate units. It was, in a sense, almost more of a town than a block of flats, containing its own shops and built around an open precinct or "lung".

A much more recent development is at **Seacroft** on the city's eastern fringe, where thousands have been housed, some in high flats on the site of what was formerly two or three villages. Its town centre, comprising shops, stores, banks, a market and a clinic was opened in 1965.

Kirkstall Abbey

Via Abbey Road (A65) Buses 24, 25, 26 and 27 from Corn Exchange. Industry seems to have grown up all round the remains of the early Cistercian buildings set amid green lawns; and the completeness of many of the walls is such that one is almost surprised not to see habited figures moving silently about the grey gritstone.

Kirkstall Abbey is an outstanding example both of Norman architecture and of early Cistercian ideals. The church is well preserved, and the layout of the monastic buildings is clear.

Kirkstall Abbey

The Abbey of St. Mary was built by Abbot Alexander, under the patronage of Henry de Lacy, Lord of Pontefract, for Cistercian monks from Fountains Abbey. They settled in 1147 at Barnoldswick-in-Craven, but moved in 1152 to the more hospitable site of Kirkstall in Airedale. The church and accommodation for monks and lay brethren (who performed the practical tasks of the Abbey), was completed by 1182. Little is known of the subsequent history of Kirkstall. In the fourteenth century, great profits were made from the sale of wool, but the Abbey was frequently in debt. On its surrender in 1540, its revenues were put at little over £500. Thereafter it was stripped of lead and other valuable materials, and slowly decayed, until in 1890 Colonel J. T. North presented it to the City of Leeds for restoration and preservation.

The church, which has lost little except parts of the roof and the tower, is in the Norman Transitional style, but without the usual Anglo-Norman ornamentation. Its extreme severity, characteristic of the first century of Cistercian asceticism, is enhanced by the dourness of the gritstone of which it is built. Ornate Perpendicular pinnacles and windows were added in the fifteenth century and the tower was heightened, in flat defiance of Cistercian rules, early in the sixteenth century. The normal range of monastic building was developed; the lay-brothers' dormitory west of the cloister; kitchen, refectory and warming house to the south; monks' dormitory and chapter-house to the east and beyond them, the infirmary and a fine residence for the Abbot.

Abbey House Museum *(daily, fee)*. The former gatehouse, which houses important material from modern excavations at the Abbey, is now incorporated in large and extensive buildings which form a Folk Museum devoted to the urban life of the Yorkshire region. As well as varied collections of costumes, furniture, toys, domestic articles and musical instruments, there are three full-scale streets of shops, houses and workshops re-erected here from in and around Leeds.

Some three miles due north-east of Kirkstall Abbey is **Adel,** where the lovely little church is one of this country's most perfect examples of Norman architecture. The church has a beautiful chancel arch in excellent condition, but most notable of all is the richly carved porch, now suffering, alas, from centuries of exposure to wind and rain. The bronze knocker on the modern doorway is also of interest.

From Adel it is a pleasant walk to **Arthington,** a delightful Wharfedale village with some fine old houses and a splendid view of the valley and the more distant moorlands from the 500-ft.-high Bank Top.

Leeds to Huddersfield

The road (A62) rarely leaves the industrial built-up areas, but what this district lacks in scenic beauty it more than atones for in character and in the delight it evokes in Brontë enthusiasts.

Seven miles along the road is **Birstall** where the church has an inscription commemorating John Nelson, a local mason who, under the influence of John Wesley, became one of the greatest preachers of his time. Charlotte Brontë's friend Ellen Nussey was buried in the churchyard, as was Margaret Wooler.

Joseph Priestley, the discoverer of oxygen, was born at Birstall in 1733. A plaque marks the site at Fieldhead on one of the hills surrounding the town. Priestley's statue performs a perpetual experiment with candle and jar, in Birstall market place.

Between Birstall and Batley, facing on to the Bradford Road, is **Wilton Park** which in spring offers a fine display of rhododendrons as a backcloth to the lake, with its small island, which may be seen from the road. Behind the lake rises a wooded hillside at the top of which is the **Bagshaw Museum and Art Gallery.** *(Open daily throughout the year.)*

Batley lies south-east of Birstall. The fine old church is said to be mostly fifteenth century, though parts of it are probably a century older. It contains the alabaster tomb of a knight of the Mirfield family. Beside him lies his wife, one of the Saviles of Howley Hall, a few ruins of which stand on a hill above the town.

Priestley was a pupil of **Batley Grammar School,** founded in 1612. It was at Batley that the method of manufacturing cloth from wool reclaimed from rags was invented, the result being christened "shoddy".

Oakwell Hall *(daily, except Friday, April to October, free)* lies three-quarters of a mile west of Birstall. It was at this charming Tudor house, now owned by Batley Corporation, where Charlotte Brontë stayed as a guest, afterwards including a description of the house in *Shirley*, where she called it "Fieldhead". Birstall itself she renamed "Briarfield".

The outstanding feature of the hall is its balustraded gallery, reached by a fine stairway supported by massive oak pillars and barred at the foot by a pair of small wooden dog gates. There is a splendid window said to contain over 1,000 panes of glass. A charming feature of the Hall is the Old English garden at the rear based on Elizabethan patterns.

Heckmondwike. Its name is probably much better known than the place itself, though Heckmondwike (about two miles from Birstall) is a worthy town with a history of self-reliance and enterprise.

Joseph Priestley once lived there, as did Joseph Curwen, the man who invented the Tonic Sol-fa method of writing music.

Heckmondwike is still known in Free Church circles for the Heckmondwike lectures, delivered annually at the enormous Upper Chapel which is visited by distinguished speakers for the occasion. In days gone by, Lecture Sunday was very much a gala event in Heckmondwike, the occasion for family gatherings and even for the baking of a special "lecture Pudding".

Neighbouring **Liversedge** was the setting for one of the Luddite riots. In 1812 at Rawfolds Mill, Edmund Cartright, inventor of the power loom, was attacked by weavers.

Mirfield (about 6 miles from Huddersfield) is a surprisingly attractive town, once you leave the A62. Its most romantic claim to fame is the traditional site of Robin Hood's grave at **Kirklees Hall** nearby. The hall is built partly from the stones of Kirklees Priory where Robin is said to have died after shooting an arrow to indicate his desired burial place.

The **Three Nuns Inn** at Mirfield is reputedly built on the site of an inn which was once the guest house for Priory visitors, the "three nuns" portrayed in its sign being the last three sisters to be living at the Priory in 1539 when it was dissolved.

Mirfield's present parish church, which celebrated its centenary in 1971, is pleasantly sited to the north-east, on the Dewsbury side of the town, next to the tower (twelfth- and fifteenth-century) which is all that remains of an earlier church, and close to the old village stocks.

Mirfield is probably best known throughout the world for the *Community of the Resurrection,* an order of Anglican brothers founded here in 1898 by the late Bishop Gore of Oxford, with the object of training priests.

The Community, which has a striking domed church among its impressive array of buildings is noted for the plays and services (Quarry services) which are periodically staged in a quarry in the community's grounds.

In recent years a Roman Catholic seminary for the training of boys for the priesthood has been established at **Roe Head,** where Charlotte Brontë met Ellen Nussey when it was a school run by Margaret Wooler, of Birstall.

For **Huddersfield,** *see* page 229.

Leeds to Tadcaster and York

The road (A64) from Leeds to York passes through interesting and attractive country. About 11 miles out from Leeds is the Bramham Cross Road where the A1 crosses over on its way to Wetherby and the north.

A diversion here can be made to **Bramham** where the church dates from the thirteenth century and has some fine carvings.

Bramham Park *(Sundays and Bank Holidays, Easter to September, charge)* is a fine Queen Anne mansion set in gardens designed in the style of Versailles. In the house are paintings by Reynolds and others.

Hazlewood Castle, a mile or two from Tadcaster, was for 800 years the home of the illustrious Vavasour family.

Tadcaster (14 miles from Leeds) is generally known for its breweries and a plenitude of pubs to match! It is said that the Romans, to whom Tadcaster was known as *Calcaria,* first discovered the merits of the water on which its brewing fortunes were founded.

Don't fail to visit the **Ark Museum.** This is contained in a fifteenth-century house near the church. The house itself is fully as interesting as its collection of curios, which include old brewing instruments as well as a wide variety of other articles of local interest.

Tadcaster was a military outpost to the Romans who had their huge camp a few miles away at York. Relics of their time in the town have been found, including horseshoes, coins and pottery.

But Tadcaster's history begins before Roman times, for it was an important centre to the Brigantes and later to the Saxons, Danes and Normans. It was raided by the Scots and figured in the Civil War.

An interesting feature of Tadcaster is the seven-arched **bridge** spanning the River Wharfe. It is said to have been built with stones from a castle which once overlooked the river. Tadcaster is famous for its quarries, where magnesian limestone has been dug for centuries. A great deal of this stone went into the building of York and its Minster.

From the bridge a fine view may be had of the riverside **Church** built of that same white stone. Mostly fifteenth century, it has an impressive embattled tower. The chancel is divided from the nave by a Norman arch. The church contains some good woodwork and interesting old stone fragments and glass.

Tadcaster is an old coaching town and some of the inns here are rich in the atmosphere of the past.

Bramham Park

Interesting places to visit around Tadcaster include delightful villages like **Bolton Percy,** south-east of the town on the north bank of the Wharfe as it winds downstream to **Nun Appleton.**

Bolton Percy has a beautiful fifteenth-century church, a late seventeenth-century rectory and an Elizabethan gate-house, locally called the tithe barn. **Nun Appleton** was once the setting for a convent of Cistercian nuns. It was in his manor house here that General Fairfax, the great Parliamentarian soldier, died in 1671. (The house has been rebuilt.) The general's tomb is at Bilbrough, four miles north-east of Tadcaster.

Towton, about 2½ miles south of Tadcaster on the A162, is remembered for one of the bloodiest battles of the Wars of the Roses, in which 30,000 men are said to have died on Palm Sunday, 1461. At **Saxton cum Scarthingwell,** a parish just south of Towton, the site of the battle is marked by a cross.

From Tadcaster the A659 leads to **Newton Kyme,** setting for Newton Kyme Hall, home of the Fairfax family, one of whom, Admiral Robert Fairfax, born in 1666, restored the home and planted some of the fine avenues of lime trees. Admiral Fairfax, who died in 1725, is buried in the village church where his monument is a ship carved in marble. The old church, parts of which are Norman, contains much else of interest.

Also of interest in the area are **Barwick-in-Elmet,** where there are some remarkable earthworks; **Aberford; Acaster Malbis,** beside the Ouse; **Bishopthorpe,** seat of the Archbishops of York, and **Cawood,** which contained their former home.

For **York,** *see* page 99.

Huddersfield

Banks. – *Barclays*, 19 Market Place; *Lloyds*, 1 Westgate; *Midland*, Cloth Hall Street; *National Westminster*, 8 Market Place; *Trustee Savings Bank*, Cloth Hall Street; *Yorkshire*, New Street.
Cinemas. – *ABC*, Market Street; *Empire*, John William Street; *Princess*, Northumberland Street; *Classic*, Queensgate.
Early Closing Day. – Wednesday.

Hotels. – *George*, St. George's Square; *Clare Manor*, Clare Hill.
Market Day. – Monday.
Museum and Art Gallery. – Tolson Memorial Museum, Ravensknowle Park. The Art Gallery occupies the top floor of the Central Library, Princess Alexandra Walk.
Population. – 131,000.
Post Office. – Northumberland Street.

Huddersfield, a hilly town, set in the Colne Valley on the edge of the Pennines, is probably equally famous for the quality of its fine worsteds and its choral singing. No place in the world makes better cloth, but although the making of worsted is Huddersfield's oldest industry, it is by no means the only one. Many branches of the textile trade are represented here, as well as chemicals, engineering and a host of others.

There is an air of stability and affluence about Huddersfield's busy streets with their abundant thriving shops and large civic buildings.

The **Town Hall,** Italianate in style, is frequently the scene of fine musical concerts, and the annual "Messiah" performed by the renowned Huddersfield Choral Society is an imperishable tradition here.

The Town Hall's near neighbour, the **Public Library and Art Gallery** in Princess Alexandra Walk is by contrast almost aggressively modern with bold sculptured figures at the entrance, representing Literature and the Arts. Sculptured panels between the windows depict many facets of life. The Gallery *(open 10–5.30 on all weekdays except Friday, when it closes two hours later)* has an extensive collection of pictures as well as sculpture by Epstein, Henry Moore and others.

Of all Huddersfield's older buildings, perhaps the most immediately impressive is the **Railway Station,** built in the Greek style. Eight fluted columns adorn its façade, which looks out on the grandly spacious **George Square.** To ensure its preservation, the Railway Station was bought by the Corporation.

Not far away in Kirkgate is the parish church, **St. Peter's.** Although in the style of the fifteenth century, the church only dates from the nineteenth. It is, nevertheless, a striking church. Among many other objects of interest it contains an inscription commemorating Thomas and Henry Parratt, father and son, who rendered a total of 90 years service as organists.

Among the newer buildings are the impressive **Civic Centre** facing High Street, the **Law Courts** and the **Market Hall** (opened in 1970) with its roof made up of concrete "shells"; it is bounded by Queensgate, Peel Street and Princess Street.

Huddersfield is rich in open spaces covering altogether about 600 acres. The chief park is **Greenhead,** near the town centre, but **Beaumont Park,** two miles from the centre, is also much valued for its rocks and woodlands in a hillside setting. To the east of the town at Mold Green, is **Ravens-knowle Park** with the **Tolson Memorial Museum** *(open weekdays* 10.30–5*; Sundays* 2–5*),* which contains among many other fascinating objects of local historical interest, some old textile machinery illustrating the development of the cloth trade. The park contains a clock tower and shelter built from the stones of the old Huddersfield Cloth Hall.

No visitor to Huddersfield should fail to climb the **Victoria Tower** at Castle Hill, Almondbury, to get a unique view of Huddersfield and the Holme Valley. Castle Hill (about 900 ft.) has been the site of fortresses of the Brigantes, the Romans and the Normans. Victoria Tower itself is of the nineteenth century.

Also at Almondbury are a **Grammar School,** founded in 1608, which has a Charter granted by James I, a Tudor house, **Woodsome Hall,** now serving as a golf club and several other old houses.

Excursions from Huddersfield

Industrial it may be, but Huddersfield is on the edge of the windswept moorland; fine open country and character-filled Pennine towns and villages are within easy reach.

Five miles from Huddersfield, **Kirkburton** (just off the A629) is a pleasantly situated town notable for its beautiful church, a good deal of which is more than 700 years old.

Denby Dale, only a few miles away at the southern end of the A636, just before the junction with A635, has a curious tradition of baking giant pies. The first one was made in 1788 to commemorate the recovery of George III from "mental affliction", the most recent, baked in 1964, had the object of raising money to build a village hall. It weighed over six tons. In between came the pie of 1846 (Waterloo year), the Great Jubilee Pie of 1887, which went bad and was buried (somewhat hastily, perhaps), and the pies of 1896 and 1928. When Denby Dale gets its periodic pie fever it leaps from obscurity, the whole world hears about it and a sizeable part of the population thereof seems to descend on the place.

Slaithwaite, about five miles from Huddersfield, is reached by the A62 which later crosses the moors on its way to Oldham. It, too, is famous for cloth and for male voice singing.

Further along the A62 is **Marsden** where the 3 mile, 63 yard-tunnel under Stand-edge (1,271 ft.) begins, to emerge at **Diggle.** Besides this railway tunnel there is also a canal tunnel $3\frac{1}{4}$ miles in length, along which bargees used to propel their craft by lying on their backs and using their feet as levers against the tunnel roof.

Holmfirth, six miles from Huddersfield is reached via the A616 and a branch road right from **Honley.** The scene of some disastrous floods, Holmfirth has a number of memorials to these cataclysms, one of them being a dual purpose monument, as it commemorates not only the height of the Great Flood of 1852 in which 78 people were killed and vast damage done when a reservoir burst its banks, but also the "Short Peace of Amiens" in 1801 which was presumably of special interest to Holmfirth, a woollen town, as the inhabitants had been engaged in producing cloth for the French armies.

Holmfirth, perhaps surprisingly, is the home of Bamforths, famous manufacturers of comic and other postcards. Even more surprisingly, this little town was the setting for some of the earliest silent films, made by James Bamforth before the first world war. Mostly comedies, the films frequently starred local residents.

Just a few miles south-west of Holmfirth, the mast of the **Holme Moss** television transmitter may be approached by the A6024, to the right of the road, about $1\frac{1}{2}$ miles past the village of **Holme.** The mast itself is 750 ft. high and the elevation of the moors at its base is 1,725 ft.

Halifax

Banks. – *Barclays, Lloyds, Midland* and *National Westminster*, all in Commercial Street; *York County Savings*, Silver Street; *Yorkshire*, Waterhouse Street.

Cinemas. – *ABC*, Wards End; *Odeon*, Broad Street.

Cricket. – *Halifax C.C.*, Thrum Hall; *King Cross C.C.*, The Ramsdens.

Early Closing Day. – Thursday.

Football. – (League) *Halifax Town F.C.*, The Shay; *Halifax R.L.F.C.*, Thrum Hall; *Halifax R.U.F.C.*, Ovenden Park.

Greyhound Racing. – Thrum Hall.

Golf. – *Halifax Golf Club*, Ogden; *West End Club*, Highroad Well; *Bradley Hall*, Holywell Green; *Ryburn*, Norland.

Hotels. – *Alan Fold*, Burnley Road; *Commercial*, Northgate; *Crown*, 41 Horton Street; *Exley Park*, Siddal; *Griffin*, George Street; *Old Cock*, Southgate; *Star*, Orange Street; *White Swan*, Princess Street.

Markets. – Held daily at *The Borough Market* and *Westgate Market*.

Museums. – *Bankfield*, Akroyd Park; *Shibden Hall*, Shibden Park.

Motor Cycle Racing. – The Shay.

Population. – 91,040.

Post Office. – Commercial Street.

Theatres. – *Halifax Civic Theatre*, Wards End; *Playhouse*, King Cross Street.

Halifax is a place dramatic in its setting in the Pennine hills and also in its contrasts between raw industrialism and rural delights; between thrusting modernity and the grace of a bygone age.

Nowhere is its impact more dramatic than at the 850 ft. **Beacon Hill**, east of the town, where you can look down into a veritable basin of industry – chimneys, gasworks, smoke – which makes it easy to understand why this view has given rise to the name: The Devil's Cauldron. Yet only a few miles away there is **Shibden Dale**, a green and peaceful valley where the only sound is often that of birdsong or the Shibden Brook. Here you could be in the very heart of the country with the nearest mill chimney a hundred miles away.

Halifax is an ancient place; it existed in Saxon times and throughout its long history it has been a producer of woollen cloth. At least as early as 1275 there was a weaver at Halifax. It was in fact the cloth trade which gave rise to one of the things for which Halifax is most widely known – the Gibbet Law and the associated saying: From Hell, Hull and Halifax, good Lord deliver us. Precisely why deliverance was to be sought from Hull is not perhaps clear, but there is no doubt that so far as Halifax was concerned, the object of dread, was the gibbet, an instrument of decapitation which anticipated the French guillotine.

Its story goes back to the mid-fourteenth century when Halifax cloth makers were plagued by thieves who stole the cloth when it was put out on frames in the fields to dry. Such a menace did these pilferers become that Halifax was granted the right to behead anyone caught stealing cloth worth more than 13½ pence. The Gibbet Law was retained until the middle of the seventeenth century and hundreds fell victim to its blade.

All that remains of the gibbet itself is its base and steps now preserved as an ancient monument and enclosed in a garden off **Gibbet Street** near the town centre.

Halifax, despite its antiquity, owes its growth to nineteenth-century industrialism. Today, in addition to carpets produced in one of the world's largest mills, it manufactures all kinds of textiles, a variety of iron and steel tools and wire.

One of the most interesting of Halifax products is the "Cat's Eyes" road stud invented by a local man, Percy Shaw, who first had the idea when, driving home on foggy nights, he was able to steer his course by seeing the reflection of his headlights in the tramlines. Also produced in Halifax are sweets, beer, stone, bricks and sanitary ware.

Although Halifax has kept pace with the changing demands of industry the modern town mingles at many points with reminders of the past. A fine example is the **Piece Hall,** opened in 1779 as a cloth market. Three storeys high, it contained 315 rooms set around a quadrangle and occupied a total of about 10,000 square yards. Now in use as a wholesale market for dealers in greengrocery, flowers and fish, it must be one of the busiest Ancient Monuments in existence.

Another relic of old Halifax is **Wainhouse's Tower,** 270 feet high, an ornate structure intended as a mill chimney but never used for that purpose. Wonderful views may be had from the platform at the top of the chimney by anyone with the fortitude to tackle its 400 steps. *The tower is open, charge, for two days at the Spring Bank Holiday and two days at the late summer break,*

Many legends have attached themselves to this structure but the true reason for the building of the tower is rather more impressive than the fables of a mill-owner who wanted to overlook his rival's domain.

Wainhouse, the owner of a dyeworks, was anxious that the smoke from his chimney should not injure the health of people living in the neighbourhood of his works. This was the reason for the chimney's great height.

The Parish Church of **St. John the Baptist,** largely fifteenth-century, has a fine Perpendicular tower. Among many items of interest is the carved wooden figure known as *Old Tristram* which stands near the west door beside the old pillar alms box. Dressed in seventeenth-century fashion, he is said to be modelled on a real beggar, well-known in Halifax in days gone by.

Heath Grammar School, an Elizabethan foundation, has been replaced by a modern building. So, too, have the almshouses founded along with the Bluecoat School by Nathaniel Waterhouse in the seventeenth century.

The **Old Cock Hotel** in Southgate contains an impressive Oak Room on the mantelpiece of which appears the date 1581. The room has splendid oak furnishings and stained glass windows depicting coats of arms.

While many of the town's old buildings have gone, much remains from the Halifax of bygone days. Most impressive of all, perhaps, in the town centre is the **Town Hall** built in Italian Renaissance style from designs by Sir Charles Barry over a century ago. The sculptured clock tower and spire rise 180 feet from ground level.

There are several parks among them **People's Park** near the centre. Others are **Belle Vue** where is the Central Library and war memorial, **Manor Heath** with notable nurseries, and **Savile Park** venue for sporting and other events.

Shibden Hall *(daily, but closed November to January)* is now a folk museum set in a delightful park. Once the home of the Lister family, this fine timbered mansion dating chiefly from the fifteenth century, contains in its outbuildings a brewhouse, as well as blacksmith's, saddler's, apothecarv's, wheelwright's, farrier's, nail maker's and clogger's shop which look for all the world as if the workmen had downed tools just a moment before and gone outside into the lovely gardens to take a breath of air. There is also a fine collection of old horse-drawn vehicles.

The **Bankfield Museum** *(daily)* in Akroyd Park is a noteworthy collection illustrating costumes and textiles from all ages and all parts of the world. There are examples of old textile machinery. A gruesome exhibit is the old Halifax gibbet blade.

A development of the emergent new Halifax is the new inner relief road scheme diverting through traffic from the town centre and thus creating a pleasant and safe shopping area in the town centre.

Shibden Hall

Excursions from Halifax

There are many pleasant walks around Halifax, particularly in the Hebden, Shibden and Luddenden valleys and in the more distant moorland areas. In most cases the local bus services serve a good starting point.

One of the most popular local beauty spots is **Hardcastle Crags,** now owned by the National Trust. It is surely a good recommendation that "exiled" Swiss in the West Riding use it for their reunion gatherings because the scenery reminds them of home.

Dean Head, Crag Vale and **Peckett Well** (a mile north of **Hebden Bridge**) are all well worth visiting; as are the moorlands at **Norland, Blackstone Edge** and **Wadsworth,** the **Ryburn** and **Blackburn** valleys and old villages like **Heptonstall, Midgley, Sowerby** and **Luddenden.**

Heptonstall, just beyond Hebden Bridge on the A646, is set on a ridge between two valleys. To walk its crooked narrow streets is to return to a village of the past. Among the several interesting buildings is an octagonal Wesleyan chapel in **Northgate** dating from 1764, a grammar school (now an old folk's club) and two churches in the same churchyard. One, built largely in the fifteenth century, is now only a shell, being dismantled in 1854 to be replaced by its neighbour, also built in fifteenth-century style.

Todmorden, about a dozen miles along the A646, has great character, as have so many small towns set amid the Pennine hills. **Todmorden Hall,** now the post office, is a beautiful house over 300 years old. Striking, too, is the **Town Hall,** with its carved pediment, where sculptures represent both Lancashire and Yorkshire, for the old county boundary once passed through this very building. Two miles east of the town is **Stoodley Pike,** an obelisk raised in 1856. It replaced a tower built in 1815 as a thankoffering for peace after the Napoleonic wars and which fell down about the time of the Crimean War.

Brighouse, six miles east of Halifax, is a busy industrial town which won for itself the title "King of the Upper Calder". The **Art Gallery** in Rydings Park contains a room devoted to the work of an outstanding wood-carver, H. P. Jackson, who was born at Brighouse in 1867.

Lightcliffe, nearby, is a very pleasant village with a "Stray" with lawns and trees occupying about 11 acres. Not far from the nineteenth-century **Church of St. Matthew** are the remains of *Crow Nest House,* once the home of Sir Titus Salt, the industrialist and philanthropist who created the model village of **Saltaire,** Shipley, for his millworkers (*see* page 241).

Bradford

Bradford is the woollen market of the world. The tenth largest city in England, it is situated on hills around a natural basin. Once the hills were covered with sheep, the fleeces from which were woven into cloth on handlooms. Then came steam and the sheep were replaced by mills and by houses for the workers who operated the new, clattering power looms. The little villages gradually coalesced and the time came when what had been a collection of peaceful if industrious communities, set among green pastures, became a grim desert of slum houses peopled by pale-faced under-nourished workers.

Fortunately, the Bradford city fathers were not content with such a situation and quickly set about improving matters. Not only does Bradford claim to have had the first school board and to have provided the first school clinic, school dentist and school baths, among a formidable list of other "firsts", but Richard Oastler made the city the centre for his campaign for the first Factory Acts, which spared young children from the horrors of exploitation in mill and mine. His statue in bronze, with a small boy and girl stands behind John Street Market. More recently slum clearance, smoke abatement and redevelopment of the city centre has achieved a pleasantness and spaciousness which might well astonish those whose mental image of the place is little more than an outdated caricature.

The **City Hall** is an impressive building completed in 1873 with statues of British sovereigns on its façade. The tower reaches to 200 feet. A carillon fills the air with music from a considerable repertoire several times each day.

The **Wool Exchange** in nearby Market Street is a worthy monument to the great industry which brought it into being.

The heart of modern Bradford is **Forster Square,** named after William Edward Forster, the Bradford M.P. who founded free national education. Now, beautiful with trees and flower beds, it is typical of the new Bradford.

The **Cathedral,** dating largely from the fifteenth century, was the parish church of St. Peter until Bradford became a cathedral city in 1920. It contains a splendid oak roof, a huge and richly ornamented bishop's throne as well as beautiful stained glass and a fine fifteenth-century font cover.

Bolling Hall

237

Petergate leads from Forster Square to the Exchange Station and, further along Hall Ings, **St. George's Hall.** Once the scene of Victorian concerts with stars like Jenny Lind and Clara Novello, it later became a cinema but is now once more the setting for live musical concerts, both by the Hallé Orchestra and Bradford's own choral societies.

Bradford also owns the **Alhambra Theatre** at the bottom of Great Horton Road, reached from Hall Ings via Princes Way. This theatre stages ballet, opera and drama productions as well as performances by local amateur companies.

Also in Great Horton Road are the **University** buildings and the **College of Art.** The University was formed from a college of advanced technology (originally a technical college) and received its charter in 1966.

Across the city at the eastern end of Hall Ings; just off Leeds Road, is the Bradford **Playhouse** (formerly the "Civic") which is one of the best known amateur theatres in the North.

Lister Park is situated in the northern part off Manningham Lane. It contains a large botanical garden and **Cartwright Hall** a splendid baroque building housing the **City Art Gallery and Museum** *(open daily)*. The Hall stands on the site of the former home of Samuel Cunliffe Lister, later Lord Masham, who founded the giant Manningham Mills. His statue stands near the park gates.

The **Industrial Museum** is at Moorside Mills, Eccleshill.

Bolling Hall *(open daily)* is on Bolling Hall Road to the south of the city. The museum houses displays illustrating local domestic life from the fifteenth to the late eighteenth centuries.

Excursions from Bradford

At **Thornton** (B6145) on the city's western outskirts is the house, 74 Market Street, where Patrick and Maria Brontë lived, when Patrick, the father of Emily, Charlotte and Anne and Branwell, was the vicar of Thornton. The four Brontë children were all born in this small terrace house on the main street of the village.

North of Thornton is a tiny hamlet with the surprising name of **Egypt,** where the road goes through a deep narrow cutting between thick towering walls of millstone grit, erected by former quarrymen, and locally called the *Walls of Jericho.*

To Haworth. Haworth is a place of pilgrimage for all Brontë-lovers, for here, from 1820 to 1861, the Rev. Patrick Brontë was the incumbent of the Church, and at the adjacent Parsonage his daughters Charlotte, Emily and Anne lived and wrote. On the whole the village strikes a familiar note to those who know their Brontë, although the church is on a quite different plan from the church of the Brontë days. A brass plate near the chancel screen marks the site of the Brontë vault, and a marble tablet in the Brontë Chapel bears the names of all the Brontë family. The old Parsonage was presented in 1928 to the Brontë Society and now houses a *Museum* of Brontë relics *(open daily,* 11–5.45, *summer;* 11–4.45, *winter, Sundays,* 2–5.45, *or* 4.45. *(Closed during Christmas week). Admission fee).*

The Brontë interest is not the only attraction of Haworth; the Rev. William Grimshaw, a famous Methodist, before the Methodist movement was separated from the mother Church, was minister here from 1742 to 1763, and his friend, John Wesley, preached often at Haworth.

There is in existence a flourishing Brontë Society, particulars regarding which may be obtained at the Parsonage Museum.

Also at Haworth is the museum of the *Keighley and Worth Valley Railway Preservation Society*, who have reopened the line from Keighley to Oxenhope and run a train service between the two places.

To East Riddlesden Hall. Reached by the A650 via Bingley. A seventeenth-century manor house, with fish pond and barns. The medieval tithe barn is notable *(N.T., open).*

To Tong. Tong, 4 miles south-east of Bradford, is a village which is reached by following a signpost, left, from Westgate Hill (the A650). This is an utterly delightful village, which is likely to remain unspoilt, having recently been declared a conservation area. **Tong Hall**, built in 1702, and now a museum, has a chimney-piece decorated with excellent and amusing carving by Grinling Gibbons. In the Church the Tempest family, who owned the Hall, had their own high box pew complete with fireplace.

Bronte Parsonage, Haworth

To Fulneck and Pudsey. It is an easy walk from Tong to **Fulneck,** the Moravian settlement on a hillside, which is part of Pudsey. The Moravians settled here about the middle of the eighteenth century to establish a base for evangelism, naming the place after Fulnek in Moravia. Here they built a church with separate "Brethren's" and "Sisters'" houses on each side which eventually became schools for girls and boys. The community's buildings form a long line overlooking a green valley. Its members are no longer self-sufficient, as in the days when they had their own weaving sheds, inn and bakehouse, but the memory of the old days is kept alive by a small museum *(Wednesdays and Saturdays)* and by ceremonies peculiar to the Moravians such as "Christingles" at Christmas, when children receive and present oranges holding lighted candles to represent the Earth and Christ, the Light of the World.

The hymn-writer James Montgomery and Richard Oastler who campaigned against child slavery in the mills and mines were both students at Fulneck school.

Pudsey itself is a busy manufacturing town, best known for producing cricketers of the stature of Herbert Sutcliffe and Sir Leonard Hutton.

To Shipley. Shipley lies a little north of Bradford. There are some interesting old houses that contrast strongly with the new town centre with its extremely modern clock tower. In the attractive **Shipley Glen** is a cable railway which climbs up the wooded hillside.

Shipley links Bradford with **Saltaire,** the model village which Sir Titus Salt created in 1853 on the banks of the River Aire in order to give his workers the benefit of clean air and decent living conditions. Sir Titus, who had foreseen the commercial value of alpaca cloth, built here the biggest mills in Yorkshire (some said in the world) and then added 800 houses, schools, a hospital, a library, baths and almshouses. A Congregational Church was built opposite the mill and in the mausoleum there lie the remains of the man who created it all, a man far removed from the hard-hearted Victorian industrialist of popular legend. Across the river in **Roberts Park** stands a statue of Sir Titus who is carefully studying a piece of cloth, while engraved on the plinth below him can be seen the alpaca goat on which his fortunes were founded.

Bingley (a few miles north-west) has the delightful **Myrtle Park** and also the internationally renowned **Sports Turf Research Institute** at St. Ives, former home of the Ferrand family. Neighbouring **Baildon,** built on a very steep hill, has some interesting old houses.

Hawksworth, north of Baildon, is a lovely village. James I is said to have slept at **Hawksworth Hall,** now a home for spastics.

East of Hawksworth is **Guiseley,** whose fine old church is linked both with Henry Wadsworth Longfellow and the Brontës. The American poet's grandfather set out from Guiseley for the New World after generations of his family had worshipped here; and Patrick Brontë was married here, immediately afterwards performing the same service for the Reverend William Morgan who had married *him* and who was being united with the cousin of Patrick's bride.

At neighbouring **Yeadon** is the Leeds–Bradford Airport. There is a large tarn at Yeadon, used for boating.

YOUR HELP IS REQUESTED

A GREAT part of the success of this series is due, as we gratefully acknowledge, to the enthusiastic co-operation of readers. Changes take place, both in town and country, with such rapidity that it is difficult, even for the most alert and painstaking staff, to keep pace with them all, and the correspondents who so kindly take the trouble to inform us of alterations that come under their notice in using the books, render a real service not only to us but to their fellow-readers. We confidently appeal for further help of this kind.

THE EDITOR

WARD LOCK LIMITED
116, BAKER STREET,
LONDON, W.1

Doncaster

Banks. – *Barclays*, Baxtergate, 3 High Street, 155 Balby Road, and Hall Gate; *Co-operative Wholesale Bankers Ltd.*, St. Sepulchregate; *Lloyds*, High Street, 209 Beckett Road, 157 Balby Road and Waterdale; *Lombank*, 12/14 Bradford Row; *Midland*, High Street and Hallgate; *National Westminster*, 12 and 47 High Street and 7 Kingsgate; *Trustee Savings Bank*, 50 Hallgate, 80 High Road, Balby and 247 Beckett Road; *Yorkshire*, 16 High Street and Printing Office Street.

Bathing. – At pools in Grey Friars and Waterdale.

Bowls. – Public greens at Elmfield Park, Hexthorpe Flats, Grove Gardens, Haslam Park and Westfield Park.

Buses. – From Southern Bus Station, College Road; Northern Bus Station, Trafford Way, North Bridge; and Christ Church.

Car Parking. – Cleveland Street Roundabout Multi-storey; North Bridge Multi-storey; Chequer Road; Dockin Hill; Duke Street; High Fishergate; Waterdale and Glasgow Paddocks and some streets.

Cinemas. – *Gaumont* and *Odeon* both in Hall Gate; *ABC*, Cleveland Street.

Cricket. – Doncaster Town Cricket Club, Town Fields. There are also many private clubs.

Dancing. – *Top Rank Doncaster Suite*, Silver Street; *Time and Place Club*, Hallgate, also in some hotel ballrooms.

Early Closing Day. – Thursday.

Football. – (Assoc.): *Doncaster Rovers F.C.*, Belle Vue Ground. (Rugby): *Doncaster R.U.F.C.*, Armthorpe Road Ground; (Rugby League): *Doncaster R.L.F.C.*, Bentley Road Ground.

Gliding. – Club at Airport.

Golf. – *Doncaster Golf Club*, Bessacarr; *Wheatley Golf Club*, Armthorpe Road; *Town Moor Golf Club*, Racecourse.

Horse Racing. – Doncaster Common, next to the Great North Road (A638).

Hotels. – *Danum*, High Street; *Elephant*, St. Sepulchregate; *Punch's*, Bawtry Road; *Doncaster Acorn*, Bennetthorpe; *Rockingham*, Bennetthorpe; *Woolpack*, Market Place and many others.

Library. – Waterdale.

Museum and Art Gallery. – Chequer Road.

Population. – 81,800 (approx.).

Post Office. – Priory Place.

Putting. – Elmfield Park; Grove Gardens; Sandall Park; Hexthorpe Flats and Westfield Park.

An industrial county borough, Doncaster (Danum to the Romans) has known human habitation since the New Stone Age. In about 70 A.D. a Roman fort was established during the campaign against the Brigantes and it is about this fort, with its accompanying township and the ford across the River Don, that the present town has grown. Along what is now Hallgate, High Street and Frenchgate ran the Roman road which connected Lincoln with York.

Discovered fragments suggest that Doncaster was the centre of a pottery industry up to the end of the period of Roman occupation. Today the town is the centre of a great coal-mining area and is also concerned with the building of railway engines and rolling stock. There are ten large collieries around Doncaster which now contains some of the coal industry's principal departments for the whole country. Other industries include numerous branches of engineering construction and building, as well as sweet manufacture. Doncaster butterscotch is renowned.

Despite this industrial basis, Doncaster today retains some of the atmosphere of the market town it became in medieval times, and those days are recalled by surviving street names like Fishergate.

The **Mansion House** in High Street was designed by James Paine and completed in 1748. The splendid ballroom with fine ceiling, musicians' gallery, white marble fireplaces and collection of paintings is a striking room.

St. George's Parish Church in St. Georgegate was built in 1858 replacing an earlier Norman building destroyed by fire.

Christ Church, in Thorne Road, is noted for its Belgian glass and for its steeple which has an interesting octagonal lantern.

A modern civic centre is being developed in Waterdale. There is the **College of Technology** and an **Arts Centre** where films and dramatic productions are presented. There also are the new Law Courts, police buildings and the National Coal Board Offices. Bloodstock sales once took place at Glasgow Paddocks but now occur at Belle Vue Stables.

Close by in Chequer Road is the **Museum and Art Gallery** *(daily)* with displays mainly of local interest. In the first-floor art gallery there is a permanent collection of British artists of the eighteenth to the twentieth centuries, together with sculptures by Epstein, Henry Moore and others.

To the south of the town is the pleasant suburb of Bessacarr.

On the northern outskirts of Doncaster is Cusworth Hall housing the **South Yorkshire Industrial Museum.**

On the east of the A638 is Doncaster Common with its racecourse where is run the historic **St. Leger,** first run (though not under that name) in 1776. The race, founded by Colonel Anthony St. Leger, was first run on Cantley Common and then, two years later, was transferred to Town Moor, where it has since remained. Held on four days in September it attracts visitors and horses from many countries.

A magnificent new grandstand was opened in 1969, replacing stands which dated back to 1778. An internal betting hall in the new building can accommodate 75 bookmakers and the totalisator on its 2½ acres of floor space. The club and grandstand enclosures can hold no fewer than 13,000 racegoers. The new stand is equipped for use outside the racing season for conferences, banquets, dances, exhibitions and similar events.

Doncaster to Goole

Seven miles from Doncaster is **Hatfield,** an old village with a lovely church, parts of which date from the twelfth century. The village stands in **Hatfield Chase** which was wild fenland, teeming with game and ruffians until Cornelius Vermuyden, a Dutch engineer, drained it during the reign of Charles I, thereby incurring the wrath of the native fenmen. About three miles from Hatfield, **Thorne** seems more suited to Holland than Yorkshire, so many canals and dykes are to be seen. The waterway called Dutch River (cut by Vermuyden) which unites the Don and Ouse crosses the flat country to reach Goole, while the road takes a more roundabout route via **Rawcliffe** (only six miles from Lincolnshire), once the home and now the burial place of Jimmy Hurst, a famous eccentric, who in the time of George III attempted, among other exploits, to fly with home-made wings.

Goole. A seaport 50 miles from the sea, Goole announces its presence from a distance by the dockside cranes which tower over the flat country. There is a maritime feeling, too, in **St. John's Church,** built by the Aire and Calder Navigation Company in 1843, and which contains memorials to ships and sailors lost at sea.

Very little of Goole is old. The oldest standing building is said to be the Georgian *Lowther Hotel* in Aire Street, but there is nevertheless a feeling of the past, for instance in the name of the *Vermuyden Hotel.* A good deal of Goole's considerable trade as a port is still done in coal, which from the first was the principal cargo handled there.

Selby Abbey

Goole to Selby

Thirteen miles via A614 and A63. An alternative would be to go south-west (instead of north) on the A614, then take the A1041 through Snaith.

Everything in **Selby** leads to the **Abbey Church,** one of the finest monastic churches in England. Surrounded by green lawns at the heart of the town, it seems to stand impressively aloof from the swirl of traffic in this busy little port and market town on the River Ouse.

The Abbey, now Selby's parish church, was built as a monastery. Hugh de Lacy, second Abbot of Selby, began the work in 1097, but the present chancel was not completed until 1340.

The chief glories of the abbey include two fine Norman doorways, the east window with its superb tracery and the tower, skilfully restored in 1909, after a fire which destroyed the roof in 1906, and further added to in 1935. The nave spans a hundred years and illustrates the development from Norman to Early English styles.

The origins of the abbey have been described as both religious and political. King William I (whose son Henry was born at Selby) needed a pacifying influence in the North, and so when the hermit Benedict, newly arrived from Auxerre, stopped at Selby on his way up the Ouse to York, he was authorised to begin the abbey. A much more recent event there was the presentation by the Queen of the Royal Maundy in 1969.

Selby is an interesting town. Ships can sail up the Ouse as far as York, and Selby even builds its own, launching them sideways into the river, which is too narrow to allow of the conventional method. Twice a year the spectacle may be observed of the high tide coming up the river.

There is a toll bridge across the river on the York road (A63). In 1970 this modern bridge replaced a timbered bridge, erected around 1791, which was regarded as the earliest of its kind in this country.

Hull

Early Closing Day. – Thursday.
Hotels. – *Broadway*, Ferensway; *Dorchester House*, Beverley Road; *Hull Centre*, Paragon Street; *Newland Park*, Cottingham Road; *New Manchester*, George Street; *New York*, Anlaby Road; *Royal Station*, Paragon Square; *White House*, Jameson Street.
Library. – Albion Street.
Market Days. – Tuesdays, Fridays and Saturdays.
Population. – 285,472.

Hull has been a thriving port since the end of the thirteenth century. Its full title, Kingston upon Hull, was first used in 1293. King Edward I, who had great faith in the port's potential, granted its first charter in 1299.

Today Hull is one of the principal British cities and ranks as one of the leading U.K. seaports. The port is also a terminal of passenger and car-ferry services to Rotterdam and Zeebrugge.

Hull was the native town of William Wilberforce, the slave emancipator, and in High Street is the house where he was born in 1759. Now a museum, **Wilberforce House** contains many grisly relics of the slave trade.

Also in the High Street is the **Transport Museum.** Appropriately enough, Hull, Britain's largest fishing port, has a fine museum of fisheries and shipping, the **Maritime Museum** in Pickering Park.

Near the city centre, **Trinity House** maintains the oldest navigation school in the world as well as almshouses for seamen and their dependants.

Other places of interest include the **Guildhall** in Alfred Gelder Street, and the **Ferens Art Gallery** in Queen Victoria Square.

In the market place there is a good fourteenth-century church, **Holy Trinity,** while the surrounding area, the Old Town, has narrow streets with such quaint old names as "Land of Green Ginger".

Running parallel with High Street is the Old Harbour area where the wealthy merchants of bygone Hull lived and had their places of business. This stretch of the River Hull served as the port before the building of the docks. The first dock was completed in 1778. After serving shipping for 150 years it was filled in and now, as **Queen's Gardens,** provides a delightful open space in the city centre.

Hull is unique in this country in having its own municipal telephone service which has been most efficiently and economically run since 1904.

Although a great industrial centre, much of the city, which suffered severely from air raids during the war, is now modern and attractive with pleasant gardens and good shops.

Wilberforce Memorial and Technical College, Hull

The fortunes of the Humberside area will no doubt receive a tremendous boost by the completion, scheduled for 1976, of the Humber Bridge, longest single-span suspension bridge (4,626 feet) in the world. The northern edge of the bridge will be four miles west of the centre of Hull and the southern end at Barton-upon-Humber in Lincolnshire.

Hull to Withernsea

Almost half way between Hull and Withernsea is **Hedon,** an ancient market town with a commanding, square-towered church called the "King of Holderness". (The "Queen of Holderness" is a church at **Patrington,** about 4 miles south-west of Withernsea.)

Withernsea itself is a cheerful seaside town with good clean sands and almost two miles of promenade. Offering golf, a pleasure park, boating pool and a heated open-air swimming pool off the South Promenade, it can fairly claim to provide for family holidaymakers. A wide variety of entertainment may be seen at the Grand Pavilion, where dancing also may be enjoyed. For the less energetic there are pleasant gardens.

Ward Lock's
Red Guides

Edited by Reginald J. W. Hammond

Complete England
Complete Scotland
Complete Wales
Complete Ireland
Lake District (*Baddeley*)
Complete West Country
Complete Devon
Complete South-East Coast
Complete Yorkshire
Complete Scottish Lowlands
Complete Cotswolds and
    Shakespeare Country
Complete Thames and
    Chilterns
Complete Wye Valley,
    Hereford and Worcester
Complete Dorset and
    Wiltshire

WARD LOCK LIMITED

Index